The Man in Blue Pyjamas

JALAL BARZANJI

The Man in Blue Pyjamas

A Prison Memoir

based on a translation by SABAH A. SALIH

THE UNIVERSITY OF ALBERTA PRESS

Published by

The University of Alberta Press
Ring House 2
Edmonton, Alberta, Canada   T6G 2E1
www.uap.ualberta.ca

LIBRARY AND ARCHIVES CANADA
CATALOGUING IN PUBLICATION

Barzanji, Jalal
    The man in blue pyjamas : a prison
memoir / Jalal Barzanji ; based on a
translation by Sabah A. Salih.

(Wayfarer, a literary travel series)
Includes index.
Issued also in electronic format.
ISBN 978-0-88864-536-4

    1. Barzanji, Jalal—Imprisonment.
2. Political prisoners—Iraq—Biography.
3. Journalists—Iraq—Biography. 4. Kurds—
Iraq—Biography. 5. Iraq—Politics and
government—1979-1991. 6. Barzanji, Jalal—
Exile—Canada. 7. Kurdish Canadians—
Biography. 8. Poets, Canadian (English)—
20th century—Biography. 9. Human rights
workers—Canada—Biography. I. Title.
II. Series: Wayfarer (Edmonton, Alta.)

DS79.66.B37A313 2011   365'.45092
C2011-905301-2

First edition, first printing, 2011.
Printed and bound in Canada by Houghton
Boston Printers, Saskatoon, Saskatchewan.

Copyediting by Peter Midgley.
Proofreading by Meaghan Craven and
Joanne Muzak.
Photos scanned by Dave Vasek/Colorspace.
Maps by Wendy Johnson.
Indexing by Judy Dunlop.

The University of Alberta Press is committed
to protecting our natural environment. As
part of our efforts, this book is printed on
Enviro Paper: it contains 100% post-consumer
recycled fibres and is acid- and chlorine-free.

The University of Alberta Press gratefully
acknowledges the support received for its
publishing program from The Canada Council
for the Arts. The University of Alberta Press
also gratefully acknowledges the financial
support of the Government of Canada
through the Canada Book Fund (CBF) and the
Government of Alberta through the Alberta
Multimedia Development Fund (AMDF) for
its publishing activities.

Several names and places in this book
have been changed to protect individuals'
identities.

Canada Council   Conseil des Arts
for the Arts   du Canada   Canada

Government
of Alberta ■

For my parents who have taught me how to make the complex simple and often prayed for me.

In this world of trickery, emptiness
It's what your soul wants.

—RUMI

I had no nation now but the imagination.

—DEREK WALCOTT

Contents

Foreword

I FIRST MET JALAL BARZANJI and his wife Sabah when he was named the PEN Writer-in-Exile in Edmonton.

The very existence of such a position throws up the eternally strange question: why do they—people of power—imprison writers, beat them up, kill them? Why do they so fear the word? This fear includes most of those with power. Of course, in the democracies what they can do is limited, but even so, those in power do somehow fear the free word and desire to limit it.

What weapon did Jalal have as a young poet in Kurdish Iraq? What weapons do any of us writers have? Weapons that kill? Economic power? Administrative power? None of these. We have only words and phrases.

I believe that ability to communicate something—not necessarily something specific—about the people in power is what creates the fear. Perhaps it is not so much the ability to communicate, as the ability to make others *feel* you can. Such a simple thing—the one thing that organized power cannot really control.

Jalal was born inside that Kurdish universe which did not fit into the official world of 19th and 20th century nation-states with their declarative borders cutting through wherever wars and treaties put them. Even as a teenager, he began to express via his poetry a world— an idea of culture—that did not match the official nation-state model. Almost in innocence, he became one of those inexplicably frightening wielders of words.

From there, in his far too lightweight blue pyjamas, he was ripped out of his family and shoved into the nightmare underworld of beatings and raw prisons. Three times over the years since then he has had to rebuild his life. The third time brought him and his family to Canada and Edmonton.

Jalal's ability to describe the life of his Kurdish world in the town of Hawler; his ability to lay out the nature of violence and the intention of power to humiliate, and the way in which individuals survive this or do not; his descriptions of the practical realities of fleeing into exile—all these things are both moving and revealing. Perhaps because he is a poet filled with poetic energy, he is able to focus in on the furtive loves of the persecuted, on the realities of the beans eaten, on the cars that break down on the way to freedom, and the minor officials who surprise by their generosity or meanness. We are literally pulled into Jalal's life and that of his family.

As he carries us with him all the way through his arrival in Edmonton, there are the moving details: the wrong shoes, the helpful officials—thank God—and the rebuilding of a life in a new language and culture.

This book is a living testimony to the Kurdish reality, but also to the reality of the writer's life. It is an illustration of why and how our country is constantly strengthened by the arrival of new Canadians who have already proved their courage, their consciousness of human realities, their ability to deal with the turbulences of life. They strengthen us because they arrive with those strengths which are essential to a good citizen—courage, consciousness, and intellectual flexibility.

I have not had to live Jalal's life, but he has drawn me into it as if the reader is one with him. This emotional knowledge he has given is now somehow part of my own imagination. It is a generous creative act, for which I thank him.

JOHN RALSTON SAUL

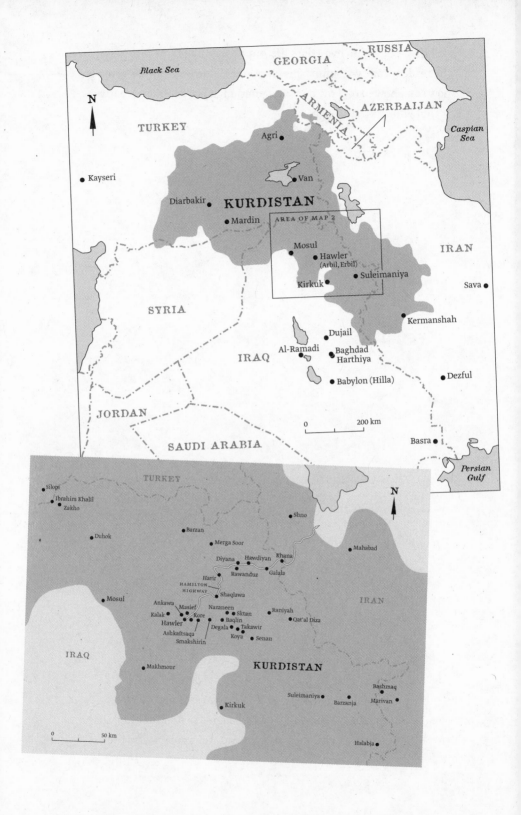

Preface

WHEN I FIRST LEFT WAR-TORN KURDISTAN, I had to cross many
borders, trusting smugglers to get me to Turkey, then Ukraine, and
on to safe refuge in a European country. My plan failed miserably, as
I was deported back to Turkey. After fourteen difficult months there,
finally Canada opened its door to my family and me in 1998. On this
long journey of crossing continents, multiple challenges and risks
faced me. My biggest concern was that I would be separated from my
passion for writing. All this time, I held my thoughts and stories in my
heart and in my memory. I also made sure I carried with me all my
notes I had written on scrap papers smuggled into my jail cell during
my imprisonment.

I soon realized that I was in a country where I could write without restrictions and censorship; there is no cost in blood or tears for
pursuing my passion. This was exciting for me as a writer from a
country in which I had not known freedom of expression. Because I
had to learn English and find work, I struggled to find time and space
to write, until a dream came true: in 2007, I was appointed as the first

PEN Canada Writer-in-Exile. I had a full year to put all my time and energy into writing my memoirs. Revisiting my past from the vantage point of exile made me realize how painful, but also how rewarding, my life has been growing up in a culture where the tragic and the comic tend to overlap continuously and where, despite decades of war, brutality, and poverty, daily life continues to be as vibrant as ever.

Acknowledgements

I WANT TO EXPRESS MY GRATITUDE to those people who have made publishing this book possible.

I am especially grateful to the famed Canadian writer and International President of PEN International, John Ralston Saul. His tireless efforts led to the creation of Edmonton's Writer-in-Exile program, of which I was the first beneficiary.

Many thanks to PEN Canada, and its executive director, Isabel Harry, and to Ted Bishop and Todd Babiak, members of the Writer-in-Exile Committee of Edmonton; the Canada Council for the Arts; the Writers Guild of Alberta; the staff of the City of Edmonton Cultural Capital program in 2007; Edmonton Public Library; the Edmonton Arts Council; the University of Alberta Press; and the Canadian Literature Centre/Centre de littérature canadienne.

My special thanks to Edmonton Mayor Stephen Mandel, whose dedication to the arts has been an encouragement for me, and also to former Edmonton City Councillor Michael Phair, who supported the idea of Writer-in-Exile program.

Thank you also to my dear friend, Linda Goyette, who has given me her unwavering support since my early days in Canada.

I am incredibly thankful to Professor Sabah Salih of Bloomsburg University for his thoughtful and excellent translation of the book, and to Linda Cameron, director of the University of Alberta Press for publishing my book. I want to thank Peter Midgley for always believing in my vision for the book, and for the great work he did editing it. Thanks also to Mary Lou Roy for her hard work during production and to Alan Brownoff for his beautiful design. Thank you, too, to Cathie Crooks and Jeff Carpenter for marketing my book.

Who can forget my dear circle of friends who have supported since my early years in Edmonton: Kelly MacKean, Yvonne Chiu, Satya Das, Shirley Serviss, Alice Major, Laura and Douglas Krefting, Linda Cook and Roger Laing.

And my beloved family: my wife Sabah Tahir, my daughters Ewar and Niga, and my son Jwamer—thank you for your support and strength through our long, emotional and moving journey.

I want to end my acknowledgments by noting my support for the brave writers who have promoted freedom of expression, who have never stopped writing in the face of personal threats, and who have refused to be silenced in the face of dictatorships, torture and imprisonment. Thank you for attempting to bring more beauty to the world and for planting a global seed of peace.

JALAL BARZANJI
Edmonton, Canada, 2011

Introduction XXI

IN THIS MEMOIR of exile and life under Saddam Hussein's tyranny, Jalal Barzanji vividly humanizes the Kurdish experience. Bitterness, finger pointing, and recrimination are kept out, ensuring the reader has, to use Henry James's apt phrase, a fair share in the narrative.

We meet Barzanji at various stages in his life: the shy but inquisitive little boy feeling somewhat distant from everyone around him; the adolescent bewitched by a female librarian who cleans the dust from books by rubbing them against her busty bosom; the soccer fan who thinks nothing of spending the entire sum he and his friend have saved from selling roasted sunflower seeds on a rubber ball; the young man who, by adding a mere umbrella to his meagre possessions, thinks he has it all. It takes as little as a window seat at school and a scallion sandwich just before dinner for Barzanji to appreciate life. Soon the joy of ball kicking is traded for the musings of poetry; fame and recognition follow before he reaches thirty. As a father, he proves to be as melting in his tenderness toward his little daughter as any Kurdish mother. Then comes the sad part: Barzanji the political prisoner facing long days and nights of isolation, torture, humiliation, deprivation, and uncertainty.

There is also Barzanji the storyteller, the eagle-eyed observer who knows what to record and when to yield his narrative to others. Everyone he meets seems to be a born storyteller like he himself is. One by one, they take us inside the Kurdish culture, which, like all cultures, can be compassionate and harsh at the same time. A hard-working man by day and a jovial drunk by night finds himself at the mercy of disapproving neighbours. A grieving father admits to his horror that he actually had never kissed the beloved son he has just buried (one of the many lives tragically lost under Saddam); sadly, he was raised to believe that kissing babies would make him look unmanly in the eyes of society. Here, imagination, not yet thinned by television and commercialism, is the prisoners' best friend. These prisoners weave story after story out of experiences that life in the West has long stopped providing. Theirs is a world in which the word still has the power to shock and entertain. We also meet men arguing strongly about religion, women, children, politicians, alcohol, love and sex, among other things.

At a more expansive level, this memoir chronicles the transformation of Iraq from a relatively peaceful and pleasant country into a modern police state where ordinary people, like Jalal Barzanji, could easily find themselves imprisoned, humiliated, tortured, and even in some cases brutally murdered simply for appearing to be harbouring thoughts the state considered incompatible with its totalitarian mindset. As such, this book will give those who favoured the continuation of Saddam's regime plenty of good reasons to reconsider their position. As the narrative unfolds, we find ourselves in a world where the state uses torture and execution not just to eliminate lives but, more importantly, to make fear of the state a national obsession—the larger purpose being the eventual elimination of individual thought. In this world, no place, not even one's home, feels safe from such fear. Even a simple modernist poem, with its fondness for symbol and image and resolute non-interference in politics, cannot be tolerated. Whether an editorial or an artwork, a lecture or a performance, words

and images and sounds all have to be unambiguous in their endorse-
ment of state thinking.

Like the land, where treeless terrain can quickly give way to
snow-capped mountains and roaring streams, Kurdish culture is a
study in contrasts. We meet women doing terrible things to satisfy
patriarchy; the next day the very same women do what they can to
undermine it. Remarkably, they usually succeed. We meet Muslims,
who without knowing a thing about the Enlightenment, project a
decidedly dialectic mindset, praying and fasting as dictated by the
faith while at the same time cheerily questioning, and even mocking,
religious faith. We meet Kurdish Freedom Fighters known as the
peshmerga (or those who face death) eager to die for the cause while at
the same time admitting how needlessly bloody and corrupt their
guerilla army has become. As one fighter puts it, "Revolution is like a
crop just harvested: if you don't get there on time, you won't get your
share." Even though predominantly Muslim, the culture is no stranger
to alcohol and other forms of secularism.

In translating this memoir, I have tried to preserve its Kurdish
flavour while at the same time keeping the interests of clarity and
precision in mind. As this memoir shows, Kurdish storytelling is nour-
ished by an oral tradition that predates modern ways of life. To use
a phrase of Edward Said's in a similar context, this tradition often
favours "allusions and indirect expression" to naturalistic detail. [1]
Readers unfamiliar with Kurdish culture can work their way through
this translation more enjoyably by taking note of that. *The Man in Blue
Pyjamas* is not just Jalal Barzanji's personal history; like the narrator
in Salman Rushdie's great novel of exile and memory, Mr. Barzanji is
"the swallower of lives" and cultures. [2]

SABAH A. SALIH
Professor of English
Bloomsburg University, Pennsylvania, January 11, 2011

NOTES

1. Cited by Michael Wood in "On Edward Said," *London Review of Books*, vol. 25, no. 20 (23 October 2003): 3.

2. Rushdie, Salman. *Midnight's Children*. 25th Anniversary Edition (New York: Random House 2006): 4.

Introduction

My life did not go smoothly from birth to childhood to adolescence to adulthood. It did not unfold as one happy, settled life in one country. Nothing moved forward in a straight line. I moved forward, I moved back. Sometimes I was thrown forward, and thrown back. I have been a refugee always on the move, crossing borders and going back again. I must present my story in small pieces because my life has been in pieces. Some of the stories in the book are captured from prisoners' words; they are retold in spirit, and smeared with my compassion.

I am beginning to understand how my time in prison affected the rest of my life. As I tell my story, I must go back and forth in time to put the pieces together. A human memory does not sort out pictures and stories in a chronological sequence, or in a straight line. We remember in sudden flashbacks, out of order.

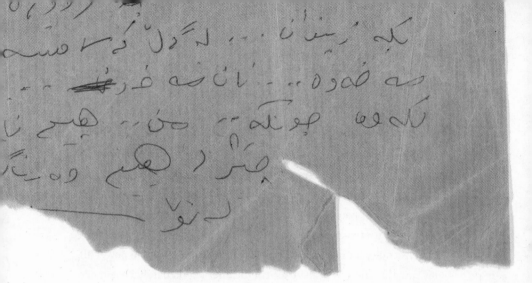

1 The First Stage of Imprisonment

A Bitter Evening

IN KURDISTAN IT IS COMMON for men to change into their pyjamas after they get home from work. Kurds even entertain familiar guests or go to the neighbourhood shop in their pyjamas. It was still cold that evening of the March 7, 1986, and although I did have another pair of pyjamas (whitish and much warmer), for some reason, I was wearing those rather thin blue ones. I think it was the colour that drew me to them. Somewhere in the back of the house, I could hear Sabah, my wife, preparing food.

As I sat looking out of the window, I could see our next-door neighbour, Amir, walking over to our house wearing his warm brown cotton robe and carrying a hot cup of tea in his hand. Amir settled by the warm stove. After a while, he suggested that this was a good night for the *peshmerga*, the Kurdish Freedom Fighters, to climb the high mountains and attack the military bases.

Our Ishtar kerosene heater had been on for nearly three hours, but the room was still rather chilly. Like most families in Kurdistan, and for that matter the rest of Iraq, we couldn't afford to heat more than one room at a time. In a country awash with oil, this made no sense. What made the situation even worse was that most people could only afford clothing made of cheap synthetic fibres, which offered little protection against the dry winter cold. We couldn't wait for the summer to arrive. I remember my mother always saying "summer is the parent of poor people." But then again, summer was always a scorcher, with temperatures reaching nearly 50°C all summer long. We had electricity for only a few hours a day, but even if we had power all day, our old fans and beat-up air conditioner would barely have made a difference against the searing heat.

Although spring in Kurdistan is short, the Ishtar heater provided some protection against the still chilled air. As I stood by the window looking at the city lights, I was, as always, slightly bemused that our heater bore the name of Ishtar, the goddess of fertility who was worshipped in the ancient city of Arbil. Heaven knows, in a world governed by Saddam Hussein, we needed all the protection we could get in Hawler, which is the name by which modern Kurds know Arbil.

Back then, Saddam Hussein's regime was at the peak of its power and glory, portraying itself as the heroic transformer of Iraq into a modern state. But in reality all it had accomplished was an efficient police state. No criticism was allowed. Problems were always blamed on the outsider. And yet this was a government that had yet to put in place a basic sewer system. Drinking tap water was a definite health hazard. Sometimes, when the water was not running, Ramo the fire-fighter drove his truck and sold the water he held in the tank. We all knew this was illegal, but people were grateful because without him there would have been no clean water at all. Cholera might have been eradicated in many parts of the world, but here in Hawler it was alive and well.

As far back as I can remember, I've always been a window person. At home everyone knew to stay clear of the sofa with its commanding view of the outside. It was my favourite spot for contemplating. And when travelling as a passenger in a car, I would always try to reserve the window seat by placing my briefcase or jacket on it. The car window had such a transformative power: looking through the window, even the familiar would seem interesting and new to me.

My mother used to tell me that when I was seven or eight years old I used to get lost frequently. My favourite place was in our one neighbour's big enclosed yard that harboured a flock of pigeons, which I loved to feed. Sometimes my mother, thinking that perhaps the fairies had taken me, would look for me everywhere, only to find me later feeding the pigeons, or hiding in the wardrobe or some other such place. I was her little angel, so she didn't have the heart to be rough with me. She told me that I had this habit of standing by the low window in our house, clutching the railings and just staring out for long stretches of time. She would often remind me how nicely all the blues—the big blue sky, the blue paint on the window frame, and the blue-bead anklet she'd made—complemented one another.

It was perhaps here by this very window, blue and without curtains, where the birds and I got used to one another and became good friends, that I developed my fondness for blue. Later, as an adult, I would stand by the window and muse about beauty and freedom. The funny thing is that when I'm by the window, I can't concentrate perfectly on my writing. For that, it is better to have a windowless room. As long as it isn't a cell.

But windows do make good places to think. And on this particular evening, my thoughts travelled far into the past. My father had been the only breadwinner in our house. After work, he would pick up a few things on the way home, and the moment he arrived at the door, we children would rush to greet him and carry the bags to the kitchen. Since my mother would often be busy taking care of the baby, my father and my brother Jamal would help with the dinner, even though this was not a common thing for men to do in our society. We were particularly eager when we knew there was *shifta* on the menu. The deep-fried veal patties were best served with Jamal's specialty—a mouth-watering onion and sumac salad.

The smell of Sabah's cooking drifted through the house. The rest of us were chatting in the living room. My mother, who loved to tell stories about food, turned to Sabah's relative, Ghafour, who was sitting near: "One night, when we were all getting ready to go to bed, your brother Jamal was hungry for meat. Your father went and got a chicken out of our chicken coop. He killed it and cleaned it and made a delicious stew, which we all ate. He said he didn't want his son to go to bed hungry. For him, food was a priority. Rather than buying a house or investing his money, he spent it all on food and other such necessities."

My father owned several farms, which he let to other farmers who did not have land to plant on. That happy time ended in 1963 when Abdul-Salam Arif sent more troops into Kurdistan to force Kurds off their land. Our family was one of the thousands who lost their land, and we had to move to Hawler, where we shared a one-bedroom house in the Setaqan neighbourhood.

There were no jobs available in Hawler besides harsh, manual jobs that my father was never able to do because they were too tough for him. After a long time, he became the school guard at the girls' public school and ended up running the school shop. I skipped my classes a few times and went with him to the shop where he sold egg sand- wiches and cookies, and other nice things. I still do not know how he got this job. But he did, and it did have many benefits for us. In the afternoon when he came home, my father would have a bag of small change with him that he would turn out on the carpet. This was our spending money.

The lack of space in our house meant that no one got any privacy— least of all our parents. In winter, we'd all squeeze into bed like sardines shortly after the electricity went out at 11:00 PM. In the summer, because of the heat, we'd all sleep next to each other under the stars on the rooftop. Except for my father, whose mattress my mother would place a little distance from the rest. But I do remember my parents waking up and going downstairs long before we did. Maybe that was their way of trying to have a little privacy. Otherwise, why would they want to miss the refreshing morning breeze coming from Mount Safeen, which was located about forty minutes' drive east of the city? On a clear day, I could see the mountain through the small window of our house, and its light blue hues, joined to the blueness of the sky, gave me hope.

By the time I got up in the morning, most rooftops would be empty. There was no one else looking out over the city except for this newlywed couple, *Mamosta* Ghazi and his wife Khonaw. Although we did not know the family personally, all the children in the neighbourhood knew *Mamosta* Ghazi because taught at the local school. Understandably, they didn't seem to be eager to rise early, and that was just fine with me: the ramshackle cloth cubicle in which they slept was the object of my intense curiosity and fantasy. Very few of the people in our district had cubicles, and I always wished we had one to sleep in, too. Being alone on the rooftop gave me a chance to spy on them and perhaps see them doing it, but sadly luck was never on my side. Whatever he and his young wife did on the rooftop stayed between the two of them.

One summer holiday we moved into the school building where my father worked, which was in fact a very fancy two-storey house in the wealthy Mustawfi district, which was about forty minutes' walk away from my old neighbourhood of Setaqan. The building that housed the school was surrounded by mansions. I did not enjoy living there. Every day, I would look outside to see whether there were any children my age to play with. But I never saw anyone and soon gave up trying to find new friends. All my friends lived in Setaqan, and every morning during the summer I would wake up early, grab my ball, and walk over to play soccer with them. In the afternoons, I would go to my uncle's convenience store nearby to get some lunch. Then I would go back to play until it was time to go home in the evening.

Those carefree days were gone now. Life in Hawler had changed. On that March evening, it was still too cold to sleep on the rooftops, but through the window I could see the children, indifferent to fear or cold, playing in the alleys while their mothers were preparing dinner. The air was filled with the smell of sautéed onions, lamb stew, and rice.

More people had arrived at our house, and my thoughts drifted back into the room and to our guests. I tried to engage in the small talk, even though they seemed to be in one world and I in another. This was meant to be a happy time of year for Kurds, as well as for Persians and Afghanis. About two thousand years ago, the story goes, Kurds were enslaved by a cruel king called Zohak, who some believed had a snake

Above: Picnic in Hawler,
Nowruz party, 1995.
Right: Jalal, lost in thought,
in his house in Hawler,
c.1980.

growing on each of his shoulders. Every day the snakes had to be fed the brains of two Kurdish children. Then, on March 21, 612 BCE, Kawa the Blacksmith killed Zohak and freed the Kurds from the Assyrian king's tyranny. After he had killed Zohak, Kawa lit a bonfire on the top of the hill to let people know that the time of darkness was over. Today still, Kurds light fires to celebrate Nowruz, the New Day, as the beginning of their year. It reminds them of their ongoing quest for freedom as much as it commemorates Kawa's brave deed.

The conversation in the background had moved on to the weather and to the upcoming Nowruz festivities, so I remarked, "This cold is just not normal for this time of the year. Nowruz is just around the corner; by now it should be pleasant, not cold."

Ghafour said, "No, *Mamosta* Jalal, winter won't be gone anytime soon—the old woman's cold is in March. I don't think there would be any relief from the cold until the first day of spring. It must be one of Khuda's miracles: that day, when you get out of the house you can easily feel there's a change in the weather. But the big change doesn't come until after Nowruz. As we say, in March the snow may reach the leaves but by evening it'll all be gone."

"You are right, Ghafour," I said. "We should not be like that old woman of long-ago stories. She was fooled by the warm days before the first day of spring. When the earth became cold again, she froze to death. You are right. We must be careful."

"I have a feeling there's going to be trouble again this Nowruz," said Kardo. "We're not allowed to celebrate. We can't build a fire, we can't dance, we can't sing. That's why some years ago, that poor girl protested by setting herself on fire." When Kardo mentioned the incident it came back to me: how that girl in Diarbakir had set herself alight in protest against the banning of this traditional Kurdish festival.

"But that accomplished nothing," Parosh replied. "I consider celebratory holidays to be Khuda's gift to humanity. It's just a wonderful opportunity for people to be able to unwind. Nowruz is our national day. I have always been very fond of it, ever since I was a child. To me, it's the symbol of rebirth and beauty. But I still don't want to see people getting hurt, let alone dying, because of it. It's a horrible thing to see a human being reduced to ashes in an instant. I see no reason why people ought not to be allowed to wear colourful dresses to welcome spring. All they ever did was go out to picnics in nature to cook, dance, and sing the day away, with a little nationalism thrown in for good measure. Where is the harm in this?"

I was no longer participating in the conversation and my wife indicated with her eyes that I was wandering off. She said, "Come back to us. Don't let the high seas snatch your boat." She knows I'm not as sociable as she is. Sometimes my mind disappears into the clouds. With guests around, I can't stay focused; my mind is buzzing with ideas and, to be honest, I can't wait to see them leave. I can't help it. When it comes to entertaining, I'm not a very good host.

But poor or not, distracted or not, I still had to entertain. Our culture was adamant about that. After keeping the small talk going very expertly—no doubt to make up for my social ineptness—my wife and our daughter, Ewar, left to see the doctor. It was a routine check-up, because Sabah was by then pregnant with our second daughter, Niga. I watched through the window as they walked down the road and then returned to the conversation. I kept glancing at the window, hoping for an escape. They had not been gone for long when I looked up for the hundredth time. A group of men with AK-47s and pistols at the ready were about to burst into the house. I could tell by their olive uniforms that they were members of the much-feared secret police.

There was no time even to warn the others. The men kicked the doors open and acted as if they were trying to capture a fortified military position; ours was a house that didn't even contain a sharp knife. The secret policemen came straight to where we were sitting. Everybody's hands shot up above their heads instinctively.

"Which one of you is Jalal?" one of them asked.

I nodded.

Then things happened fast. The man reached over and grabbed me by the arm. The men started punching me and kicking me all over, calling me a million names. They hastily handcuffed and blindfolded me and dragged me out to what appeared to be a waiting truck— I could tell that by the way I was dumped into the back. The cursing and kicking continued once the truck started moving.

When the truck stopped some twenty or so minutes later, the men
dragged me out and pushed and kicked me, still blindfolded, into what
I sensed was a building. The floor felt uneven, and when they kicked
me particularly hard, I lost my balance, fell down, and rolled, hurting
myself just above the left eyebrow. In the darkness behind the blindfold, I couldn't tell what time it was or whether there was blood, but I
knew I was in the cell for twenty-four hours because five times I heard
an Imam leading the call to prayer over a nearby mosque intercom. I
was feeling a lot of pain all over my body. Around me, I could hear the
cries of other prisoners being tortured. The pungent smell of urine was
everywhere.

At one point, I could tell some people were passing. Their voices,
though faint, seemed familiar. I was certain some of those voices
belonged to my mother, Zerin; my sister, Ruqya; and my brothers,
Jamal, Kamaran, and Peshtewan. I could not hear my younger brother
Kamal's voice, and I wondered what had happened to him. What was
especially hard for me was that before I could let them know where I
was, their voices went quiet. Later, I learned that they, too, were blindfolded at the house and brought to the prison.

Even today, whenever the subject of our ordeal comes up, my
mother blames it in part on her inability to lie. When the security
police asked her where her children were, she told them they were at
school. She still believes that if she could have brought herself to tell
a lie or two, her other children might have been spared the torment,
especially the two younger boys. Minutes before the junior high school
day was over, and while Kamaran and Peshtewan were putting their
books and pens into their backpacks, waiting for the bell to ring for
home time, the secret police arrived at their school and pulled them
out of class.

Our family was no stranger to arrest. My father was arrested in 1963
when Abdul-Salam Arif sent the feared Haras Qawmi, the military
police, into Kurdistan to force Kurds off their land. The Haras Qawmi
would enter peoples' houses and arrest both old and young and take
them to prison. My father was passionate about the Kurdish revolution and made his views known. But not everyone in our family agreed
with my father's views. My uncle, for instance. He had moved to

Hawler ten years before we did and became a real city man. He dressed well and shaved every day, and you could smell his cologne in the air. He worked as a gardener at a local landlord's house, got married and had three children. Whenever my father began to talk about the revolution, my uncle would leave right away. So, when the police came to arrest him the day after my arrest, he was very unhappy. My brother Jamal remembers him telling the officers, "It's been about twenty years since I visited them! Jalal, he's my stepbrother's family. I'm not like him. I joined the military for two years."

His protestations did not help. Punishment under Saddam Hussein was collective. When someone was arrested, the entire family and all close relatives would be arrested, too. So would anyone who happened to be visiting at the time. The guests I had that evening all ended up spending four days in jail. It was extremely fortunate that my wife and Ewar had left and gone to the doctor just minutes before the secret police arrived. But that was no guarantee of their safety. The secret police were known to come back to round up any remaining family members. I worried a lot about Sabah and little Ewar. Later, much to my relief, I found out that the police, most unusually, did not return. They made no further inquiries about them.

I was still blindfolded when they came for me in the crowded jail. Another round of cursing, kicking, and slapping followed. At one point, someone pushed me and I fell down what felt like a floating stairway. My legs got stuck, but they pulled me back, punched me some more, and then shoved me into a waiting vehicle, which quickly drove off. I knew I was still in Hawler, because it didn't take long for the truck to stop and for me to be dragged out and kicked anew.

Finally, I was taken into another building. What happened next was a surprise: the men removed my blindfold. I was in a fairly large room. There were some chairs and metal desks and about a dozen or so olive-uniformed intelligence officers loitering around. I could see several other families sitting on the floor, waiting. I'd been standing for no more than a minute or two when I saw my mother, sister, and brothers, all blindfolded, being led into the room.

The minute their blindfolds were removed, my mother noticed me. "Oh, Jalal, my dear, dear son," she whispered. "I'll give my life for you.

Why is there blood on your forehead? Did they beat you? I'll ask Khuda to break their hands. Oh, my son, I thought I would never see you again. This is unbelievable. Prison or no prison, it's so nice to see you again."

When she tried to walk over and hug me, one of the men pushed her so hard that she fell backwards onto a black sofa.

"If you move, we'll feed you shit," he barked at her in Arabic.

I felt utterly powerless and ashamed that I couldn't defend my mother against this brute. It was a good thing that my mother did not understand Arabic. When she was seven, her grandfather had made her memorize enough Arabic from the Qu'ran for her to say her prayers and although she has never missed a prayer in more than fifty years, beyond those words she knows no Arabic. At that moment, her lack of understanding was a blessing, for it offered her some protection from the insult.

Like my mother, my father, too, couldn't read or write. However, unlike her, he seldom concerned himself with religion. Nor did he invest a penny in anything; feeding his family well was all that mattered to him. Occasionally, under pressure from my mother or some relative, he would pray for a day or two and then he would stop. He didn't care for Friday prayers at the mosque. He would say, "I can't go and listen to some stupid mullah rambling about the same things for two hours week after week. Besides, I don't know any Arabic. I don't want to lie to God and pray in a language that I neither speak nor understand. He's in charge, not these stupid men, and I see no reason why God would want to send me, or anyone else for that matter, to Hell just for not praying. I love my God. I don't think He is in need of my fasting or prayer. I believe He owns the earth and the sky. He is greater than these minor things."

After all the years of living and after reading many books, I still cannot respond to my father! All I know is that God is not a stranger to me. He is in the sky, in the blueness around us. I can see him more than anything else. And, like my father, I do not need anyone to help me pass my love, or prayers, to him.

The man who had insulted my mother turned to his companions. It soon became apparent what they were planning to do. The officers brought five young men—or I should say boys, for they all seemed to be younger than eighteen—into the room. They were blindfolded and shackled together. I was still trying to figure out who they were when the shooting began. Within an instant they were all gone. Right there in front of their parents.

One mother, weeping and beating her chest uncontrollably, said to her husband, "This was our son, Nawzad." Then she turned to the officers: "I beg Khuda to come and blind you all."

Her husband, old and unable to see well, asked calmly, "Is it really our Nawzad? He was just a boy. He would cry like a child when hungry. He was too afraid to go to the outhouse by himself at night. I had to go with him and wait until he was finished. Lord, where's the justice? Where's the justice?"

Another mother identified her son as Burhan.

We were all crying, even as the officers were trying, rudely and aggressively, to make us stop. Crying, I suppose, was our only way to fight back. They made us watch the slaughter in the hope of crushing our spirits as Kurds. They failed. We were crying and they couldn't stop us.

Just before I was blindfolded again, I managed to see through a little window part of the stone façade of Erbil High School. I knew that building well, as I used to see it almost every day. I now realized where we were: at the headquarters of the secret police. The school stood right across the street from Hawler Public Library, a place that for years had been like second home to me until Saddam Hussein turned it into a prison.

A Deathly Quiet Cell

Handcuffed and blindfolded, I was dragged away and kicked and punched and finally thrown onto a hard surface. A door was shut, and I could no longer hear my mother's and other prisoners' soulful cries. I could tell I was back in a military vehicle. As the vehicle started moving, the biggest worry in my heart was the image of the young people shot in front of me and my mother: how she was going to take it and what might they do to her?

I had no idea where we were heading. I was rolling about in the back of the vehicle and a blow to my head nearly knocked me out. Why was I still handcuffed and blindfolded? This was surely to torment my soul, I said to myself. But I wasn't going to let them do to my soul what they had done to my body. They could confuse me about my whereabouts, but they couldn't break me down. I couldn't escape, I knew, but my soul couldn't be conquered.

I was in the midst these thoughts when suddenly they removed the blindfold. Perhaps they wanted to make me see something horrific again, I thought, so I kept my eyes shut. But when I opened my eyes, I was in a van with two secret policemen standing over me. They must have been the ones kicking and punching me. As though to confirm this, one of the men kicked me really hard in the chest, calling me many names.

I returned the insults.

Enraged, the other guy kicked me so hard that I fell on my back and nearly fainted. I had no energy to sit or stand, but I was conscious enough to look through the van's rear window and through the window on the driver's side. The hue of the sky told me that it wasn't night yet.

As we drove, I forced my mind to think of other things. I recalled the road where students would work on their homework by the roadside because they did not have room in their own homes. In my junior year (Grade 11), I had been one of those children by the roadside.

When the vehicle stopped, I was blindfolded again. In my mind, I was trying to prepare myself for the long haul, thinking that perhaps I would be languishing in prison for years to come without trial, without ever being allowed to see a lawyer. Perhaps I would die under torture. But I didn't entirely rule out the power of bribery. A hefty bribe, I thought, was all that was needed to put an end to my misery.

Even before my arrest, it was very hard for me not to think about what it would be like to be imprisoned in the secret police headquarters. On my drive south along the main thoroughfare through Hawler, I could see the police headquarters, and my mind involuntarily tried to get behind those walls. How did the prisoners manage under torture? How did they pass the time? What it was like to be kept in isolation and in the dark? Just pondering such questions would make me feel like a prisoner already, although even without such thoughts it was very hard not to feel imprisoned. People were being watched everywhere, and even if they weren't it didn't matter because people felt spied upon regardless, even in their bedrooms.

Every so often, my friends and I would go for a walk, which would usually culminate in a visit to the civil servants' club in the evening. Located in the city centre, the club's sprawling rose garden, surrounded by huge eucalyptus trees, was an ideal place for drinks and a conversation about the arts and literature. In winter, the inside of the club, with its floor-to-ceiling windows, offered an even better refuge from the ever-present ears of Saddam's regime.

The civil servants' club was where teachers went to discuss their classes, but when the government took it over it became a garage. Later still, after the collapse of Saddam's regime, it became Nishtimani Mall. Part of this new mall was built on a large old cemetery, called Sheikh Allah Cemetery. I don't know whether the reason for the mall's unsuccessful sales had to do with the fact that it was the first mall in Hawler, or the fact that it was built on top of a cemetery in which some of the loved ones of the shoppers were laid to rest.

Sometimes we would meet at an old tea house called Majko, which was located in the heart of the old city. Every evening, writers from the city would go there to see each other, drink tea, and discuss various topics. Since Majko was more intimate than the club, it was easier for us to vent our frustrations against the military dictatorship, even though there was nothing we could do to change the situation. Getting together like this was indeed a big relief for all of us, even though it made us more aware of how little freedom we had. Talking about freedom was like talking about something that we could never get or find. We were aware that life could not be enjoyed without freedom and that without freedom truth was impossible. We knew our freedom had been taken away from us, but it wasn't until I became a prisoner that I began to realize how horrific life behind bars was. Nothing had prepared me for the cruelty of being taken away from my wife and child.

Somehow I had always known my turn would come. You see, Saddam's regime was not the type that would be satisfied with leaving

Jalal browsing the bookshelves in the entrance of the Majko tea house.

literary types like me alone. The regime wanted to take over everybody. I wanted to have an independent existence, but the regime wouldn't allow it. That's why I knew it was only a matter of time. Still, it was quite a shock when they came for me that chilly evening. I was planning on taking a much-needed bath and then going to bed. It was hard to believe I was being led away like that, blindfolded and handcuffed with nothing on but my flimsy blue pyjamas.

Since I was blindfolded most of the time I was in the vehicle, I was unable to keep track of time. But my mind was active: one moment, I would seriously believe my mind was capable of transforming the prison into an island of freedom and tranquility; another moment, however, I would become desperate and consider myself a fool.

What was happening to me was not something new or different. It had happened before to others. And it would happen again. Saddam would imprison people and then release them. Before their release, the prisoners would be given a pep talk about their responsibilities and how much harsher their penalties would be if they returned to their old ways. They would be told they would be kept under constant surveillance. The aim was to keep the people in a constant state of paranoia. Saddam did not invent the art of imprisonment and torture; he merely perfected it. That's why after their release many would try to find a way to seek asylum overseas. But that wasn't easy. Ordinary Iraqis were not allowed to have passports. The only way to leave was to be smuggled through difficult and dangerous terrain, a practice that over the years claimed many lives.

A year before my arrest, a man in our neighbourhood called Safeen was one of those prisoners Saddam released. As was customary in our culture, people went in droves to visit him when he came out of prison. Listening to Safeen tell his story made me wonder if I could endure what he had endured. He was hung from a ceiling fan and beaten daily with a thick cable. His fingernails and toenails were pulled out. Cigarettes had been stubbed on his chest, and he had been made to sit naked on a bottle. Lying there in the back of the vehicle, I tried to tell myself that I would be all right, but inside I wasn't so sure.

I was trying not to mind my pains when the vehicle suddenly stopped. I was blindfolded once again and punched twice so severely that I fell. I was kicked repeatedly until my body became numb. I was like a punching and kicking bag for these men. I was alert enough to wonder why they had so much anger towards me; they had never seen me before. I blamed their cruelty on the dictatorship. They were, after all, men trained to be cruel by the regime.

I was dragged out of the vehicle and pushed with such force that I fell onto the ground and bruised my head. Then they picked me up and dumped me into a very narrow room, so narrow in fact that I couldn't stretch my legs or arms. With the blindfold and handcuffs removed, I now saw that I was sitting on a dirty old blanket on a concrete floor. I was still wearing my blue pyjamas. I checked to see if I was bleeding. A drop or two fell on the pyjamas, and I wiped off the rest with my sleeve. The drops of blood left a big stain.

It was very cold. I remember wondering why I had changed so fast the previous evening. If I had remained in my black pants and grey coat I would not have been so cold. When I moved the blanket a little, I saw traces of blood and hardened human waste all over the floor. I tried to think of things beyond this tiny room. Nice things, like Fridays.

Friday was the most anticipated day of the week when we were young. On that day, everyone cooked a delicious meal. My father would chop the head off a chicken in front of the house. I used to be happy that the chicken was being killed in a moral way, but I could never stand to watch and always closed my eyes so that I didn't have to see the blood. Now my own fresh blood mixed with the dried blood of other prisoners who had been here before me. My entire body hurt. I worried a lot about my mother, how devastating it would be for her to see me so weak and bloody in this, the second prison I had been held in since my arrest. I thought of what Safeen had told me and realized, given all the moaning and crying I was suddenly hearing, what lay ahead.

A yellow light burned constantly in the cell. The switch was outside the door where I could not reach it, so I could not tell whether it was day or night. Suddenly the tiny iron window above the cell door was opened from outside and a small loaf of old bread and a bottle of water were thrown down. With the place being so small, they landed on my lap. The cap of the bottle opened from the impact and half of the water spilled out. It was warm and smelly; the bottle had been filled and refilled with tap water. Even though I had not been given any food until now, I had no desire to eat. When I tried to stretch my right foot a little, I revealed some markings and dates and numbers that previous prisoners had left on the wall. What was most startling to me was that these people had used their own blood to leave traces of themselves behind. Perhaps this was their way of trying to lessen their pain and remind themselves that the cruelty they had been subjected to could not go on forever. But somehow the idea of using blood as a means of communication revolted me. My forehead was still bleeding lightly, but I just couldn't bring myself to write with the blood.

I was still reflecting on what was on the wall when suddenly the door was flung open and two men with powerful shoulders and arms dragged me out, handcuffed and blindfolded me once again, and led me away, kicking me repeatedly from behind. A few minutes later, they ordered me in Arabic to stop, removed the blindfold, and made me sit on the bare floor. All around me were tools of torture: on a steel desk there were cables, bottles, pliers, and hammers; electric wires were snaking out of the wall; a black rope was dangling from the ceiling, under which was a chair. I wondered how many innocent throats had been strangled in that room.

Safeen's words were painfully vivid in my mind, and I realized that I was here to be tortured. They undressed me with such a force that they nearly tore up my pyjamas and the shirt I was wearing. At least they let me keep my underwear on. Then they turned on me with the cables. Everything became dark before my eyes, and I started to faint, but somehow I remembered what my friend Abd had told me about the way his father had described the fires of Jahanam. I wondered which was worse, being in Hell or being here. I remember, vaguely, at one point they were lifting me up to where the ceiling fan was. I must've fainted completely shortly afterwards, for when I regained consciousness I was back in my cell. I could hear the loud cries coming from other prisoners being tortured. I was blue and black all over now. My knees hurt the most, and I was feeling a little cold, but as I was too weak to put my pyjamas back on, I wrapped myself in the dirty old blanket.

As a child, I had hurt my knees playing soccer. Back then, my mother helped me clean my wounds and soothe the pain with home remedies so that I was able to sleep that night. There was no one to soothe my injuries this time. But the biggest annoyance was the strong ceiling light, which was constantly on. It made my wounds burn painfully, and it kept me permanently disoriented. In the midst of all this, thinking about writing and about more pleasant memories gave me a glimmer of hope.

My torturers were two men. I couldn't tell whether it was morning or evening, day or night, when they came for me, but it seemed to be every other day. One of them had a face full of pimples and a small tattoo in the shape of a dot perched on the tip of his nose. His thick moustache seemed to have been dyed jet black in the fashion of the times, but I think his heart must have been blacker. They never got tired of torturing me; they treated my body as though it was a carcass.

But it was the guy with the pimples who did most of the torturing. He would start with the cable, and after several blows he would shout, "Now admit your guilt. Who are these people who write against our revolution?" I always said the same thing, that I was a poet and that I was only writing about human desire, peace, and beauty. Then the beating then would continue. Afterwards I would be as good as dead. Back in my cell, I would slowly return to consciousness.

One day, I heard someone tapping on the wall, and when the tapping continued, I realized it was from the adjacent cell. I never discovered who was in that cell, but through tapping we kept in touch and made our concern for one another known. It was a small thing, I know, but tapping made us feel connected.

I had been left alone in my cell for what I thought was several days when one morning two different men came for me. I tried to put my torn blue pyjamas on, but they dragged me out before I could do so. Once they had taken me out of my cell they blindfolded me, wrapped the old blanket around me, and shoved me away to what felt like another part of the prison compound. When they removed the blindfold, I found myself face-to-face with an officer dressed in an olive uniform. His desk was cluttered with papers.

He fired off questions and comments in a business-like way: "How many poems have you written under a pseudonym attacking our great revolution? We know you write for underground publications. We know that your brother, Kamal, instead of turning himself in, fled to the mountains. Obviously, he has something to hide."

The news about Kamal caught me by surprise. At the time of my arrest, my younger brother was finishing high school at an evening school. That evening, Kamal had arrived at school as usual. His English teacher, Ali Jukil, pulled him aside and told him that the secret police had come looking for him. At once Kamal grabbed his books and fled to the Setaqan neighbourhood where one of our relatives, Bawakir's son, arranged his escape to the village of Senan in the Smaquli Valley southeast of Hawler. There he stayed for a while with my aunt and her husband, Sayyid Salih, and then joined the *peshmerga*.

The officer continued: "Let me make it clear to you: you can spare yourself further trouble by coming clean. All you need to do is to tell us who these people are who attack our revolution in *Shakh*, the subversive underground magazine. They publish this in the mountains, so how do they get submissions from people here in the city?"

I had indeed written a few pieces in the 1980s under the pseudonym Zamand for the then underground *The Kurdistan Writer*, the organ of the Kurdistan Writers' Union. But since they didn't mention this, I decided they probably didn't know about it. But what if they had the publication right there in the drawer? I told him that the information they had on me was not accurate and added, "And as for my brother, Kamal, well, I'm a prisoner. How could I know his whereabouts? I am a family man. He's only twenty years old; he doesn't live with us. He's responsible for himself; I'm responsible for myself."

The officer who interrogated me told me to shut up and said that I was not in prison to argue or give explanations. I had been arrested only to admit my crime.

Only, I had committed no crime.

The officer was not happy with what I had to say. He said they would get everything out of me by force. I was blindfolded yet again and taken back to my cell. On the way I was kicked repeatedly; twice I came close to slipping on the stairway. I had a feeling they knew I was innocent, but that it mattered little to them. I was afraid I would die under torture and that my family would be forever kept in the dark about it.

My friend Safeen was released on Saddam's birthday after doing five years, and what he'd told me about his experiences gave me some clue about what lay ahead for me. If I could bear the torture for a few months, I might turn out to be all right. Sentenced to die without a trial was of course a possibility. Ending up languishing in Abu Ghraib or Badush, two of Saddam's most notorious prisons, for years to come was another. I hadn't done anything wrong and I was determined to tell them that the next time they took me for interrogation. I also wanted to tell them again that as poet I only wrote about peace, love, and beauty.

I knew I had lost some weight because my pyjamas were very loose. I also was covered in rashes. I was desperate for a bath and for some good food. Imagine nothing else but bread and water every day.

I had cramps in my stomach and was constantly constipated. But to be denied pen and paper was simply beyond endurance. I wanted a complete record of my imprisonment, but I was afraid I couldn't rely entirely on memory. Pen and paper would've been my salvation.

I don't remember exactly when, but one day I realized I had not been tortured for days because my wounds were healing. I was allowed two visits to the toilet a day. The other prisoner and I were still tapping on the wall to stay in touch. The sound of doors opening and closing nearby made me realize that there were people all around me. Then one day, or one night, two men I had not seen before appeared. They blindfolded and handcuffed me.

One of them said, "The bastard's wounds have all healed."

"With these bastards the gun is the only answer," responded the other.

Like before, some punching and kicking followed as I was led away to what felt like a vehicle. No more than ten or fifteen minutes later the vehicle stopped. I had no idea which prison I was being brought to this time. There were hordes of prisons in Hawler that had been built by different sectors of government and military. It could have been any one of these. For some reason they decided I didn't need to be blindfolded anymore. Now I could see that we were at a police station. Inside, the handcuffs were removed and I was asked to wait. They gave the police officer in charge a slip of paper and I was then taken to room number four. He had a set of keys hanging from his army belt. He took the keys out, opened the door with one of them, and pushed me into a rectangular room. A group of people stood to my left and I could see their faces change the minute they saw the secret police.

The first three halls we passed were jam-packed with prisoners who all seemed to be talking at the same time. These ears of mine had no choice but to listen. Little sacks containing peoples' belongings were hanging on the walls. I saw some men knitting, making footwear or other things. Room number four could hardly accommodate twenty people, but they had put fifty in it. Many were forced to stand. While waiting by the door, I noticed how dirty my pyjamas were. They no longer looked blue, and one of the pockets and part of one knee, along with all the buttons, were missing. I thought if I had been arrested in my cream pyjamas, which were thicker, I would have been better off, especially now that fall was approaching.

Five men were standing near the door, and I had no choice but to stand next to them. For how long? I wondered. I asked one of the guys, and he said they had been standing since the previous day. There just wasn't any room to sit. The policeman said all the prisons were full and that since we were prisoners of the secret police, there was really nothing they could do to lessen our ordeal. He then locked the door and left. That was when I realized that I would have to spend the entire night standing.

Hope Fading

The guard opened the door and ordered us to move into a small open space to the left of the one door in the room. I wanted more than anything to be able to sit down, but there was no space in the over-crowded room. As in the previous three prisons I had been held in, prison number four also made it impossible to tell whether it was day or night.

From the minute we arrived, people were fighting with one another over space to stand in the room. Two fluorescent lights burned down on us permanently as we slept standing up. The old timers, those who had been in the room for a long time, slept on the floor. They lay on their sides, head to toe, packed in like slaves on a slave ship. A few had sunk onto their haunches because they were tired of standing but could not find a place to lie down. The crowded conditions made it difficult to see anything, but not long after I arrived, I discovered a little hole in the ceiling where the hallway met the courtyard, fifteen or so metres away. It was covered with iron mesh, but even without it a sparrow couldn't get through. It seemed as if it had once been a large window, but that someone had closed it in to make the opening a little smaller so that it would fit the criteria for a prison window. I noticed the hole sometimes looked pitch black, while at other times it looked grey, and this subtle change made me realize that I could now actu-ally tell when it was daytime or nighttime. I was thrilled. That window offered something to distract me while we stood.

The older prisoners didn't like waking up in the morning, but we
newcomers did. Those who had an urgent need to go to the toilet had
their hands on their stomachs; it looked like cramps had kept them
awake all night.

The only thing we would look forward to was the freedom to go to
the washroom. Some who were really anxious to go would not sleep
through the night; the desperate ones were forced to relieve themselves into plastic bags they smuggled in. In the morning, they would
line up at the door with their bags as soon as it was opened. They were
careful not to spill anything on the floor. Once, *Mam* Hawez, a restaurant owner from Koya who stood right next to me when I arrived,
accidentally spilled his bag and the security police tortured him for
two hours and then made him clean up the floor. That night, I had to
find myself a bag.

Those prisoners who did not need to relieve themselves and had
nothing to look forward to except the boredom and agony of another
day in prison lingered under their blankets for a little longer, their
faces showing disappointment and bitterness. Even the stories we
shared had to do with people relieving themselves. One of the stories
the prisoners were fond of telling involved this man Karim. It was just
a few minutes before midnight on December 31, 1986, and the prisoners were in the courtyard for a little celebration. Karim suddenly
decided to do something different: he squatted and started relieving
himself into what used to be a water fountain. As he did so, he declared
proudly, "The dump I'm taking will take two years to finish."

That first morning after our toilet break, we were all asked to gather
in the courtyard, where we joined the regular prisoners and other
political detainees. We were given a piece of bread and a cupful of
lentil soup, which I soon discovered was our food for the day. For water,
I had to borrow another prisoner's tin cup until I got my own. After
breakfast, we were ordered back into our rooms, and not much later,
a policeman appeared with a piece of paper in his hand. He asked the
two men whose names he read to follow him, and the men quickly
obliged, walking briskly behind the officer in their vests and sherwal,
traditional Kurdish trousers. They left behind their shirts for whoever

wanted them. We who remained behind could only speculate about
where they were taken or what became of them.

"Maybe they were taken for interrogation and the guards will
return them soon."

"Maybe they took them to be tortured."

"Maybe they took them to an isolated place where they will be
gunned down and their bodies will disappear without trace."

"Maybe they're releasing them, or just taking them to another
prison." Because we had been ignored for so long in prison, we wanted
to have our names called, whatever the reason.

We had been entertaining these and other possibilities for a while
when two other policemen came and ordered us to line up in the
hallway. They returned to the room in which we were being kept. I
craned my neck to see what they were doing. I could just see them,
pencils in hand, going about the task of dividing floor space up by
drawing a system of lines. I slowly realized then that they were giving
us our own space to stand in: each prisoner had to squeeze himself
between two lines less than thirty-five centimetres apart.

It occurred to me that my pyjamas no longer looked blue at all; dirt
had taken over the colour. I remembered how blue they were when
they were new, and how much bluer they looked under the spring
sun when I would go and pick grape leaves in our little garden for my
wife's dolma—rice, spices, and minced meat all stuffed together in a
vine leaf.

As the two policemen emerged from the room after marking the
floor, one of them threw me the blankets that had belonged to one of
the two guys who had just been taken away; that was upsetting in
itself, but even more so was not knowing what had happened to them.
It saddened me to realize that I could have easily been one of them.
Then they ordered us back into the room, to our assigned spaces. I was
still thinking about these two men who had recently joined us when
one of the other prisoners standing near me greeted me. He looked
calm and rather handsome with his salt-and-pepper beard.

"I'm Hanna," he introduced himself. "My brother is Priest Yusuf."
From that, I knew right away he was a Christian.

It was as if Hanna's introduction made it easier for others to speak to me, for another prisoner interrupted: "From your clothes and liverish look, I can tell you've been here long. How long?"

"I really don't know. I don't even know what day it is," I responded. He grew silent.

Hanna was very calm and humble. He, too, was wearing pyjamas— white ones with broad brown lines. I noticed his black cap was a little too small for his head. As Hanna spoke, I learned he was his forties and was a priest from Shaqlawa, a beautiful tourist town half an hour's drive northeast of Hawler. He had been arrested in church, he told us, and even though he had a serious heart condition, the secret police didn't let him send for his medicine. Since we had no access to a doctor, all Hanna could do now was pray and hope he would be all right. Hanna would talk to me often, telling me about his life.

I also came to know Haider. He was one of the prison old timers who looked older than his forty-five years and was still in the same brown suit and red shirt he was wearing when they arrested him at his office about six months previous. He had, however, taken off his white tie.

Haider constantly railed against his son-in-law. "I'm here because my son-in-law and his wife have taken refuge in Sweden," he would complain. "Now, what I want to know is how the government found out? Tell me, who says it is bad to be a son-in-law? Just look at mine: he fucks my daughter and gets me arrested."

As the days passed, we got to know each other and our surroundings better. We would occupy our time telling each other our stories. It upset me to know that any one of these stories could be my own, and I worried for my family. Now that I had been assigned my space, the hole in the roof was almost directly opposite me, and the water fountain was in the opposite corner of the room to the left. Whenever someone needed a drink, he would have to take his cup and negotiate his way over to the fountain and back. Prisoners would lean outward, creating a parting along which you could shuffle. If someone was sleeping, you had to step over him carefully. Waking a sleeping prisoner would only start a fight.

The man who stood a few squares away from me, Kanabi, wore the same shirt and shawl as Haider. Kanabi had a farming background and told us about things that I, as a city person, had not known before. The story that sticks in my mind is the one he told us about the day his son was arrested.

"My son fled the army, and members of the secret police were everywhere looking for deserters. We built a spider hole in our court-yard," he confided in me. "There my son, Dler, would hide all day long; he even ate there. He would get out only at night. His younger brother would be outside until bedtime, looking out for military vehicles.

"I don't know how it all happened, but that day I had a feeling something awful was going to happen. I had just finished my morning prayer, and Dler had just gone back to his hole. The tea was brewing inside, and Dler's mother was preparing a breakfast of yoghurt and black-eyed beans. She put the food on a little tray and was about to ask my daughter, Ghazal, to take it to him when suddenly we heard a commotion outside. I could tell the men were speaking Arabic, even though I didn't understand a word. They kicked the outside door open and, with their Kalashnikovs at the ready, went straight for the hole. They kicked away the rug concealing it and had their Kurdish trans-lator ask Dler to raise his hands and come out. He was blindfolded and handcuffed, pushed and kicked several times before he was taken away.

"I had no idea where they took him, but the rumour in town was that army deserters would be taken to Harthiya near Baghdad, which was a horrific prison run by military intelligence. I found out about the place just before my arrest at the funeral for Salar, a man who had spent time there. I was a friend of Salar's brother.

"Salar was a soldier who didn't like where he was stationed in the Iran–Iraq war. Understandably, he didn't want to be killed in a point-less war. So he fled, but unfortunately for him, he was caught at the bus station and taken to a prison in Harthiya. He was made to stand on his feet for an entire month. He and the other prisoners were given just enough room to stand. Bread would be thrown to them from a hole in the roof. Frequently it would land on their shoulders. They had to manoeuvre it to their mouths with their heads.

"Drinking was even harder. Hoses would be lowered from the ceiling; if the person was lucky, the sprays of water would land near his face. But the most gruesome part of their experience was that they were not allowed to go to the toilet; the prisoners literally had to stand in their own shit and urine, day in and day out."

At least we still get water in a cup, and can go to the toilet, I thought to myself as Kanabi continued with his story. My thoughts drifted to my own family, and I wondered what had happened to them after that night when I heard them at prison number one. I forced these thoughts out of my head and listened to Kanabi finish his story.

"Salar's family finally managed to get him out by paying an exorbitant amount in bribes. When he got home, he told us that they would let the bodies of those who didn't survive in prison rot before removing and throwing them to the stray dogs roaming around the prison compound. The dogs seemed to be doing quite well on human flesh," Kanabi said wryly. "It was too scary to look at Salar when he got out. His family had to carry him everywhere. They took him to all the big-name doctors, but in the end his gangrene-infested legs had to be amputated from the thigh down. I think it was this, losing part of his body, that eventually killed him."

Kanabi looked at me with an expression of great pain in his eyes. "Maybe that's where my son Dler is. That morning when they took my son, the secret police also arrested me and told me I should've informed them about what Dler had done and where he was hiding."

On the day Kanabi told his story, a miracle happened—well, sort of. We had grown accustomed to our assigned spaces, and we resented it when the guards brought in new prisoners to share the little space we already had. After Kanabi's story, we receded into our own thoughts until the guards opened the door to shove a few more prisoners into the space by the door. I could not believe my eyes! One of the new prisoners was my brother, Jamal. I still do not know how I moved myself through the mass of bodies in the room, but the next thing I knew we were hugging and kissing. I immediately began to negotiate with Haider and managed to get him to agree to exchange places so that Jamal could be near me—about halfway down the wall to the left of the doorway. It was really nice to have him next to me. Jamal didn't have much news, but he did not have to say much since his story was familiar to all of us. I looked him over carefully: he looked healthy enough.

We did not talk long at that first meeting, but I knew that people who came into this room did not leave soon. There would be plenty of time to talk. I stood in silence for a long time. There were too many thoughts drifting through my head. The other prisoners gave us two brothers time for ourselves. When we had done talking, we just stood there, wrapped in our own thoughts.

Eventually, Hanna looked at us and said quietly, "I was deep in prayer when they came for me. I was praying for peace. They told me that my son was a member of the Iraqi Communist Party. I told them I was a man of faith; I had nothing to do with that. But they just shut me up and took me away."

Hanna had been in the room for five months and after that amount of time, words can no longer tell the whole story. Having spoken, he returned to his own thoughts.

••• All of us in the room were classified as political prisoners. There were also quite a few conventional prisoners; they were housed in a separate area. Some of the charges against the conventional prisoners were serious: manslaughter, sex with a minor, and rape; others had committed petty crimes. One of the serious crimes involved three guys raping a girl at a cemetery; she was left there completely naked. The most hated prisoner was Haji, a notorious child molester. Among the petty criminals was one who had sold photographs of a naked behind, claiming it belonged to Suhair Zaki, an Egyptian belly-dancing star. In the end, it turned out the photographs were of his own backside.

There was an old man among us by the name of Soran who was well versed in the history of the city. Soran had seen the building we were in before it was converted to a prison.

"This used to be an inn," Soran told the prisoners who had gathered to listen to his story. "In the summer, villagers would come to the city with their loads of fruit, mostly grapes and figs, as well as snow that they had stored in the mountains since winter. Their donkeys and mules would rest here for the night. All around were open fields in which the animals roamed and grazed freely. This water fountain," Soran said, pointing to the tiny water fountain in the corner of the room, "used to be a lot bigger. It was for the animals." He remembered one incident when a horse had refused to drink from this fountain and they had to take it all the way to Pirdoka Creek on the other side of town.

"The way Soran describes it, it is obvious the animals had more rights than us; they certainly had more freedom," reflected Wasman, who stood to my left.

"Absolutely," Soran continued. "Back then Iraq was a monarchy, and the government was basically decent and civil. But under this current regime even the animals have suffered. The farmers make donkeys and horses work really hard and then, once they become old or sick, they just abandon them. Some have become wild. Without these animals, the farmers cannot supply all the military outposts the government has built on every hill and mountaintop. Some of the farmers got tired of the daily routine and committed suicide after the uprising. Shepherds and hunters found many mouldy bodies in the valley."

We were largely unaware of many of the catastrophic events that were taking place outside the prison walls. But later, after our release, it would become all too terribly real as the resistance to Saddam's regime intensified.

Knowing this prison was once an inn made me think about what all the poor donkeys and mules had to endure and how little they got in return. How were we any different than these animals, I wondered.

I must have drifted off in my own thoughts for a while because when I returned to the conversation, Soran had finished his story and had gone back to his spot. To escape the ever-present gaze of the fluorescent light, I covered my face with the blanket and dozed off.

A Hill of Blankets

When the cell door opened and we were taken to be given our usual piece of bread and cup of soup, I realized how much I missed not being able to go for walks. We had to wait in the corridor for a while before being allowed to go outside, so I tried to walk a little in the corridor, but with it being so narrow, I just didn't have the energy to push my way through a crowd of prisoners. At last we moved down the corridor and into the courtyard. As I leaned against the courtyard railing, I noticed that I could see the top of the city's only microwave tower, which helped me realize where I was: within the proximity of the governor's office complex, the *Kurdistan Press*, and all those streets I had been so fond of walking. It was that time of the day when people headed home. The sight of the barbed wire was like a knife cutting through the sky. Beyond the barbed wire, two clouds hung in the sky. Because they were so far away, I could barely see that they were moving. As the clouds gradually turned orange in the fading sun, my mind filled with romantic thoughts.

We tried to ration our conversation and talk about the things that would make us look forward to one day at a time. That is how it happened that I had been in prison number four for almost two weeks before I overheard some of the prisoners talking about visiting time. I wasn't expecting any visitors myself, for I wasn't sure if anyone in my family knew where Jamal or I were being kept.

The news about visitation surprised me. "But I thought we were not allowed visitors," I remarked to Haider, the man who was rude about his son-in-law.

"That's true, but regular prisoners are allowed visitors. You arrived here just after the last visit, so no one talked about that subject again until now. The regular prisoners are allowed visitors once every two weeks and some people come pretending to be visiting them when in fact they come looking for us. The regular prisoners know that but they don't mind."

Haider continued. "We begin visiting day by piling all our blankets on top of one another. We take turns standing on them to look through that hole in the ceiling to see if any of our people have come. The idea is to try to make eye contact with them."

Haider was, of course, pointing to the hole I had discovered shortly after my arrival. From where I stood along the opposite wall, I wondered how much a pile of blankets would help anyone to see a thing through that hole. The hole was about fifteen foot off the ground and barely a foot wide. It was covered with a mesh grid. This could be interesting to watch. I shrugged and began the long wait for the morning.

In the morning everyone got up energetically and passed their blankets to the prisoners who were standing beside the hole. Shabib, the man appointed by the security police as our leader and mediator with the guards, took control of the affair, directing everyone. The prisoners standing around the hole piled the blankets up until they formed a wall about five foot high. And then we waited. Shabib reminded us that because there were now six prisoners more than there were the previous time, each person would get to stand on the pile of blankets for no more than a minute.

"A minute will be more than enough," Haider remarked. "All one can do is look and gesture a few times." He then added, "I can't understand why killers and child molesters are allowed to spend time with their family and we're not. I miss my little daughter so badly—they took me away from her before she learned to call me *baba*."

As we waited, we talked about many things. Soon, however, the conversation returned to how people had ended up in this prison. Today, Uncle Mustafa, the resident apostate, had his turn. Uncle Mustafa was fifty years old and wore a black coat and green pants. As usual, he railed on about what he would do when he was free and about how he had lost his faith. He was put in prison because his son had run away from military service and joined the *peshmerga*. "My biggest regret," I heard him say piously, "is that I didn't turn my back against Islam sooner. What can prayer and fasting accomplish? Nothing. I have had it with religion. The moment I'm out, I'll be keeping company with my old friend Magha and his drinking buddies and will have nothing to do with religion anymore."

I have mentioned that I am a bad host and a bad listener. I had heard this story before and so instead of listening to Uncle Mustafa drone on in the background, my thoughts drifted to my friend Abd. One thing about Abd was that he knew how to make a good story last. Before I came to the prison, he always used to tell us about his authoritarian father bullying him into fasting during Ramadan. He was only seven years old when it started.

"I don't recall my father ever calling me by my name or using a polite word with me," Abd always began his story. "He would drag me out of bed just before the morning prayer for our only meal until sundown, and make me eat two *nawsers*, whether I was hungry or not. In winter, my mother would deep-fry the thin pastry-like flatbread in the same room where we slept. It made everything and everyone smell awful. After we'd eaten, my father would make me drink plenty of water before ordering me back to bed. By noon I would be hungry, but breaking my fast was out of the question. That would result in my being send straight to Jahanam, my father would say.

"When my grandmother found out about my fasting, she tried to talk me into giving it up. 'You're not eight yet; you're not required to fast,' she said. 'You can break your fast by midday every day, and I'll sew up your half days into full days without any problem.' I liked her idea, but I was still reluctant to break my fast. Father had told me that eating anything during Ramadan would taste like eating your own flesh, and that once in Jahanam there would be no escape; the burning in hell's fires was never ending. I believed him."

Even thinking about Abd telling us this story made me long for my friend's company. I knew how the story went from here: Abd would tell us how his sister, Kalthoum, was only six years old when their father forced her to wear a head scarf and sent them both off to madrasah at the mosque. What I always found most amusing was when Abd told us what lessons he had learned at the mosque, and so I would listen eagerly as Abd reached that point in his story. "Young as I was," Abd would tell his listeners, "I realized there was money to be made through religion, and then I did not mind Kalthoum having to cover her head and us having to go to mosque together. You see, my father never gave me—or my sister—pocket money, not even during the big religious holidays, like other fathers did. It was during one of these holidays when I realized I could put my meagre knowledge of the Qu'ran to good use.

"The day before Eid-al-Fitr, Sheikh Omar Cemetery would be teeming with people. Everyone wanted a man of religion to come and recite a few passages from the Qu'ran in memory of their dead. Even though I was still a kid, no one seemed to mind if I stood in for the cleric. I could smell the blue smoke of burning cyclamen in the air as worshippers burned cyclamen on the graves. Through the scent of the *bxor*, I could hear the sound of women crying in memory of the dead. As I approached, they would call on me to read a passage in the Qu'ran for those occupying the graves that surrounded them. As I began reading, the sound of the verses from the Qu'ran made them stop crying, and they felt good as they headed home to celebrate Eid. I was also happy, because they paid me one dinar for each reading. That was easy money for me—all I had to do was read the passage and take the Qu'ran back to the mosque in a rush before going home to eat my Eid dinner and celebrate."

Just like Abd, I had grown up poor, and in many ways, his story reminded me of fragments from my own childhood. Whenever Abd reached the part where he would tell us about how his family raised chickens so they could eat them on Eid, my mouth would water. And after that, he would say, "The celebration of Eid started early in the morning as people ate their big meal in the morning. My father didn't buy me a new set of clothing every Eid, which is what happened with the other kids; instead he bought one set every two Eids. I would tuck them away carefully so I would be able to wear them again. To make them look as if they were new, my mother would wash my clothes two days in advance and tuck them away under a pillow because we did not have an iron. Although I had tried everything I could to make them look as if they were new, I still felt a little embarrassed in the morning as I walked towards my friends. But that embarrassment would soon disappear when we got to spend money on sweets, games, and going to the cinema. As there were kids from a variety of backgrounds, I was not the only one with an old set of clothes.

"The highlight of the morning was going to the movies. I was just crazy about any movie with Hercules in it! He was my hero," said Abd.

I, too, liked to watch movies when I was a teenager. My favourites were Indian movies, love stories where the two lovers never ended up together and were left broken-hearted. I remember the most powerful love story of all—it was called *Sangam* and ran for three months. It left all the boys coming out of the theatre with tears in their eyes.

But Abd's story did not end with the movies. His distrust of religion came from other experiences with the mullahs. "Whenever I was at the mosque," I remember him telling me, "I noticed that Mullah Nasser was in the habit of rubbing his body against mine when we sat down on the carpet for my lesson. He would press his thigh against mine and place his mouth so near to mine that I could smell his awful breath. I was too shy to tell him to back off or make him realize he was hurting my thigh. I also thought that since the mosque was supposed to be God's home, no harm would come to me. I didn't tell my father about this because he would not have believed me. But the word spread anyway, thanks to a junior mullah who was living and working in the mosque. One day, Mullah Nasser was there no more. People said he had gone away for a while because of poor health, but he never came back."

In 2005, after my release from prison and after we had settled in Canada, I returned to Kurdistan, where I met up with my old friend Abd. He asked if I remembered Mullah Nasser. I needed some prodding.

"The man who molested me," he noted. I still looked vague, so Abd just continued: "Well, after the collapse of Taliban in Afghanistan, he escaped to the Iranian border, and now he is leading a group of extremists, brainwashing youth to commit suicide, and paying children money to slingshot unveiled women."

Mam Mustafa had reached the end of his story. Kno, the prison buffoon whose ignorance about his surroundings was astounding, applauded. "I'm forty-five years old," he said. "Not even once in my life have I prayed, and I'm determined to stay out of religion. But I cannot blame Allah for where I am. Imprisonment, after all, is a man's verdict, not Allah's. I started drinking when I was sixteen. Back then there were only two kinds of beer, Shahrazad and Lager, and for a while I was hooked on Shahrazad. Then I discovered Baghdad arrack, which was quite potent, and I loved it. When that became scarce during the Iran-Iraq war in 1980, I switched to this other brand called Haddad, which came from Jordan. But I just couldn't afford it. Then someone told me about bootleg arrack made by the Christians of Ankawa. It was cheap, but good. Night after night we would get so wasted at a very nice club called Nadi Tijara [Commerce Club]. Access to this club was restricted to traders and you needed an ID to get in. We could not go in, but always went with our friend, Jami, who did have an ID and knew the man at the reception. They had a very good shish kebab and every night, I would have a quarter litre of arrack and two shish kebab. By the time the club closed we were so wasted we had to be taken home in a cab.

"Some of my neighbours didn't approve of my drinking. They would sometimes instigate the neighbourhood boys to chase after me with stones and filthy words, and one time they beat me up really bad. I had bruises all over. What a way to raise children! Instead of teaching them how to play ball or fly a kite, they made them behave like common criminals. But none of their tricks would stop me."

On Fridays, Kno told those who were still listening, they would all get into their friend Bijou's car and head for the highway leading to Masief, which was situated in the mountains some twenty minutes' drive from Hawler. At that time, Masief was still a tourist attraction. Before the military coup in 1958, King Faisal built some cabins and hotels with swimming pools there, and visitors from all over Iraq would go there for vacations and honeymoons. During the uprising in 1991, however, all the cabins were destroyed, and Masief ceased to be a tourist area.

"By late afternoon," Kno continued, "both sides of the road would be jammed with people like us. The drinking and the lamb barbeque would continue well into the night. It was on one such night, after I got home and was unwinding to the voice of Majko, my favourite singer, that the secret police came for me. They dragged me out of my house and kicked and punched me as hard as they could. My hangover dissipated instantly.

"The only reason they came for me was because of my son. He was a big liar. He spent the better part of his time taking care of his flock of pigeons instead of finishing high school. When he turned eighteen, he had to report for military service and was taken straight to the front-line near Dezful, the area that had seen some of the fiercest fighting in the Iran-Iraq war. In 1986, he managed to get a few days off by bribing one of his superiors. When he got home, he decided not to go back.

"The next day his mother arranged for him to go and join the *peshmerga* near Koya. She would go and visit him regularly in secret, making sure he was well supplied with food and cigarettes. You know, when I look back, I wish my son was more like me. Had he been a coward like me, he would not have become a *peshmerga* and I wouldn't be here today. That day I was captured, the traffic was calm and the streets almost empty, but I wish it had been a Friday so that there was a traffic jam. If that was the case, I would have gotten home later and the police would have taken me later and I would have been in prison two hours less."

And so the stories continued until about mid-morning, when we heard a commotion in the courtyard. Visiting time had arrived.

Shabib was the first to get on the pile of blankets. He stood right across from me in the room, straight under the hole. The young man swung his tall muscular frame onto the pile of blankets. He stood up straight and stretched his arms above his head, but even then he was still about a metre shy of the grid. His dark face grew serious as he bent his head back to see through the hole. "There are many visitors today," he reported.

When Shabib got down, he immediately began to organize the prisoners in an orderly way, as he always did. He timed them carefully and precisely, making sure no one stayed up on the blankets longer than the allotted one minute.

When it was Uncle Rostam's turn, he said, "Let me remind you, fellows, I have two wives and eighteen children. I therefore deserve to stand here twice as long as everyone else. I need the extra time because so far I've been able to see only my younger wife."

Everyone laughed and teased him about that. "Now we know why you're always in a hurry to get out of here, Rostam," they shouted.

Rostam waved his chubby arms and his brown pyjamas flapped in the air. "I miss my wife," he replied. "She is only twenty-seven. I only have five children from her—I used her mostly during nighttime."

Uncle Rostam tried to lift his short legs into the blanket pile, but his stomach got in the way. Uncle Rostam was very fond of his food and always hurried to get out of the cell in the mornings. After struggling for a bit, he turned to the prisoners behind him. "Come on fellows, give an old man some help." Two of the prisoners pushed him from behind. Uncle Rostam leaned on their shoulders as he teetered on the pile of blankets. When he regained his balance, he pushed himself up.

Mam Rostam spoke into the hole, saying to his younger wife, "Sewey, how are you with Xarman? Don't tell me that you two are fighting!"

Sewey shouted back in the hole loudly enough for us all to hear, "No, since you have been imprisoned, we have stuck together like sisters and have no problems."

Mam Rostam did not respond to what she said and asked instead, "Who is that child beside you?"

"It is your son, Magdid," Sewey replied.

"He has grown big!" *Mam* Rostam replied with surprise.

As Uncle Rostam continued talking, I could not help thinking how difficult it must be balancing two wives, especially when one wife is younger than the other.

Before Uncle Rostam could ask any more questions, Shabib said, "*Mam* Rostam, your time is up." Uncle Rostam put his one hand on his turban and jumped down. Haider, who was next in line, steadied the old man as he landed.

Haider climbed onto the hill of blankets. He spoke into the hole, to someone we could not see. It must have been his wife, because Haider's first question was to ask whether his son's grave was still intact. "Who is the shepherd who now takes care of the sheep?" he asked next.

"I couldn't hear anything," he complained when he jumped down at the end of his turn.

And so it went, one prisoner after another. When it was my turn, I jumped up and looked into the patch of sky above me. As I expected, I didn't see anyone I knew, but the sight of all this great food— kebabs, dolma, yoghurt, salad, and much, much more—the visitors had brought along for the regular prisoners made me want to jump through the hole and grab some. Fortunately, the other prisoners always found a way to smuggle some of the food into our cell. I spoke to anyone who happened to be near the hole, and it just happened that I was lucky enough to find someone who could at long last send word to my family about my and Jamal's situation.

Some Shocking News

There was very little space left in our room with all the new prisoners who had been brought in. Sleeping sitting on one's haunches or lying on one's side on the floor was no fun at all. In addition to various kinds of skin rashes, sleeping on the floor day in and day out and always on the side, and with nothing to sleep on except a couple of dirty old blankets, gave us all kinds of aches and pains and made us feel terribly depressed most of the time.

Just across from me was a man called Abdullah, but we all just called him Sharbat because when he was still free, he sold *sharbat* for a living on the streets of Koya. *Sharbat* means "juice" in Kurdish and Sharbat made his juice from grapes, which was very popular. More than anything else, Sharbat used to tell us, it was the smell of the blankets he couldn't stand. And he was right, the blankets were filthy and stinky.

"It'll be like a dream getting into a clean bed again," Sharbat told me one day. "For me, a clean bed and good food comes before anything else. Even as a child I liked these things—everyone in my family knows that. My daughter must have known I would be arrested one day because a month before I was arrested, she began to cook dolma, kebab, and kofta for dinner every week. She didn't care about my high blood pressure. She was only interested in fattening me up more than I already was," Sharbat joked about his weight. "She also set aside a clean cotton *doshag*, a pillow, and a blanket, all tied neatly into a bundle, for me to take along when the dreaded day came. To make the clean smell last longer, she sprayed them all with her favourite perfume.

"The perfume she used always reminded me of this one particular evening in 1983, when they brought the body of Doctor Azad back to Koya. He was another casualty of the Iran-Iraq war. They kept his body in a freezer at the hospital for weeks, but for them to get it back to Koya, they had to take it out. The family tied the coffin to the roof of a Toyota and drove like that for ten hours from the south of Iraq to Koya with the corpse in the hot sun. In the mosque, they opened the coffin and we all had to cover our noses. This was of course something embarrassing to do, but the smell was just too overpowering to bear—absolutely horrible. Until then I had no idea how terribly awful the human body could smell. The situation made me realize how easily we can all be deceived by vanity into thinking that we can always be in the best of shape and condition.

"The men from the mosque went about their task without delay. They took out the body, washed it thoroughly, drenched it with rose water, and then wrapped it neatly in a plain white sheet before placing it on a wooden stretcher for the men to carry to the cemetery. It still smelled awful. Now when I smell blankets, I can only think of Doctor Azad, and not my daughter's kindness."

Sharbat paused for a while as we all took in what he had told us. Death was not an unfamiliar thing among the Kurds, but it hit home when you describe it the way he did. It became personal.

After a while, Sharbat started telling us more about his arrest. "My son, Aza, joined the *peshmerga*. He was in the 21 Kirkuk Battalion, so I knew it was only a matter of time before I would get arrested. I didn't have the energy to join the *peshmerga* again. You see, I was a *peshmerga*, too, from 1965 to 1970, the year our revolution suddenly crumbled. For all of us, that was too much to bear. So I threw my rifle into the Choman rapids and returned to the city a broken man. Later on, the government arrested me along with thousands of Kurdish people and sent us south to Al-Ramadi. Being sent away from Kurdistan to the heart of Wahabi Iraq was bad enough, but then they put us in the hands of the local authorities, who kept us in a detention centre for two years before letting us come back to Kurdistan. After we were released from the compound we lived in all that time, some of my comrades sought refuge in Europe, Canada, and the U.S., but I saw no point in going into exile in a Western country.

"You see, you can't fight a government that oppresses your people with a gun alone. You've got also to have international backing, and not just from any country. At least one powerful country needs to be there for you, and not just for tactical reasons, as was the case in our situation, but for the right reasons. Ours has been a painful situation: today this country says it's with us, and we trust it; but tomorrow it stabs us in the back. Isn't that what Iran and Iraq did to us in 1975 with help from Henry Kissinger?"

Sharbat was of course referring to the Algiers Accord signed on March 6, 1975. It was an initiative led by the Algerian president, Houari Boumedien, the Shah of Iran, and Saddam Hussein. According to this agreement, the Shah would withdraw Iranian support for the Kurdish revolution. As a result, the resistance collapsed.

Sharbat paused to regain control of his anger before getting back to his story.

"Aza and I were doing some renovations on the house after my wife passed away. One day we decided it was time to go for a major overhaul. The renovations kept us busy for a while and our next-door neighbour kindly offered to help by making the pasta for us that summer so that we could work on the house. Like every other family, we usually made enough pasta during the summer to last us through the winter and spring.

"I was always hoping to keep myself out of jail a little longer, so I would not sleep in the same house twice in a row. Wherever I would be for the night, my grandson, Zimnako, would be by my side, and he would quickly go and fetch the bedding my daughter had put aside for me. I hoped they would let me take the bed with me, but when they came for me that one night and started kicking and punching me, I knew that was not going to happen. I did manage to put my tablets for high blood pressure and stomach ache in my pocket before they pulled me out of the house. Fortunately, they did not search my pockets."

It was already very late, and Ako, one of the other prisoners in a space near ours, stretched his neck out from under the blanket and asked, "What are you two talking about? I thought I heard you talking about us being let go. Well, maybe I was just dreaming or just hearing things. Maybe this time round there's some truth in the rumours floating around. Maybe our release is near."

By now, more people had woken up. Uncle Sharbat, however, was tired and closed his eyes. A fellow whose name I can't recall said, "Sooner or later, the day will come when we can put all this behind us. They can't keep us here forever."

The man's words pleased Ako, and his face glowed a little. He said, "Sweet words come from heaven."

Release was always on our minds; we never got tired of talking about it. It was seldom absent from our dreams. Sometimes we actually felt it was going to happen by just talking about it. This made our disappointment all the more bitter. Sharbat and I carried on talking quietly, and twice more Ako stretched his head out from under the blankets. Finally Wali, another prison neighbour, asked him if he was going to sleep at all.

In reply, Ako simply said, very softly, "I miss my children all day long, but at night I only think of my wife. It is just so hard for me to be without her. I can tolerate the day, but not the night."

It was very late already when Ako finally grew quiet. Ako came from a village that had neither electricity nor running water and he had been married to his wife for thirty years. Even after all those years they had spent together, his feelings for her were still remarkably strong and he missed her terribly. He loved to tell us details about his private life. His biggest complaint was that luck was seldom on his side.

In Kurdistan it is very rare for a husband and wife to sleep in one bed. In 2003, when my oldest daughter came back from a visit to Kurdistan, she asked her mother, "When will you and Dad sleep in separate beds?" So it was not strange for us to hear about how Ako and his wife had slept in their separate beds.

Ako would tell us how he and his wife had had to share the room with his parents, two younger brothers, and a twelve-year-old sister when they got married. Only a curtain separated the newlyweds from the rest of the family. Every day, his mother would enquire about the events of the previous night. "So what happened?" she'd say. "Where's the white piece of cloth I gave you? Still no blood on it?" Ako told us how embarrassed he was by his mother's questions and how he always would say, "Mother, be patient. Tomorrow night, I promise." He just couldn't do it with all those people around him.

Ako woke up again. Since I had been thinking about his marriage story, I asked him to tell it to us again. "From where you say 'Tomorrow night,'" I prompted him.

Ako sat up with a sad look on his face and began his story. "On the fourth day, early in the morning, I saw an opportunity. My brothers had gone to school, my little sister, Shno, was outside playing with other girls, and my father was enjoying the morning sun. My mother was out somewhere—I can't remember where. Quickly, I pulled my wife into the room, grabbed a foam mattress, and began fondling her. She was shy and nervous, and didn't seem to be interested. She was afraid someone might come. I had reached a point of no return. I forced her legs open, pulled down her undergarment and my sherwal. I was shaking everywhere.

"But I must say this was nowhere as risky as the time when I was teenager and I did it to a donkey. I placed some rocks under my feet in order to reach the hole, but even though I couldn't reach it, I still managed to have a strong orgasm. It was at this exact moment, as I was trying to pull up my sherwal, when I lost my balance and crash landed on the rocky ground below. I went home with a broken hand. This time around, the situation was definitely much better."

At this point, Uncle Sharbat suddenly woke up. He seemed to be in a good mood. "You know what I'd like?" he asked.

"What?" I asked.

"I'd like going back to my village, Nazaneen. I imagine lying down in a clean bed on the rooftop of my little mud house, which my family built in the middle of our pomegranate orchard, and I imagine my hand stretching into a tree and then returning with a juicy sweet and sour pomegranate. I remember when I was a child, my family and I would spend the whole summer in the orchard. We could reach out and pick pomegranates and figs right from where we slept."

"Thanks, *Mam* Sharbat, once again your speech took me off into a cloud," I whispered.

I could tell it was somewhere around four o'clock in the morning because outside, a muezzin was calling the faithful to prayer. The floor of our cell room looked like a deserted battlefield with the dead and the wounded left behind. I forced myself to crawl in under my blanket. It felt like being buried under a pile of trash.

The smell from our blankets had become so bad that one morning our guard, Sergeant Hassan, felt it necessary to do something about it. "Quickly, take your blankets to the rooftop," he said. "Leave them under the sun and let them air out for the day—and come down immediately."

Just going onto the roof was an exciting change for us, for even though we were not allowed to linger there, just seeing the big sky for a moment or two was a delight. Someone said that he saw a caravan of cars on the main thoroughfare, indicating that a wedding was in progress. Another said, "What do you expect? Do you really expect life to come to a standstill because of us?"

Zrar responded, "I doubt that anyone beside our families are thinking of us."

"But why do you think we're here?" another man asked in exasperation. "We're here because we want to liberate our people from oppression! Every one of them down there owes us a big debt of gratitude."

For me, the most satisfying thing about the rooftop trip was to be able to have one good look at Mount Safeen. From afar and through the summer dust, it looked majestically picturesque; dark blue. I am a writer, and even in prison poems took shape in my head. I would memorize the lines so that I'd know them when I once again knew the joy of holding a pen. That night, the lines in my head were:

The prison walls are high,
My memories are intimate.
I can bring life through these walls, into this place.
Here,
Frequently,
The policeman comes,
A pile of keys in his hand,
And while still walking,
And quickly finding the right key,
Locks us all behind without delay.
Here,
Death is always behind the door.
They imprison a nation by prolonging death.
Which way do you come?
Through the wall?
Through memories?
Or through my soul?

It was our dream in prison to be called to throw away the garbage. Whenever the policemen needed to dispose of the garbage, they always called on four prisoners to do the work. The prisoners would fight each other for the task because it meant being able to spend a little extra time outside.

Two or three days after our rooftop visit, a policeman entered the room and said simply: "In two hours you'll all be gone from here. The order has come from the Directorate General of Security." We stood there in shocked silence as the policeman ordered everyone in the room to gather their meagre belongings, fold their blankets, and wait. We were afraid and bewildered. As I folded my blanket, I remembered that this blanket had once belonged to a man who was called away by the police.

When the policemen returned, they had us walk towards the back door, where a huge covered truck was waiting. We got in as fast as we could. The sluggish ones were kicked and pushed and two of them ended up with bruises on their noses from falling face down.

As soon as the last prisoner got into the truck, the driver pulled away. We couldn't tell exactly where the truck was heading.

Prison Number Five

There was still a general feeling of apprehension among all of us when the truck pulled up behind what seemed to be a newly constructed cinder-block building. A narrow pathway led to a fairly spacious court-yard, but the high walls, surrounded by barbed wire, made the place look forbidding. The speed and eagerness with which the prisoners got out of the vehicle made Sharbat, who took his time to get off, wonder if the prisoners really thought they were about to be released. "Why the rush, fellows?" he asked. "It's just another prison."

"Be thankful. At least they didn't take us to be executed," someone behind us shouted.

Following a brief lineup in the courtyard, we were taken into a room with a rather small door. We were told to stand against the wall and lay our blankets down in front of us. That was all. When they had finished giving us the instructions, the guards locked the door and left abruptly. As we unfolded the blankets, we noticed that the room was actually spacious enough for all of us to be able to sleep on our backs, something we hadn't been able to do in the previous prison. This extra space felt like a luxury to us.

Lying down on his back, one of the prisoners, Zahir, remarked that the whole thing felt like a dream. "I can't believe this is me," he said. We all felt the same way.

It took us a while to get used to sleeping on our backs again. However, this little luxury was not to last. Little by little, more and more prisoners were brought in, making the place as crammed as the previous one. So once again, we had to modify how we slept.

Even today, some twenty years later, here in Canada, I still find myself sleeping at the edge of our double bed. I think this is how I came to have this sharp pain in my right leg; doctors tell me nothing can be done. Thank goodness for painkillers.

Basic facilities, including sanitary ones, were in awful shape in all of Iraq's prisons. This one, though fairly new, was no exception. There was no heating or cooling system to speak of, just one tiny window high above the door. Inside, it was oven hot in the summer and ice cold in winter. The fan hanging from the ceiling turned day and night, but it only succeeded in making a disturbing noise and spreading the same dirty old air around the room. This new prison did not have a hole in the roof like the previous prison, and from time to time I missed the fresh air that came in through the hole and the ability to see when it was dawn. In the new prison it was not as easy to see what time of day it was.

At night, we could hear the Army firing their guns nearby, so I knew we had to be somewhere in the west of Hawler in the area controlled by the government. The area was littered with secret police buildings, training camps, and prisons. In this prison, we were allowed into the courtyard every day. Some evenings when the officer in charge, Colonel Rayid, was away, Sergeant Hassan would let us stay out a little longer. It was the perfect time to watch the sun going down behind the tree in the courtyard. I always looked forward to that and also to seeing a flock of birds high up in the sky. It gave me a strong sense of relief to see the outside world, and it made me want to get out of prison more than ever. The beauty of the night sky mingled with the sadness I felt about my surroundings. But at least being outside allowed my mind to soar beyond the prison walls, with the birds.

Sergeant Hassan's whistle meant that the sun had gone down and that it was time for us to go in. It was usually around this time when Haider would have something to say.

"*Mamosta* Jalal," he told me sadly as soon as we were in, "I'm going crazy—absolutely crazy. I'm getting desperate for my children. It is not just one or two: there are ten of them, and most of them are still too little to understand what's happening to their *baba*. I don't deserve this; I have done nothing wrong.

"You know, my father was a shepherd all his life—that's how I came to be one myself. I also learned how to play the pipe from him. Once he told me, 'You won't learn how to play the pipe until you become a shepherd. Once you become a shepherd, you also begin to appreciate nature a lot more. The moon and the peace and quiet that comes with being all by yourself for hours on end creates a special bond between you and nature.'

"I must have been sixteen when my father decided he could trust me with the task of looking after the flock, and as a token of his appreciation for my work, one day he gave me his own old pipe, which I had been eyeing for quite a while. I would take our sheep to the hills not far from the village and sit down to play my pipe. In my imagination I saw all the animals dancing. One night, we were all caught in a heavy downpour. I sat on a rock, tucked my pipe in my waistband, and took cover under my overcoat. I was afraid I might get hit by lightning. There was no let-up in the rain, and as I was pondering my options, I heard my father calling out for me. He was on horseback holding a lantern. He put me on the horse and took me home. 'What about the herd?' I asked. 'Don't you worry about that,' he replied. 'The dog is with them. They'll be safe.'

"When we got home, my mother had the wood stove ready. I lay down before the fire, and before long I was fast asleep. I think it was the exhaustion. Next day we found the herd at the village cemetery; they were still drenched.

"*Mamosta* Jalal, I cannot tell you how much I miss that day. I know, I know, it can never be brought back. But I miss it."

Secret Funeral

Not knowing when, if ever, our families would be able to find out where we had been taken was a big concern. Our hope was that they would get the word somehow through the people we left behind in the previous prison.

Zirak, a tiny young prisoner who had come from prison number four with us, was wearing a red T-shirt and strolling along the streets of Sirwan, wishing to see a girl when he was arrested. "It is not enough for them to know that we've been moved," he said, "they need to know where to."

Himdad, who seldom spoke while we were in the room, said, "They did have some idea that as prisoners of the secret police we would eventually be moved. It may take a while, but ultimately they will get to know where we are. The secret police are experts in keeping the whereabouts of their prisoners secret, but I think our situation may not warrant a measure this extreme."

Of late, Haider had been thinking a lot about the loss of his *peshmerga* son.

"Only two days after Azad was killed," he told me one day, "they came and arrested me. They did not even let me have a secret funeral. Word came through some of our relatives in the country that he had been shredded into pieces by a helicopter gunship, and that even though the area was a no-go zone for civilians, somehow they managed to get there and bury his remains. People had come to pay us their condolences when they came for me.

"Some of my relatives thought there might be a way to get me released since my son was no longer alive. They went to see the head of this Kurdish mercenary group, *Jash*, that had turned on the *pesh-merga* and had been working closely with the government. They had, of course, to pay him a handsome bribe. He suggested that they should go and dig my son's remains out, take a few snapshots, and show them to the secret police. The idea was that once they could determine that my son was no more, they would release me."

Sapan, a quiet prisoner who lived in Hawler, interrupted Haider. "That makes no sense," he said. "The secret police have files on everyone, the living and the dead. It is inconceivable that they didn't already know what had happened to your son. If they pretend otherwise, it is because they don't want to release you."

Haider lowered his head and began talking softly to himself. "They didn't even let me have a funeral or tamp down the soil on his grave to make it waterproof for the winter. Last winter was unusually wet, and nothing had been done to stop water from getting in. Azad was ever so careful not to put himself in danger; he said it was too risky to come and visit. He never saw his home again."

What had happened to Haider was not unusal. When Saddam Hussein was in power, funerals for those who had been killed during torture in prison and those who were *peshmerga* were forbidden. Families of the deceased would hold a memorial service in a secret room.

When we felt a little more comfortable around Sergeant Hassan, we begged him to get us some medicine for our persistent itches and rashes. At any one time, nearly everyone was scratching, not surprisingly, of course, considering we hadn't had a shower for months. He did get us some cream, but it had little or no effect.

One day, when Sergeant Hassan was by the door, I asked him if he would be kind enough to get me a pencil and some scrap paper. When he said, "I'll try," I couldn't believe it: pencil and paper were not allowed. But Sergeant Hassan kept his word and brought me what I had asked for. It meant so much to me. He could have easily gotten into a big trouble over that. I knew the consequences would be quite severe for me, too, but that's the way writers are: they seldom think about the consequences of what they do or write.

2 Early Childhood in the Age of the Village

Unknown Birthday

THE MOST DIFFICULT TIME IN MY LIFE, the most tragic for me, began on the day I was arrested. That is why I gave the incident priority, and made it the first chapter in my book, in the story of my life. Only then could I return to my unknown birthday, and childhood shadow, and from there again to what I remember of the journey of my life.

Before I came to Canada, I hardly thought about my birthday. This was because in Iraq and Kurdistan, hardly anyone celebrated birthdays. Except of course for Saddam, who celebrated on everyone's behalf, all seventeen million of us. Every year the government would spend millions of dollars on Saddam's birthday. The day was a national holiday. There would be official celebrations throughout the country, with one particular theme song leading the rest in popularity. Its first line, "With our soul and blood we sacrifice ourselves for you, our Leader-President," carried more weight than the national anthem. For several days nothing else would be shown on television except the celebrations, which would often feature Saddam appearing in a white suit, receiving gifts and adulation from the ruling party faithful and school children. Every citizen knew this wasn't a day to be ignored.

After the collapse of Saddam's regime, some of his private affairs came to light, among others that he sometimes changed his suit five times in one day. Or that high-placed officials who went to say happy birthday to him in person were afraid to get close and shake his hand. They would kiss him on the stomach or kissed the air between them. But they seldom touched him.

Whenever Saddam visited a village, people became very nervous and sacrificed many sheep in front of his feet to show him how they were celebrating his arrival. They baked fresh firewood bread, which he ate with the special long shish kebabs they made for him.

For the rest of the year, and during times of war, life was very diffi-cult for the Iraqi people. Yet through all poverty and shortages of all kinds of food, people dreamed of the long shish kebabs that had became a trend. After the collapse of his regime in Kurdistan people would go to restaurants and say "Can you make me Saddam's shish kebab, please?"

What made Saddam's birthday celebrations all the more bizarre was that there was something utterly false about birthdays in Iraq to begin with. My family's situation illustrates the point. Whenever I ask my mother about my birthday, all she can say is that my older brother Jamal is three years older than I am, and that he was born in the fall and that I was born in the spring of 1953. My wife, Sabah, is two years younger than I am; according to her mother she was born when there was still snow on the ground. And yet, on official documents we all share the same birth date: July 1. So do millions of other people in Iraq. This is a government-imposed date and it has nothing to do with our and other people's actual birthdays. What makes our situation all the more absurd is that, now that we're in Canada, where people do know their birthdays and birthdays do matter, we're stuck with our false birthdays, in all likelihood for the rest of our lives.

Ashkaftsaqa didn't have a birth registry, so none of the people in the village had any of these documents. Not that it would have

The Man in Blue Pyjamas
A Prison Memoir

Jalal Barzanji / Based on a translation by Sabah Salih

John Ralston Saul, Foreword

In his far too lightweight blue pyjamas, Jalal Barzanji was ripped out of his family and shoved into a nightmare underworld of beatings and raw prisons. Three times over the years since then he has had to rebuild his life.... The Man in Blue Pyjamas *is a generous creative act, for which I thank him.*

—John Ralston Saul, President of PEN International

From 1986–1989, Jalal Barzanji endured imprisonment and torture in an Iraqi prison because of his literary and journalistic activity. It was not until 1998, when he and his family took refuge in Canada, that he was able to consider speaking out fully on issues of peace, justice, and freedom. Ever an acute observer, Barzanji offers readers detailed portraits of life in the ancient Kurdish city of Hawler; in prison, he grounds readers with his ability to find moments of compassion and humanity amidst the relentless assault of Saddam Hussein's regime.

In 2007, Barzanji was appointed as Edmonton's first PEN Canada Writer-in-Exile. This poignant literary memoir is the product of that residency. *The Man in Blue Pyjamas* is his first work in English.

The style of my book must be in small pieces, as my life has been in pieces.

—Jalal Barzanji

Jalal Barzanji is a highly respected Kurdish poet and journalist. Since 1970 he has published seven books of poetry and numerous critical columns. After his three-year imprisonment by Saddam Hussein's regime in the late 1980s and further political repression into the 1990s, Barzanji and his family fled to Turkey. They remained there for eleven months, eventually immigrating to Canada.

288 pages • 34 B&W photographs, translator's preface, foreword, map
Wayfarer Series
6" × 9" • $24.95 (T) paper
ISBN-13-978-0-88864-536-4
Memoir/Human Rights/Kurdistan

Also available in ePub:
$19.99 (T) ePub
ISBN-13-978-0-88864-611-8

The University of Alberta Press

For more information or to obtain books for review or examination, please contact:

Cathie Crooks
Sales/Marketing Manager

The University of Alberta Press
Ring House 2, University of Alberta
Edmonton, AB, Canada, T6G 2E1

P: 780-492-5820
F: 780-492-0719

E: ccrooks@ualberta.ca
W: www.uap.ualberta.ca

Orders: GTW
Toll Free: 1-877-864-8477

E: orders@gtwcanada.com

mattered if there was one. My mother, like most mothers her age, can't read or write. She only knows when nature changes the colours of the earth, and the simplicity of life. Maybe that was one reason why she had a hard time getting used to the city. I couldn't help noticing how calm, energetic, and happy she would become every time we visited Ashkaftsaqa, where she was born and where my grandpa still lived. Her personality would undergo a dramatic transformation. I guess this was because she felt this was where she belonged. The place made her intimate with her past, making it easy for her to be herself and share her many interesting stories with us.

I remember when we all piled into Jamal's Land Rover to go to Ashkaftsaqa for Uncle Zenden the shepherd's reburial, twelve years after we had left the village. As we neared Ashkaftsaqa, my mother's facial expression changed from confusion to relief as her surroundings became more familiar. She knew the sky and the names of all the mountains, and where most roads led. It was the first time I saw my mother guiding us. As we came around a bend in the road, she made Jamal stop the vehicle.

"Come," she said, and led us down the steep embankment by the roadside and into the valley. There, hidden from the roadside, lay a magnificent field of wild flowers in full bloom. After a while, we returned to the car and proceeded up the winding road that led to Ashkaftsaqa. A little farther along, she showed us the ancient pomegranate trees in a secluded vale. From there, she took us to the hill where she remembered camping in the summer. During the summer months, when the homes of Ashkaftsaqa became unbearably hot, villagers would camp near a spring at the foot of the hill. Not far from the campsite we came across a copse of blackberry bushes where we grazed until we'd had our fill.

But with all her knowledge of local places and traditions, my mother did not know her birthday, or mine, or anyone else's for that matter. Our birth certificates all say July 1. When I moved to Canada at the age of forty-five, I quickly realized that here nothing was as central to a person's identity as a birthday. When I turned fifty here in Canada, my co-workers at our office bought a cake and had a small surprise birthday party for me. I even received birthday cards. It was the first time in my life that someone had made a fuss of my birthday. After that experience, I made a concerted effort to see if I could finally liberate myself from this lie by determining the actual date of my birth. I knew that my mom doesn't know when she—or I—was born, but still, one day I called her in Hawler and asked her if she could do her best to find out when exactly I was born.

She said, "My son, all I remember is that when you were born, the grass was green, and the animals were ready to go to the grassland. They were lambing and every evening our shepherd, Ali Puchal, would bring the lambs in his bag. For days, we had fresh milk. You didn't like milk, but your brother Jamal did."

I still don't like milk. I remember when I was in Grade 4, the school had a program where they would provide the children with milk every day at break time. Every student had to take cup to school. Some teachers forced the students to drink it. I also took my cup to school and stood in line for my milk. But when our teacher turned his back, I spilled the milk on the ground and covered it with soil.

"You were born shortly after dawn, that I do know," my mother said. "Aunt Naxsheen was the midwife who cut your cord."

My mother's stories always took a long path home, and so she began to tell me how much my father loved parties. "Before you born, Mamand Agha brought two singers to the castle every year. One of the singers was called Jalal. When he sang, his voice was very powerful and was heard from every home in the village. Your father loved to listen to him sing. Your father loved his voice very much and decided to name you after him.

"The night before you were born, your father went to a nomad wedding. My mother told me your grandfather bought him a rifle for fifty dinars, and that he sold it for twenty-five so that he could give the money away as tips to the singers during the wedding. He loved nomad weddings and parties. Your aunt Kaje told me that even before we got married. When he came back from the wedding and found out you were born, he was so joyful that he sacrificed a sheep to celebrate. And because he had spent a night listening to singing, he decided to name you Jalal, after his favourite singer."

So I know where my name came from, but I am forced to continue to live with the lie that the Iraqi regime forced on me. One thing is certain, though: I was born during the spring, and it is nice to come into the world during spring.

A Fire in the Village

When I was young, the village of Ashkaftsaqa consisted of about fifty houses that were made of mud and rocks. The village was about eight hundred years old and had been ruled by seven chiefs. Ashkaftsaqa lies in an extremely beautiful area, but the design of the houses was not so beautiful. Back in those days, when someone built a house the entire village would help to put on the roof, and afterwards the owner of the house would have a wonderful feast to share with the helpers. This celebration was a time of enjoyment for the children of the village, but, unfortunately, the adults ate all the good meat and the children were fed the leftovers.

I was young at the time and did not need to go to school quite yet, but I remember when our village got its first school. I was seven years old when one afternoon a big truck turned off the main highway and headed for our village. When the truck stopped, villagers began to surround it. Inside, I could see a driver and a man wearing a vest sitting in the passenger seat. They climbed out of the vehicle and the man introduced himself as the new teacher of the village. He said: "A school will be opened in Ashkaftsaqa." This news came as a surprise to the villagers. Many of them were not aware that Shimadi Ghazal, the wise man of the village, had been to Hawler many times to plead for a school in our village.

The new school didn't have a building yet, and so I wondered what the teacher was going to do about that. Fortunately, my father had two extra rooms in the village, so he offered them to the school. One of the rooms became a classroom, while the other became a bedroom for the new teacher. He covered the walls with big sheets of paper to make them look clean. Two days after his arrival, people begin sending their children to be registered for the school. My dad took me and Jamal. As we were walking, he kept saying, "Hurry. You must go to school so that you and your brother don't become blind like us."

On the day the school began, there were fewer chairs than the number of students in the class. The teacher, *Mamosta* Mosher, asked those who were standing and those who were sitting on the floor to bring an empty can to sit on the next day. The following day, the students brought their cans, but they still had no desks. I was lucky: I had a space in the middle of the class.

Each morning, the parents, after sending their kids off to school, would come and linger for a while. They were curious about the male teacher's clothing (a white shirt and dress pants, quite unlike the more traditional attire of the village men) and his Elvis hairstyle. They had never seen anything like it. Nor had they ever heard the national anthem, which we had to sing each morning before classes started.

The villagers had plenty of respect for the teacher and took turns inviting him to dinner. They made sure he was never without fresh eggs and yoghurt. One day in class, the teacher said, "Eggs and yoghurt are piling up under my bed! Please thank your parents for me, but tell them not to send me more, at least for a while. I don't want any of it to go to waste."

I was not particularly interested in school at first. I didn't like being kept in class for forty minutes at a time. I wanted to be outside and free. But a big change in attitude came when I learned the alphabet and some stories. Each school day was now like a new journey and I could hardly wait for the next day.

The new teacher also brought other oddities with him besides his dress, like a new soccer ball. No one in the village had played soccer before, but now, thanks to the teacher's obsession with the game, many of the younger men became hooked on soccer. Every afternoon, the men would roll up their sherwals, take off their cheap rubber shoes, and play barefoot until dinner-time. Children and women acted like cheerleaders; the elders seemed indifferent. For my part, I thought there was too much aggression in the game, but that was because I was little boy and could not get the ball and got in the way of the adults who were playing. Getting hurt was a real possibility, and I did not like that. There were other boys who felt the same. We would go and stand a little distance behind the goalkeeper, acting like a second line of defence. It was very exciting to see the men, youth, and children of the village playing together.

To the west of Ashkaftsaqa there was a river that started running when the snow melted, but as the summer progressed, the water almost dried up and the villagers had a hard time watering the crops they had planted. Even though the grass had turned yellow and there was dryness in the village, in summertime the sound of the water coming from the river brought a feeling of joy to the farmers.

People would have to line up to get some water. The villagers had erected two wells along the riverbank—one for the men and one for the women. Because there were no showers in the houses, villagers would have to wash in the river. As a young boy, I would run off to the river early in the morning while the mist still clung to the edges of the valley. I would settle myself on the edge of the river alongside the stone wall that marked off the well area and watch the fish fry play in the clear shallow eddies around the well. Every now and then, a frog sunning itself on the bank would leap into the water. I would look up from my play to see the men dunking their faces into the fresh cold water. As the morning traffic increased, the water would become murkier and the fry would flee into the safety of the reeds. This was my cue to return home, for the water no longer tasted as crisp and clear as it had earlier when no one was around.

At the women's well, the activity included washing clothes. Every person in the village only had one set of clothes, so once they had washed their clothes, the women would hang them on the tree branches to dry. On the days when they washed the men's clothing, the men stayed home and wrapped themselves up in blankets.

One summer evening, as we wandered back from the well, we could see a fire on the slopes of Mount Korader to the east of Ashkaftsaqa. Mount Korader forms part of a range of mountains that starts in *darbandi gomaspan*. The range runs south from Mount Korader until it rises to form the peak of Mount Bawaji. In Koya, each peak of the mountain had a name, and each name had a background story. The peak facing Ashkaftsaqa is called *Gali wasman kujray*—the place where Wasman Agha was killed.

I heard the story of *Gali wasman kujray* from my grandmother, who was a good storyteller. "The story behind its name," she said, "begins a long time ago in the time of the Ottoman Empire. Wasman Agha was the brother of Ismail Beg and he was the chief of Ashkaftsaqa at the time. One day, a general called Saleem Se Tanga set up base on the narrow end of the mountain and the people automatically assumed the group belonged to the Ottoman Army. When Wasman Agha died, his brother, Ismail, married his wife and took over as chief of the village. Wasman Agha's son, Pusho, could not adjust to his uncle becoming his father and he refused to live at home. One day, he took his father's sword, and killed Ismail Agha while he was hunting in mountains. Pusho told his mother what he had done, and then he ran off to the army base. He stayed there for three months because he couldn't come home for fear of revenge from his uncle, Kato, who was now chief of the village. When the army finally left, they took Pusho with them. After the death of her husband and disappearance of her son, Pusho's mother spent all her time knitting in front of the door of the castle, looking onto the mountain where she lost her new husband and her son."

Every time I looked towards the mountain, I would see a red section. I was thinking the redness of the mountain resembled blood that had been dried on the mountain. I didn't like looking at the mountain, but our house was right across from it and our door was always open. I had no choice but to see it.

The fire on Mount Korader troubled the residents. In Kurdistan, fires were used for communication, as they had been since Kawa the Blacksmith had lit the fire to communicate his victory over the evil king Zohak. In modern times, fires meant someone was in trouble. Men from our village often went to gather firewood along the slopes of Mount Korader and so a fire there was a cause of some concern. Whenever there had been an accident, it was a common practice for wood-gatherers to light a small fire to let the villagers below know that help was needed. We soon established that no one from our village was missing and so concern soon gave way to fear among the villagers. Fires seldom brought good news.

Summer evenings in our village involved a certain ritual. Just before sundown, as the day started to cool off, we would head to the rooftop to have dinner and begin making sleeping arrangements. As there was no electricity, all this had to be done before it got dark. My mother would go up and down the wooden ladder at least a dozen times, carrying stuff; I would only go up when dinner was ready because I was terrified of climbing the ladder. After dinner, my mother would go down and bring the tea that had been brewing slowly on the leftover embers from the day's cooking. My father did the pouring; the aroma of the tea filled the air. Lying down on our *doshags* under a big starry sky made us all very happy. Everything smelled like nature itself. At tea, my mother always made a point of reminding me and Jamal to limit ourselves to just one cup, as she didn't want us to pee our beds.

But that particular evening, the fire was making everyone uneasy, so one after another, families decided to leave their rooftops—just as a precaution in case the fire reached the village. This was all very confusing to me. I couldn't understand why we couldn't spend another beautiful night on the roof. Back then, Ashkaftsaqa was the only world I knew, and I knew it well. I knew all the pathways leading to the village, all the alleyways, all the people, and all the cats, dogs, and cows. I even knew the trees. I knew the best places to find friends and the best places to be alone. I also knew under which walls our chickens laid eggs. Sometimes I would run off and find an egg when my mother was baking bread. She would put it in the fire for me and I would eat the baked egg with a fresh piece of bread. I couldn't think of a better meal at the time. Ashkaftsaqa was a peaceful, safe place, and the disruption caused by the fire upset me.

That night we slept downstairs because of the fire. In the morning, I was relieved to hear my father tell my mother, "The fire is gone. However, just to be safe, we aren't letting the shepherds take the flocks out today." I only really listened to the first part. Finally, I could go outside and pee in peace. I say outside because we had no toilets or plumbing of any sort. A nearby spring, in a somewhat secluded area, was where the women went for their daily needs. Some distance upriver there was another spring, which was where the men went.

Children like me went to the nearest wall. I didn't like it; it was disfiguring the village, but it was a common practice. When I finished peeing, I walked up to the area near our house where one could see the mountain better. I looked to see if there was any life left in the fire, but the strong sun didn't allow me to see anything. Everything looked blurry.

My nervousness about the fire was fuelled by local superstition that said that a fire on the mountain predicted disaster. Among the many stories about fires was one about a woman called Fatima whose brothers would go hunting every day and when they came home from the hunt in the evening, Fatima would start a fire. One day, Fatima was unable to get the fire started; however, she had seen a fire far against the slopes of the mountain and so she decided to follow the light. When she got near the light, she noticed that there was a monster in front of the door of the cave from which the light shone. The monster captured Fatima and took her inside, where he forced her to give him her finger to suck on until she dried out and died.

Being firm believers in local legends and myths, the villagers of Ashkaftsaqa didn't consider it appropriate to go and investigate a distant fire. For most people, going up Mount Korader was simply out of the question. Because of the fire, this day resembled a public holiday. People were everywhere except at work. There was still a great deal of talk about the fire, but some people were also getting bored by it, or at least seemed indifferent. Some of the boys my age took a rope and headed to the big mulberry tree not far from the spring where the men went to relieve themselves. I went along. We ate some of the sweet and sticky fruit that had fallen, then we hung the rope around a strong branch and took turns at swinging. We didn't head home until lunchtime and not before getting our fill of mulberries—the fruit seemed to taste a lot better when picked right off the tree.

That evening, we noticed the fire again. And again we slept inside. Not being able to take his animals out for the second day running made the shepherd, Zenden, furious. Zenden, my uncle, had been a shepherd for twenty-five years and thought the situation was unfair to the animals, and also to himself. Years and years of solitude in the hills made him jittery and uncomfortable around people. By sundown, the

fire was visible again and villagers ate dinner a little early just in case
something bad happened.

That night, sleeping downstairs made me feel a little safer but I was
still afraid. I pulled the cover over my face but remained awake until
midnight, when my father got home from his deliberations with the
other men of the village. When I heard him telling my mother that
the fire had been put out again, I felt a lot better. I thought about the
mulberry tree and the swing. My brother Jamal was sleeping soundly,
but I could hear my mother breastfeeding my sister, Ruqya. I don't
remember anything else from that night, so I guess I must have fallen
asleep at some point. I felt good in the morning. I wasn't thinking of
the fire at all. I was ready to go and play.

By the time I got outside on this, the third day of the fire, people
were already talking. Now they were eager to see the mystery behind
the fire resolved. They wanted to go back to their daily routine. The
teenaged boys of the village were especially keen to see the woman
with the knife, better known as Fata, resume her work of circum-
cising the girls. Female circumcision has been widely practiced in
Kurdistan for as long as anyone can remember. Today, there are people
who are trying to stop the practice, but tradition dies hard, especially
in the smaller villages. Fata lived in a nearby village, Baqlin, and two
or three times a year, as the occasion demanded it, she would walk to
Ashkaftsaqa to perform the ritual. Fata would apply her knife to girls
under ten without mercy, slicing off a good portion of the clitoris.
When she had finished, she would throw the pieces away like they
were nothing. The teenaged boys would then go and gather them, and
use the pieces for masturbation before burying them.

As the sun set on the third day, a man we called Baldar was happy
that the fire was more visible than the night before. Baldar was one
of the few people who wanted to go and investigate the fire. Zenden
smiled and offered to accompany him. It made the villagers happy
that Baldar was willing to go. Although Baldar had grown up in
another village, the people of Ashkaftsaqa had grown to trust him
after his marriage to a local girl. Baldar's real name was Ahmed, but
he had earned his nickname, which means "The One with Wings,"

61

because he had once travelled from Ashkaftsaqa to the town of Koya and back in one day—a distance of about fifty kilometres. I recall my father recounting that feat often: "All the villagers were surprised, and we went to his house to welcome him. He had brought with him a pair of shoes and some cucumbers, which he and his wife served to their guests that night."

But as I have mentioned, the people of Ashkaftsaqa were superstitious. On our way home Uncle Smile stopped and held up his finger in warning. "Do you fellows hear the owl? This is a bad omen. Our forefathers knew how evil this bird is. Its call will bring calamity to whatever settlement the bird targets. It means nothing but ruin for us." Uncle Smile got many of us very scared. If only he knew at the time how true were the words he had spoken.

The villagers took their concerns about the fire to the village chief, Mamand Agha, to decide what to do. The consensus among the villagers was that we ought to wait another day before sending a team to the mountain, but they needed the agha's blessing for their plan. Mamand Agha lived in an ancient castle with a front door that overlooked the village and a back door that faced the two springs where villagers went for their ablutions. The agha loved folk songs, and almost every night he would have men from the village sing late into the night. My father took me there one evening and I still remember the house in detail. The reception room, furnished with Persian carpets and round cushions, was fairly spacious and comfortable. There was a big samovar by the door.

I thought it was odd that the agha shaved his moustache when most of the men in the village took pride in their moustaches, but I liked him all the same. I noticed how glittering his cigarette case was and I hoped to have it after he was done with it. I had never seen anything like it. The agha was paralyzed from the waist down, and according to his servants, it was this that drew him to arrack. He would order the stuff by the case from Koya.

The news that Mamand Agha was finally on the verge of making a decision got Zenden very excited. He thought the ordeal for him and the animals would finally be over. "Tomorrow will be four days since I last took the animals out," he said. "It has taken its toll on the sheep and the goats. They have been surviving on very little. They need to be taken out to the hills, and soon." Zenden's concern was a very practical one: it was too early in the season to give the animals dry feed, mostly hay and barley. He had to make use of the good pastures while food was still plentiful. And so we headed off to home and to bed anticipating the agha's decision.

The Mystery Solved

On the fourth day, just after sundown and before Mamand Agha could put his plan to send Baldar and Zenden to explore the origins of the fire into action, some of the sharper-eyed men swore they could see people coming down the mountain. Mamand Agha went inside his house and returned with a pair of binoculars. All this time, I had no idea that Mamand Agha actually owned a pair of binoculars. He looked into the darkening distance and confirmed what the villagers thought they were seeing: a column of men was heading towards the village. But who the men were no one could tell.

The news spread like wildfire. Everyone was looking in the same direction in silence. As they came closer, the villagers could distinguish dozens of men walking single file. At the head was the leader, an imposing figure with a bushy salt-and-pepper moustache and beard. He was wearing a thick red and white turban and he had a pistol tied to his waist. A traditional Kurdish dagger stuck out prominently from his waistband. The bandoliers criss-crossing his massive chest were full; the walking stick looked firm in his hand. As he approached, he greeted us all and went straight to our agha. He shook hands and introduced himself as Hamad Agha of Merga Soor. "We're *peshmerga*," he said. "We've been in the area for a few days."

"So you're the ones responsible for the fire," said our agha. Hamad Agha nodded. Having settled that issue, our agha gave the visitors a warm reception and everyone in the village made them feel welcome, even though none of us knew who the *peshmerga* were. All I remember as a child is that the men looked impressive with their rugged demeanour and weapons. Most of them, we soon learned, carried Kalashnikovs, but a few of them had other, heavier, guns. Children gathered around them and women gazed fondly from rooftops; these were the men of their dreams, so it seemed.

No one knew what the men were up to, but that didn't stop people from inviting them to their homes. Two of the *peshmerga* stayed with us. My parents felt so honoured by their presence that my mother had them sit on a special wool carpet my uncle's wife had made my parents as a gift. I was always amazed by my aunt Haybat's carpet-designing talent. She had never attended school or design training, yet she had taught herself to make the most beautiful handmade carpets.

My father quickly killed a chicken, cut up some firewood, and went about energetically helping my mother prepare chicken stew with cracked-wheat pilaf. The men looked battered. When one of them tried to remove his socks, I noticed they looked like they'd been glued to his feet, and they smelled awful. They ate like they hadn't eaten a hot meal for days.

That night we all slept downstairs; we gave the men the porch, which after the roof was the coolest part in the house. We slept inside, and even though it was hot in the house, we all slept better knowing that the mystery was behind us.

When I woke up in the morning, my mother was baking bread. The smell of smoke from the burning wood mingling with the aroma of fresh bread was enough to make any young boy's stomach growl in anticipation. As I opened my eyes, I noticed that the two *peshmerga* were getting ready to leave. My father tried to talk them into staying for breakfast, but the men insisted that they had to leave the village at once. My mother folded two pieces of fresh bread into quarters and handed it to them. As they took the bread, one of the men said, "That's all we eat most of the time: bread and bread and more bread." They then went outside and joined the rest of their group. I watched as the men quickly disappeared into a valley west of Ashkaftsaqa.

And so the *peshmerga* became part of life in our village.

Half of Ashkaftsaqa Dancing

By day, the *peshmerga* would wander around the surrounding hills and valleys. In the evening, they would return to the village and spend the night with their hosts.

One night after dinner, about a fortnight after their arrival in Ashkaftsaqa, the two *peshmerga* who were staying with us set about meticulously cleaning their guns; as soon they finished, they abruptly got up and announced that they were leaving. They offered no explanation, and my father didn't ask for one. But it wasn't just them; the entire force took off. About an hour or so after their departure, as we were getting ready to retire for the night, we heard gunfire. It continued nonstop for about half an hour, then grew very intense before dying down. We hadn't heard anything like this before, but we knew the shots didn't come from Mamand Agha's hunting rifle. Everyone hurried downstairs. It was eerily quiet for a long time, then we heard footsteps outside. It sounded like a crowd was approaching. Before long, the village was full of *peshmerga* again—except this time it wasn't just them.

It turned out the *peshmerga* had indeed been up to something. They had gone to attack a strategic police position in the Gomaspan area, not far north of Ashkaftsaqa. The fifteen policemen inside, all Arabs from the south, had apparently surrendered without a fight. The *peshmerga* told them they were free to go, but with transportation not being available, the policemen had to be put up in our village for a night or two.

The *peshmerga* billeted a man named Kamil from the city of Babylon (Hilla) just south of Baghdad. He was dark brown and was still wearing his police uniform, but he didn't have his military cap on because he had dropped it during the raid. He looked terrified at first, but when he saw the food and realized how kind everyone was to him despite our lack of Arabic, he started warming up to us.

Kamil seemed surprised that no one could speak Arabic. All the men of my father's age had gone to military service and could therefore speak at least some Arabic. My father tried to explain why he didn't speak any Arabic, but he couldn't make Kamil understand. I was also curious to know why and so I asked. My mother turned to me and explained: "Your grandfather, Sayyid Habas, was a highly respected village elder. Like so many people who came from the town of Barzanja near Suleimaniya, he was a Sufi, even though it was haraam to be one under Islam. The people in Ashkaftsaqa didn't care about that, though. They just respected his wisdom. Whenever there was a conflict, he was the first person the villagers would go to for help. He owned a mill in Degala, and the business made him rich enough to afford paying the government five hundred dinars so that your father could be exempted from military service. That's why your father doesn't speak any Arabic; he didn't have to be sent to the south to serve in the military."

Kamil, who spoke only a few words of Kurdish, looked at my father and then drew his forefinger like a knife across his throat and said the government was no good. My father interpreted the motion for the rest of us. "Kamil knows he's free to go," he said, "but he's terrified of what the government might do to him. He thinks the government will execute him because he surrendered. He was supposed to back up the main Iraqi force, and withdrawing like he did almost certainly means execution." Despite his feelings about the government, Kamil was aware he had no choice but to leave. Every day, he would go to the road leading from Koya to Hawler in search of a ride into the city. It took about three days before he and the rest of the policemen managed to squeeze themselves into a crowded Land Rover that ran between Koya and Hawler once a day. A few days later, the *peshmerga* disappeared as suddenly as they had arrived.

With the Arab policemen and the *peshmerga* gone, we thought at long last life was returning to normal in our little village. But that was not to be the case. Another group of *peshmerga*, led by the duo Said Masiefi and Anwar Jokheen, soon arrived. For a while, it was the same story all over: the men would spend their days in the hills and return to the village by sundown. They were personable and friendly and, at times, fun to have around, like when they would sing and dance.

This second group of *peshmerga* loved to sing and dance, especially the one man nicknamed Ahmed Tokarev, after the Soviet heavy machine gun he carried. He always walked around with so many bandoliers slung around his shoulders that one could hardly see the colour of his T-shirt.

Ahmed Tokarev was also the lead singer of their group, and his folk songs were hard to resist. His songs were a big hit with the youth, who sat mesmerized as he danced, his bandoliers jingling and coming alive with the rhythm of his body.

Many of the village men joined in the dancing, but the women were allowed only to watch from the rooftops—the villagers did not consider it right for their women to be seen holding hands (which Kurdish dancing requires) with men who were still essentially outsiders. The dancing became so frequent that for a while I thought the *peshmerga* had come this time to teach our people how to sing and dance.

One evening, my mother told me about the dancing that had taken place when Mamand Agha's brother got married. The festivities had lasted for seven days, and every day the villagers slaughtered many sheep. The women prepared several pots of rice and soup and the smell of the cooked food drifted through the whole village. The men would ride on their horses and fire shots of celebration into the air.

Little by little, the *peshmerga* settled in and became part of village life. Baldar let them use one of his rooms, which they converted into their official headquarters. They also found a few more rooms. They cooked their own food and stayed on friendly terms with everyone. Day and night they were there. Everyone was impressed by how disciplined they were, and some of our families became good friends with the *peshmerga*.

Leaving Ashkaftsaqa

Thanks to the *peshmerga*, dancing became a normal part of the evening's activities. Following evening prayer, the village would come alive. Even the young man from the mosque who was studying to become a mullah couldn't stay away. As he put it, "I know my first and foremost duty is to serve Islam, and I think in this regard I've been quite faithful. But I must also admit that when I hear this guy singing and see the men dancing, I can't help it: I have to come and join in."

Every night a thick layer of dust could be seen rising from under the men's feet. The women would have made the dance more beautiful in their bright dresses, but instead they watched from the rooftops and kept a watchful eye on the dirt road leading to Koya and Hawler. One night while watching the dancing, some of the women suddenly detected an unusual column of vehicles approaching. They started screaming. Instantly, the dance stopped, and the men rushed up on the roof.

Masiefi, the *peshmerga* leader, wasted no time telling everyone what they needed to do: "This looks like a military convey. We need to pack and leave for the hills this very moment. It is not safe for anyone to remain in the village. I have a feeling it will be bombed from the air first thing in the morning."

For their part, the villagers were not sure they believed him. Some wanted to pack a few things and leave; some found the idea of abandoning their homes and properties unthinkable. Pounding the ground as hard as he could with his right foot, Sabir made it very clear he was not going anywhere. This was his home and he had no intention of leaving the place of his birth. But others found this kind of posturing beside the point.

"Lives are at stake," my father said. "We need to get to the mountain caves before daybreak," he told my mother, as they got ready to leave. My mother put all the bread in the house in a bag while my father stuck his hand deep into his bed roll and pulled out the money he had hidden there. He cast one look around the place before opening the door and stepping out into the coolness that settles in just before daybreak.

Like the majority of the people, we left on foot. It was a very hard for me, a mere seven-year-old, to rise before dawn and keep up with the adults running to the mountains. From time to time, my father, realizing the walk was hard on me, carried me; many other parents did the same with their young children.

Even though the rushing was very stressful, I was nonetheless excited about the exodus. The mountains, especially at sunrise, always looked mysterious to me from afar. I had always wondered where the sun came from when it rose from behind Mount Korader; now, I thought, I was about to find out.

••• As the village faded into the distance behind us, I heard an unusual sound—a deep, thunderous noise that was repeated again and again. I stopped and turned around to see what had happened, but my mother grabbed my arm. "Walk!" she said, and dragged me along in the direction of Mount Korader. As the attack on the village intensified, she and my father picked up the pace. When we reached a protected gully in the Valley of Korader, the sun had just risen and the landscape was awash with brilliant colours. There we ran into Meena, a neighbour, who began to speak almost before we'd come into earshot. He said, "Sabir's wife, Amina, decided to stay. She started her morning as usual, baking bread. She said she wasn't afraid of the military. 'Why leave when everything is in Allah's hands?' she said calmly. But the moment the shells started falling, she fled."

Because of the shelling, we decided to walk around to the other side of the mountain, where we would not be visible from Ashkaftsaqa. Finally, I was about to see where the sun came from! I was slightly disappointed to see only more hills and valleys, but no nice bed for the sun. The caves, too, were a bit of a surprise. I had imagined them as tiny holes in the mountainside, big enough for a deer or a rabbit, and I wondered how we would all fit into them. As it turned out, they were much bigger and we could squeeze about fifteen people into one. I was small enough to walk right in, but the adults had to stoop and remain squatting on their haunches.

Throughout the day, the attack on Ashkaftsaqa continued. From the safety of the crowded caves, we could hear the roar of warplanes and loud explosions. As the day wore on, the cave felt smaller and smaller, and I began to wish I had remembered to bring the thick woollen cord with me so that I could tie it to the big tree outside and swing. Just after sunset, when we were certain we could no longer be spotted by the soldiers scanning the ridges of the mountain, we emerged from the cave. Outside, we could see thick smoke rising from our village and several other locations. The adults in our company shook their heads with the realization that everything they had known had changed in the course of a day. After standing quietly looking at the destruction throughout the valley for a long time, my mother took me by the hand

and began to search for food so that we children could have more than bread to eat. Fortunately there was a clean spring nearby, so getting fresh water was not a problem.

I cannot find a better word than disbelief to describe how we felt. My father said, "This is the beginning of an end for us. Today they've burnt down our village; there's nothing left to return to. We have no choice but to move to the city—for good. I know this won't be easy. Generations of our people have lived here in Ashkaftsaqa. We're all defined by this place and we've gotten so used to its sky and air and everything else. I know it is going to be hard to leave, but I'm afraid that's what we have to do."

My uncle Mamad also thought it was time for action. He favoured walking towards the Koya-Hawler road. He dug in his pockets as he spoke and pulled out a cigarette, which he stuck in his mouth as he spoke. When he finished, he struck a match and raised it to his mouth. No sooner had he lit his cigarette than two artillery shells landed nearby; the sound was deafening but luckily caused no harm. He quickly put out his cigarette and told us not to panic: "Whatever weapons the government uses against us, they're no match for these rocks. They will protect us."

Those of us who had reached the cave safely were worried about some of the villagers, like Zenden, who had left town with his flocks before the military arrived. He had been gone for a few days before the attack and no one knew where he and the animals in his charge were. Bapir, Zenden's father, remarked that his son was too stupid to even know where he was. Stupid or not, my father and Uncle Mamad argued, it was our responsibility as fellow citizens to go and find him and the animals and then head straight to Hawler while it was still dark.

But Bapir was in a fighting mood. Nothing anyone could say would lift his spirits or convince him that going to the city was a good idea. "All city people are stupid," he said dismissively, but he didn't object to the idea of finding his son before heading to the city.

I stayed alongside my father as we headed into the darkness to look for the missing shepherd. Before long we did find Zenden, not far from the Koya-Hawler highway. His sheepdog was sitting next to him and some of the animals around him were dead; the rest were standing almost motionless in the moonlight. I didn't know what to make of the scene until the women started moaning and crying, some hysterically.

My father covered Zenden's body with his headgear. I was too frightened to look at the dead man. These were the war's first casualties among our people. Zenden's mother wanted the body to be taken with us to Hawler, but my father and Uncle Mamad convinced her that, since he would never have agreed to be buried in the city, it was better to bury him in the area. It wasn't too far from the village, and we could come back later and rebury him in the village cemetery.

My uncle used his pocket knife to cut down a few branches from a tree. He sharpened the ends and handed these rough-hewn implements to the men around him. They set about the task of digging a grave in silence. It took them a long time and the grave was shallow, but under the circumstances it seemed adequate.

"*Insh'allah*," the men said in unison as they buried Zenden. Then my uncle ripped a piece of cloth off his belt and tied it around the grave stone so that it would be easier for the relatives to find the body in the future.

We were all very sad, but Father said it was crucial for us to try to make it to Hawler while it was still dark so that we could avoid being seen by the authorities. I didn't have the slightest idea what Hawler was like, but in my mind it had become synonymous with safety.

So it came about that one day in 1963, just before daybreak, we fled to Hawler, leaving behind most of our belongings. Our only means of transportation was a donkey, which in the confusion my father had failed to saddle properly. We took turns riding the animal, and although I couldn't keep up with the adults, I preferred walking rather than sitting on an animal I didn't know how to manage. Besides, I didn't have the heart to be rough with the donkey. Every time the animal would linger to get a mouthful of dry grass along the side of the dirt road, the men, realizing they couldn't afford to slow down, would yell loudly to make the poor creature move.

We made it to Hawler by early morning. The city was slowly waking up to its daily routine. I liked this time of day. The city lights in the street were on and I'd never seen lights like that before. Already, there

were many cars on the road, and although I didn't know the models
or names, they impressed me. At the time I'd only seen Waisi Afnas's
small Jeep, which would come to the village a few times a year to carry
some products like tobacco and wool. In the mornings after we arrived
in Hawler, I would go on the roof of the house to look at all the cars
down below.

The style of the houses was new to me, and each one had lights
burning inside, just like the big street lights. I soon discovered that in
Hawler, each house had its own electricity. This was something very
new to me, as I had never encountered electricity before.

We walked along in silence and I marvelled at the sight of the
ancient citadel. The imposing walls on the hilltop loomed over us and
seemed to be watching over our journey as we passed by. Since I did
not know any better, I also assumed that was where the governor's
mansion was.

We were heading towards the Setaqan neighbourhood, where my
father's cousin, Khazal, and her husband, Bawakir, lived in a house
not far from the ancient citadel. The streetlights were still on, and the
city, with its ancient citadel rising majestically above an endlessly flat
land, seemed like a giant bubble of dust. My father had lived in the city
before, following some dispute he had with his village agha, but when
things cooled off, he went back to Ashkaftsaqa at my mother's urging.
Now we were moving back to the city, and not by choice.

Our new life in Hawler was about to begin and my parents were
nervous. My mother never quite got used to it, never. However, I wasn't
like my parents, and the city became a part of me.

Even though we all got to the city safely, we were not safe. The
following day, all the adult men in our party were arrested. When my
father was released from jail he would take me for kebabs once in a
while. For a long time I was afraid to go farther than a few blocks away
from home. I used to live in a small village close to nature with fresh
air. Being in the city was a big change for me and my family.

My father did not forget the people of the village easily, nor did
he forget our guests. When my father was released, he tracked down
Anwar Jokheen and he became a frequent guest in our house. We all
liked him. He always looked so sharp in his Kurdish outfit. After I began

to write my memoirs here in Canada, my mind often returned to those days in Ashkaftsaqa and Hawler and I wondered where Anwar Jokheen was now. It bothered me that now that Kurdistan is semi-independent and getting rich, the government hasn't done much for the likes of Anwar; after all, the *peshmerga* did put their lives on the line for the Kurdish cause. One day, I called Kurdistan and told my brother Jamal about this particular episode in my memoir. He said, "Just recently, Anwar Jokheen and I were at a tea house together. We were talking about those days. Anwar said, 'Revolution is like a crop just harvested: if you don't get there on time, you won't get your share.'"

The interesting thing is that this is exactly what Anwar's name means: "a crop just harvested."

Our First Days in the City

Bawakir, Khazal and their two sons lived in an open-style house of several rooms. When we arrived, Siyamand, Bawakir's son, put our sheep in the room where they kept their chickens and tied the donkey to a pole alongside the grass behind the house. Bawakir had Khazal cut up some watermelons and cantaloupes for us and asked his son to take the peels to the donkey and to be sure to leave the animal enough water. I was glad Bawakir didn't forget about the donkey's needs. At first glance, it seemed to me that things were mostly the way they had been in the village.

Bawakir's house had a spacious courtyard, at the centre of which stood a fairly large mulberry tree. In the morning and in the evening, its branches were laden with noisy little birds, mostly sparrows. I remembered these birds from our village and noted how easily the bird could adjust to its surroundings and how it could be found everywhere and anywhere. I spent my first day admiring all these wonderful new sights. When it was time for me to use the toilet for the first time, I was pleasantly surprised I didn't have to do it behind a wall. There was also no need to wipe off my behind with a stone—here, there was a proper toilet and running water to clean with. I also noticed that Siyamand, who seemed to be a couple of years older than I was, had a collection of toys to play with, something I had never had in the village. He carefully explained to me what was what and how everything worked. I was especially intrigued by his tricycle, which I could not get enough of once I had figured out how to ride it.

There were other luxuries, too. On my first day in Hawler, I discovered ice cubes, something I had never seen before. The city people put these little blocks of ice in their yoghurt drinks; I thought that was a nice way to cool off.

Until now I had only seen paper money, which my parents kept in a little fabric sack under a *doshag* in our bedroom. Now I saw coins for the first time, and I struggled to figure out how to use them. In the afternoon of my first day in the city, Siyamand showed me how I could use these to get soft drinks, sweets, and baklava, among other stuff. With a little coin I could even buy myself a skewer of grilled sheep spleen. My mother was like me when it came to coins. She had to rely on Khazal to understand how paper money converted into coins.

Slowly, I learned the names of the coins: the little coins were called flis. There was a one flis coin and another for two flis, four flis, five flis and ten flis. One hundred flis made one dirham. The dirham coin had a wide flower engraved on one side and had "Republic of Iraq" engraved on the other. Then there were coins for a quarter dinar, a half dinar. One dinar came in a note, as did five dinar, ten dinar and twenty-five dinar. I needed to take ten flis to school to buy a sandwich or ice cream. During the war on Iraq, Saddam cancelled the currency and had new currency printed that had his face on the twenty-five dinar note.

Bawakir and Khazal and their children were very good to us. They really made us feel at home, but it was hard not to feel out of place. For a long time afterwards we continued to think that the ordeal of moving to the city was just a terrible dream. When my mother told my uncle and aunt how Zenden was killed, they broke down and cried. We cried, too. Bawakir said he had seen a big military force heading towards Koya a few days earlier. He knew they were up to something, but that he had no idea it would be so terrible, or that his own family would be affected by it.

This sudden and quick transformation of our lives was especially hard on my grandpa and Uncle Mamad. To be a refugee in their own country was something neither was prepared for. But here they were at least safe, they kept saying. They could not have been more wrong, for trouble was on its way. The afternoon following our arrival, Siyamand came running home with some really scary news: "Haras Qawmi vehicles are all over the neighbourhood! They're saying there's going to be a curfew from 5:00 PM to 7:00 AM. Anyone who violates the curfew will be shot!" he reported, and leant forward to catch his breath.

Bawakir gave his son some money and asked him to go and get a few things before the shops closed. Then he turned to us: "Haras Qawmi men are real brutes. They harass, imprison, and beat up people for no reason. They impose curfews at least twice a week. Everyone is scared of them."

Bawakir was still trying to explain what a curfew was when several of the brutes stormed into the house with their guns drawn. The women huddled together in fear, keeping their covered heads lowered. The men stood on the other side of the room trying to remain calm. I huddled with the women, as I was still a child. I watched in horror as they took the men outside. From inside the folds of my mother's clothing, I heard the women begin to wail as the Haras Qawmi marched the men off. It was the same story in every household on the block.

Zenden's mother took the triple loss of her home, her son, and her husband exceptionally hard, and after two weeks she slipped into a deep depression. The arrests were especially hard on the women, since, as housewives, they relied heavily on their husbands for food and supplies. When the curfew ended the following morning, I went outside to see the street was full of children and women, most of them crying. Seeing everyone wandering the streets aimlessly made me forget about what had happened the previous night.

Uncle Bawakir was released a month later, but my father, Bapir, and Uncle Mamad were detained for three months. We stayed with Bawakir and his family all that time. When they were released, my father and Uncle Mamad couldn't thank Bawakir and his family enough for letting us stay with them for so long. Even though Bawakir told them they were welcome to stay much longer, they decided that it was time they each had their own place.

Life in the city certainly was a big change for all of us and I realized very quickly that I would have to adjust, just like the sparrows on Uncle Bawakir's mulberry tree.

Resuming School

Fortunately for us, there were many places for rent at affordable prices. My father found us a new place in the Setaqan neighbourhood, not far from Bawakir and his family. Life soon developed its own routine. My schooling in Ashkaftsaqa had been rudely interrupted by the arrival of government forces, and now that I was living in the city, the time had come for me to resume my studies. I don't remember much about my first year at Korrack Elementary for boys, except that it was located on one of Hawler's main thoroughfares and that it was big building. I remember that I found this most exciting because in our village, the school had been a single room.

I remember more about our new home. I do recall quite vividly a particular piece of furniture that my parents acquired soon after coming to the city. It was a wardrobe-dresser combination, about two metres wide and one-and-a-half metres tall. It was handmade by a local artisan and every household had one. Like other families, we used the top for stacking up our *doshags*, blankets, and pillows, and the compartments for storing clothes and other such things. Ours had two mirror doors; it was endlessly intriguing to be able to see myself for the first time in the mirror. Another attractive feature of the unit was that the compartments were big enough for me to hide in, something I frequently did when mother's friends and their noisy children came to visit.

One of the doors had an animal painted on it. I couldn't tell what it was; neither could my parents. All we could establish was that it definitely was a four-legged animal. It did partially resemble a horse. My mother asked the wife of the local mullah about it, and she said this was supposed to be a depiction of the sacred winged animal that took our prophet Mohammed up to Allah. When I first heard about the wings of this strange animal, I began to dream about conquering the sky with my own wings one day.

My middle school, Republic Middle School, was just across the street from Hussein Agha's imposing mansion, which later was taken over by the secret police and turned into a house of horrors. I could see the house clearly from my classroom window, but I never imagined that one day I would be kicked and punched and imprisoned in its basement. The window in our classroom was broken, but despite the cold winter wind, I liked being by the window. *Mamosta* Ghafour, who was always dressed in a black suit with a white tie, would always tell me not to look out of the window and he punished me many times because I would not listen. In the end, he had no choice but to move me. I hated it when he moved me. Classes now felt longer, and I felt miserable, but *Mamosta* Ghafour said his decision could not be reversed.

A bigger headache, not just for me but for all the boys, were the toilets: there were only two student toilets for all 1,500 pupils at the school. As a result, they were always clogged up. When we peed, we had to be extra careful not to let the excrement fly all over from the impact. The classroom next door smelled like an extension of the toilet; its door had to be shut at all times.

There was a man called Rasho who cleaned the toilets. He would empty the excrement out into bucket, which he then put in bags tied onto the back of his donkey. At the end of the day, he would pour the contents of the bags onto Farmer Kidder Kar's field as fertilizer. I knew this because after school some days, my mother would send me to buy fresh radishes and onions from the farmer so that she could add them to the tomatoes and boiled eggs we would have for lunch the next day.

Most days after school I would wander along the banks of the Saidawa River, which flowed through the city. I would sit on the stones beside the river and watch the different kinds of little fish swimming in the shallow waters. I never ceased to be amazed at how they managed to survive against the powerful waves. Sometimes, I would climb onto the branches of the trees that reached out over the river, pretending they were vehicles that would take me home to the hills of Ashkaftsaqa.

Just north of Setaqan lay the neighbourhood of Saidawa. I seldom ventured into this area, for the kids from Setaqan neighbourhood didn't get along with the kids from the Saidawa neighbourhood. Due to lack of hobbies and recreation centres for children, sometimes the children from the different neighbourhoods behaved like they were mortal enemies, fighting all the time. But winter was different. That was the rainy season in Hawler and the river would flood its banks and I became very jealous of the Saidawa kids. Saidawa was built around a dip about a hundred metres wide, which was prone to flooding. Almost every time it rained the children from Saidawa didn't have to come to school. They were the lucky ones, I thought. They got to wander along the flooded riverbank, gathering treasures. It was incredible how quickly they forgot about the rivalry and became our friends at this time of year. Whenever the floods came, we acted like we were the best of friends. This made me even more jealous!

An Unlikely Continuation of My Story

I had disappeared into my own thoughts after telling my fellow prisoners about the attack on Ashkaftsaqa, but Sharbat yanked me back to reality. "You know, he said, "the force that came and attacked Ashkaftsaqa later came and attacked Koya, the town where I grew up, and then went on and attacked a cluster of other towns, burning them all down.

"I was only twelve at the time. Fall had just arrived; school was not open yet. Since the harvest was already over for the year, the owners would let people go and pick the leftovers. One day, some boys and I went looking for pomegranates in one of the orchards. There was this particular pomegranate high up in the tree and I had to climb all the way to the top to pick it. It was big and plump, split open from the top, bigger than anything the other boys had found. Its sweet and sour taste was a delight. My sherwal got torn a little from the climb, and that made me worry about how my mother would react. This was, after all, the only pair I had, and I knew my mother couldn't afford to buy me another pair. For that I had to wait a whole year.

"As we were heading home, I was thinking about how delicious the pomegranate would be with a little salt when suddenly a frightening roar overhead made us all fall to the ground. I forgot about the other boys, but not about my fruit. It rolled all the way down the valley below. When I lost sight of it, I became so sad. We were still on the ground when we heard the roar a second time, but this time it was followed by a big explosion. Lifting my head, I saw plumes of smoke rising above the city. As I looked up, I saw two planes circling above, but they were not like the ones I had seen in our school book: you know, like the ones in the story from our Grade 2 readers. The one with the picture of the girl holding two planes, one in each hand, saying she was going to hide them in the orchard. Well, nothing like that, I tell you! When the planes could be heard no more, we got up and headed straight home.

"In the morning, it became clear what the military commander in the region, the infamous Major Taha Shakarchi, had in mind for the people of Koya. He had thirteen local men tied to concrete columns supporting a big building in the town centre before he had them all gunned down in cold blood. He even forced the townspeople to come and watch the massacre."

Sharbat's story reminded me more than ever before that my story was somehow connected to the stories of everyone else in Kurdistan.

3 A City Boy

My Sun Rising Above the Citadel

FROM WHICHEVER DIRECTION you come to Hawler, or in whichever neighbourhood you live, you are bound to see the heart and soul
of this city: its ancient citadel. Nothing looms larger than the citadel,
not even the ancient minaret. When I look at the walls of this ancient
place, I begin to wonder about the strength and resiliency of the
people who built these thick strong walls with their bare hands and
shoulders without the help of modern-day technology. The citadel is
built on a mound that rises thirty-two metres above the rest of the
city. Only once you have cast your eyes up to the top of the mound do
you begin to see the walls of the citadel, which rise a further twenty-
six metres above that. It is an imposing structure that covers 102,000
square metres, or about ten hectares (twenty-four acres). People have
been living in the citadel since time immemorial. The first settlement
dates from at least 6000 or 7000 BCE, although recent discoveries have
unearthed signs of a settlement dating back 150,000 years. Hawler is
indeed a city of wonders. And as a young boy seeing the beauty of this

Citadel in background on return visit in 2009.

View of the repaired statue of Ibn al-Mustawfi, which had been partially destroyed by a bomb in 1996.

city for the first time, I was struck by a sense of wonderment, as I still am today.

The first citadel was built during the time of the Assyrians. It used to have three gates, one of which was reserved for women entering the citadel. The Greeks, Persians, Mongols, and Muslims, among others, all had fought ferocious battles on the plains nearby. They all had a tough time capturing the citadel. That's why some call the citadel the Hulagu Route, after Hulagu, Ghengis Khan's grandson, who was unable to penetrate the wall of the citadel.

As a child, I would take a break from my soccer game and look up at the citadel in the distance. Towering high above the rest of the buildings was the old water tower that supplies the city below. I would wonder how the water got to the top of the tower.

When I returned to Kurdistan in 2005, I took a walk through the citadel, determined to discover where the water came from. As I entered the massive walls, I was engulfed by a labyrinth of unpaved dusty streets. Few of the small stores I remembered seeing there as a child remained. After the collapse of the Kurdish Revolution in 1975, families displaced from their rural homes took refuge in the ancient homes inside the citadel. Low rent and proximity to the city centre made the citadel an ideal place for such destitute people. But despite the poverty of their daily living, they had brought many of their traditions with them to the city. The citadel came alive with the display of tradition. Every Eid, we would go to the citadel to shop and chat and experience some of the older traditions that were being lost. During the Eid festivities, the entire citadel became a giant bazaar, and we would wander from store to store, enjoying the music being played by the vendors trying to sell their wares from their carts.

By the early 1980s, the citadel was in disrepair. By then most of the old timers had left, having built themselves spacious modern homes in suburbia. The municipality began demolishing these small stores around the citadel and replaced them with concrete roads. Now I again walked through the alleys, but the music was gone and the streets were empty and smelly. The bustling bazaars had disappeared and what remained was a ghetto where the poor had become a living monument to years of neglect and abuse.

As I made my way deeper into the citadel, I passed by the ancient *hammam*. Public baths have a long history in Kurdistan. Few of the older homes had their own hot baths, and the *hammams* became places where the people of the city would gather and gossip while they cleaned themselves. It was at the *hammams* that much of the daily business in Hawler happened. I poked my head into the building and marvelled at the beautiful arches of the *barrani*, the outer hall. Beyond these arches, I knew, lay the *wastani*, the middle hall, where the water was warmer. At the heart of the building, right beside the furnace, was the *jawani*, the hot and steamy inner hall. The water that supplied the baths was drawn from an ancient well reaching more than sixty metres down into the heart of the citadel. Even in its state of disrepair, the light shining in through the round glass windows gave the building a magical feel.

Until the 1970s, the ancient *hammam* built by Qasim Agha Abdullah in 1775 was still used by locals. But as the destitute people of the citadel were left to rot in their misery and as newer suburbs, each home fitted with a hot bath, began to spring up, the need for public baths disappeared. And so did the culture that surrounded them. People no longer came to the *hammam* and, like the people who lived in the neighbourhood, it was soon forgotten. The ancient *hammam*, once a hub of activity, was left to crumble along with the rest of the citadel.

After the *rapareen*, or uprising, of 1991, Kurdish political parties put some effort into restoring parts of the citadel, including the baths. City authorities cleaned up the building and built a statue of the mediaeval poet and historian, Ibn al-Mustawfi, in the front. Ibn al-Mustawfi was a leading scholar whose contribution to Kurdish intellectual activity was vast, yet he is best remembered today for his four-volume history of the ancient city of Erbil.

Stepping back outside, I looked at the statue. Children were climbing all over Ibn al-Mustawfi's statue, or what remained of it. During the civil war that raged between the two Kurdish parties, the Kurdistan Democratic Party (KDP) and the Patriotic Union of Kurdistan (PUK), in 1996, a bomb destroyed Ibn al-Mustawfi's shoulders and he was maimed, like many of the other survivors of various wars.

In another attempt to rescue bits of the citadel's history, the authorities restored the house that belonged to the Al-Mufti family, who had made the citadel their home since the Middle Ages. For generations, the Al-Muftis have supported and nurtured the cultural and intellectual environment of Hawler. The family library contains one of the most impressive collections of rare books written in Kurdish. Among the treasures of this library is an old copy of Ibn al-Mustawfi's history of Erbil, *Tarikh Erbil: Nabahat al-Balad*. The Al-Muftis exemplified the spirit of the citadel—until they, too, moved in the 1970s.

But rather than turning the Al-Mufti house into a museum that could stand as a testament to the achievement of these stalwarts of Kurdish culture, they turned it into a TV station. And, as is often the case, the houses that surrounded it, the houses belonging to the common people, were left to collapse. Their numbers continue to diminish and now have turned into dust in the streets that no one bothers cleaning up.

More recently, there have been renewed efforts to recuperate the citadel and have it declared a World Heritage site. In 2007 hundreds of families who remained in the ghetto were moved to a new suburb to the east of Hawler, to a place they call "The New Citadel." One can only hope that it, too, is not left to crumble with neglect.

Finally, I reached the water tower. Up close it is even more awe-inspiring than I remembered. But somehow, it no longer stood out as a monument that provided life-giving water to the people of the protected city. Now, it was a hollow reminder of a glorious past. And I still have no clue how the water gets to the top.

For a long time we lived in the eastern part of Hawler—I suspect mostly because the road leading to Ashkaftsaqa happened to be nearby. In all the forty years I lived in the city—minus, of course, the years I was in prison—I don't think I ever failed to see the sun rising and setting behind the citadel. To me, this natural cycle defines the city.

Hawler of the 1960s was also a place where you could hear the train announcing its arrival from Kirkuk every day. You could almost set your watch by the loud piercing whistle. The track was not far from our house, and as young boys, my friend Kh and I would go to see it at

every opportunity we had. The minute we heard the train announce
its approach, we would run to the track as fast as we could. Our
goal was to put a one-flis coin on the track before the train arrived.
Out of breath from the running, Kh would scramble in front of the
approaching train and carefully lay a flis on the track. I never ceased
to be amazed by what the train could do to a coin! It could magically
turn a simple flis into one the size of a ten-flis coin. Once the train had
disappeared into the distance, Kh would pick up the squashed coin
and run off to the ice-cream vendor. Hama Ali, who was half-blind,
would rub his fingers against the coin to determine its worth. He
always accepted it as a genuine ten-flis and handed us our ice creams.

In the 1980s, train service to Hawler was terminated. Little by
little, the once beautiful station began to resemble a junkyard. Scraps
of iron joined the handful of carriages left there when the government suspended the service. There was no real reason for leaving the
carriages, as far as I could see. They just looked lonely and dilapidated,
waiting in vain for travellers who would be amazed by the view from
the window as the train made its way through the mountains leading
to Kirkuk. While visiting Hawler in 2005, I walked past the station one
morning. The grand carriages that I remembered from my youth were
rusted and overflowing with garbage.

The visit to the station frustrated me. The most awful thing of all was
that the station complex had been converted into, of all things, a prison.
Most of the open acreage where people used to come and have picnics
in the spring had been taken over by a giant mosque, called Safwan. It
seemed that everything I had held dear, like the library and the station,
had become prisons in which my memories could languish. I tried to
remember the whistling sound I had heard when I was child, but I
couldn't. As I turned my back on the station, I could not help wondering
what other things I would not be able to remember on my next trip.

An Overplayed Ball

My years in elementary school went by quickly, and so did the middle-
school years. Almost without noticing, I had changed from a village

kid to a seasoned twelve-year-old city boy. During the summer break following my graduation from middle school, the fondness of soccer that I had developed in Ashkaftsaqa quickly turned into an obsession. It began with Bawil who had a rubber ball. Initially it was just the two of us playing in an open field near our homes, but soon we were joined by enough boys to form a team. We had one big problem, however: the boy with the ball was in the habit of suddenly picking up his ball and breaking off the game, saying, "I've got to go. My dad bought me this ball on the condition that I'd always be home before sundown."

Bawil's knack of ending the game just when everyone was beginning to really enjoy it frustrated us all. At some point during the summer, I decided on my own that the time had come for me to try to make some money. I teamed up with my friend, Zengena, who lived a few blocks down the road from me, and started a little venture of our own. We bought a kilogram of roasted sunflower seeds for seventy-five flis—just less than a dirham—and began selling it to anyone who would buy from us. I would carry the seeds around the streets in a deep dish while Zengena walked ahead advertising our wares and luring potential customers to our business. Within four days, we managed to sell it all. By this time, my pockets were heavy with the small change we had collected from our sales.

That night, I took the money home with me. I ran upstairs and emptied the coins onto my pillow. I counted them over and over: three whole dirhams! I had not seen so much money in my life. I hid the money under my pillow and tried to go to sleep. All night long I thought about the money. Before I finally fell asleep, my mind was made up: I wanted to spend it all on a medium-sized rubber ball. I knew the money was not entirely mine, but the thought of owning a ball of my own for playing soccer was just too good to resist. I knew that the ball I wanted cost exactly three dirhams because everyone called it the three-dirham ball.

At daybreak, I took the coins out and, after counting them again twice, went straight to *Mam* Osman's shop. I told my mother what I was going to do, but when she asked if I had told my partner about it, I pretended I didn't hear her and walked away briskly.

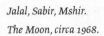

High School team.
Jalal is #4.

Jalal, Sabir, Mshir.
The Moon, circa 1968.

The shopkeeper was just opening as I arrived. He seemed preoccupied and somewhat confused when I asked him if he had any of the three-dirham balls left.

"I don't know yet, boy," he responded curtly. "Be patient; let me first get a little organized and then I'll look." That was the way *Mam* Osman always was. Angry and rude. When he had finally finished his opening routine, he did find two of the balls in a box. Without hesitation, I pushed the coins across the counter and hurried home with one of the balls. On the way I gave the ball a few kicks, and felt completely satisfied. I told my mother I didn't need any breakfast. I wiped off the ball nicely and went to see Zengena.

Zengena admired my purchase. "Where did you get the money for it?" he asked after he had turned it over several times.

"With the money we made selling sunflower seeds," I responded innocently.

He looked at me in disbelief. Finally he smiled gently and said, "I can't believe it! You've ruined the business."

He didn't seem to be too upset, though. Soon we were in the field, playing. We carried on playing until we could no longer see the ball in the lengthening shadows. Now that we had our own ball that could not be taken away at sundown, everything else in our lives was eclipsed by soccer. When I picked up the ball after the game was over I would take note of how tired and worn out it felt. I would wonder to myself how a ball could take so many shots. When we were not playing with the neighbourhood boys, we were at the stadium watching our favourite teams.

Soon I was playing like a pro and caught the eye of one of the older boys who played on the school team. When school started again that fall, he told our PE teacher how well I played, and the teacher made me a member of the school team. I was player number 11.

When I finished school, I played for a team called The Moon, whose members included the poet Fareed Zamdar and the artist Abdullah Rasoul.

I don't remember how many times we won, or how many goals I scored, or how many shots I missed. I do remember all the joy I would get from playing, though.

Throughout my playing days, I kept a close eye on the professional players in Hawler. Mursel was my idol. He was a terrific soccer player. Mursel may have looked very quiet, but on the field he was very sharp. He was number 10 and the closeness of our numbers made me dream of stardom one day. Mursel wasn't very tall, and he always shaved his moustache, which was quite strange, as moustaches were very fashionable back then. They still are in Kurdistan. When I watch the news from Kurdistan now, I still see the rows of men with shiny bold moustaches gathering for meetings around the countryside. Rumour had it that imported black polish was in high demand, for keeping these bushes well groomed was essential business.

In the 1980s Mursel joined the *peshmerga* group led by the Patriotic Union of Kurdistan. Sadly, he was killed in an air raid. His death was a big blow to me. It drove home the point I had realized very soon after Saddam came to power: in his world, everything was controlled by fear and blood. Every aspect of civilian life was replaced by the military and there was very little room left for individual expression. Now the time young men used to spend playing soccer was spent doing military training, where they could be brainwashed and prepared for the wars that were occurring more and more frequently. It did not take long before all the soccer fields were abandoned and the grass in the fields dried out.

Perhaps, Peace at Last

Since we had come to the city when I was still quite young, I did not have many memories of my own from Ashkaftsaqa. And yet the village was never far from our lives. Our house lay near the road that led to Ashkaftsaqa, and we had remained in contact with many of the people who had come to the city with us on that dreadful day in 1963. My most vivid memory of Ashkaftsaqa was of the lonely tree at the entrance of the village.

It was different for the people who were older. For many of them, the city was a temporary place to be until peace came to Kurdistan. They longed to return to the village and to life as they had known it for most of their lives. For some, that day seemed to arrived sooner than expected. The Kurdish resistance that had started on September 11, 1961 continued almost uninterrupted for the rest of that decade. Although the Ba'ath Party had made a concerted effort to end Kurdish resistance when it came to power in 1968, resistance continued. However, international pressure from Russia and the growing tension with Iraq led to a more serious attempt at brokering peace. On March 11, 1970, the Iraqi government finally signed a ceasefire with the *peshmerga* led by the popular leader Mustafa Barzani.

All hostilities ceased and people were overjoyed. Festive celebrations went on for months. Instead of going to work or school, the people of Kurdistan took to dancing. Not a single soccer field in Hawler stood empty. There were dances everywhere and children often had to give up trying to play soccer and watch the dancing instead. I, too, watched the dancing with a sense of déjà vu. Only this time, rather than watch the dancing from the rooftops of Ashkaftsaqa with my mother, I joined the line of adult dancers. Finally, I was dancing the dances of my early childhood!

In the midst of these festivities, *Mam* Bapir and his wife Meriam bought some sheep, goats, a cow, and a donkey, and one early morning they rented a truck and returned to Ashkaftsaqa. There, they lived in a makeshift shelter until a couple rooms and a porch had been built with locally made mud bricks and timber from a nearby forest, which hadn't been harvested for some time. With the agha being away from the village, the project moved forward without intervention.

Once he had settled down, Bapir's priority was to give his son, Zenden, a proper burial in the village cemetery. It had now been twelve years since Zenden had been killed. Bapir returned to the site where we had buried his son on our way to Hawler and placed the few pieces of bone that were left of his remains into a sack so that they could be reburied in the village cemetery.

I went with my family to attend Zenden's funeral and on the way to the village, I recall being overwhelmed by the sky and the calm of the mountains. I also noticed that lonely tree that had looked so large as a child now seemed quite a bit smaller. It was an intensely emotional ceremony, and afterwards Bapir slaughtered a sheep for the occasion.

For many summers afterwards, Bapir made it a habit of offering
travellers between Koya and Hawler free yoghurt drinks in Zenden's
name. Thirsty travellers greatly appreciated Bapir's generosity and
found the shady area he had created a welcoming place to rest. Of
course, Bapir could have made good money selling the yoghurt, but
as he put it himself, "As long as I live, my yoghurt and cheese will be
given away in Zenden's memory."

Whenever Bapir came to Hawler to visit us or to do business, he
often slept at our home. He was much loved by all of the refugees from
Ashkaftsaqa and so he could not stay with us every time. We had to
share his company with the others. Every time he was in town, he
would bring us a dish of yoghurt and a few heads of fresh cheese. For
our part, we would never send the cooking dish back empty.

In 1988 the Iraqi regime, in a systematic campaign to depopulate
rural Kurdistan, began the forcible evacuation of thousands of villages.
Once the Army had forced the people out of their homes, they burned
the villages to the ground. Ashkaftsaqa, which had lovingly been
rebuilt by the people who returned there from Koya and Hawler, was
one of the villages that was destroyed during Saddam's purge. Once
again Bapir had no choice but to return to Hawler. He and Meriam
lived in an apartment he'd bought years before, but it never felt like
a real home to them. He spent most of his days standing at a nearby
intersection watching military convoys moving in the direction of
Koya, hoping against hope they would soon withdraw from Kurdistan
for good. He never gave up on Ashkaftsaqa. He was desperate to go back
and spend the rest of his life there. But one day he collapsed at his
intersection. A heart attack ended his dream.

Unlike Bapir, my father opted to stay in Hawler, and until he
became seriously ill, I had no idea how much Ashkaftsaqa meant to
him and that he, too, longed to return. Of course, by that time it was
impossible to take him there—not just because the village had been
destroyed, but also because the government had declared the whole
area a no-go zone. The best we could do was to take him out along the
road to Ashkaftsaqa and stop at a spot where he could easily see the
ruins of the village from afar. Even at that distance, the change in him
would be instant and dramatic. His chronic stomach pain and the

intense aches in his left arm would just disappear, or at least that was what he told us. On occasion, he told us, "This area by the stream used to be all trees. When I was young, I used to go there with the other men to cut grass for the animals. We would return in the evening with loads of grass. Boy, it smelled so good, and looking at the sun going down was always breathtaking."

My father knew he was not going to be around much longer, but he tried to conceal his fears, even as his breathing problems worsened. On the evening of April 11, 1978, we were all sitting in our grassy front yard when he started complaining about the heat. My brother, Jamal, said there was enough daylight left to go for a ride all the way to the foothills near Ashkaftsaqa. My father seemed to like the idea, but something didn't seem to be right with him. He looked like he had trouble getting up and his breathing became a lot heavier. When we tried to get him into the car, he fell. So instead of taking a drive to see Ashkaftsaqa, we rushed him to the hospital. It took the doctor no more than a few minutes to say, "He's gone."

We all broke down. It was impossible to hold back the tears. The women among us wailed and beat their chests as the hospital staff took the body for autopsy. We buried my father near Bapir's grave in the Sheikh Ahmed Cemetery in Hawler.

The Illusion Ends

I finished school in 1971. I had applied, and had been accepted, to the University of Baghdad, but over the summer following high school, a new Teachers' Institute opened in Hawler, and I enrolled there instead. It was cheaper and also meant that I could be closer to my family. The Institute had an additional attraction—it was the first post-secondary institution in Hawler to have co-ed classes.

As time went by, it became very clear that the peace that had ensued after the ceasefire was an illusion. For the Iraqi regime, it was just a break and a time-consuming effort and they had grown tired of the situation. By the mid-1970s, the intentions of the Iraqi regime were becoming increasingly clear: not only was the regime going back on the promises it had made to the Kurds in the March 11 Manifesto, it was also preparing for war against them. The regime began with a campaign of terror, targeting shops, restaurants, and tea houses in Kurdish cities, in particular Hawler.

One of the first targets was the popular tea house, Bakour, in the centre of downtown Hawler. The tea house was located right by one of the gates to the citadel, and from the balcony you could look out at the magnificent structure. It was about half an hour's walk from the campus, but it was worth it. As you walked up the staircase leading to the door, you could hear the laughter and fun inside. There were always students there, and before and after class my friends and I practically lived at Bakour, playing dominoes and *tawli* late into the night. On cold evenings, the owner lit a stove in the middle of the lounge and we would huddle close to enjoy its warmth as the sounds of Kurdish music filled the room.

One afternoon late in the autumn of my first year, I was at Bakour, enjoying the company of my good friend, Farhan. I got up to go to class, but Farhan decided to stay. "The music is too much fun," he insisted. He tried to convince me to stay a while longer and enjoy a lazy afternoon rather than go to class. As I left, I motioned to him one last time to join me. He shook his head.

It could not have been three minutes later, for I had not even reached the bottom of the hill leading away from Bakour, when an explosion shook the ground underneath me. People on the street turned and looked back in horror. I could see smoke rising from the rooftops of what I knew was Bakour Tea House. I ran back. It was horrific. Debris was lying everywhere and the place was engulfed in smoke. It seemed as if there were many casualties, but the shock of the unexpected bombing left people milling around in shock. We lost many friends that day, including Farhan.

About a week later, another bomb went off at a local kebab restaurant, Farouq's. The restaurant was just up the road from where the Bakour Tea House was situated. The bomb went off at lunchtime when the place was jammed with locals. Among the many dead was the owner's only son, Bashir, who was a primary school teacher. The loss was too much for his father, Farouq, to bear and he went crazy. Because at the time there was no such thing as a mental health hospital, those

Shaqlawa field trip with other students from the Teacher's Institute, early 1970s.
Left-to-right: Bakir, Mustafa, Faik, Aziz, Jalal.

Bakour Tea House with friends, 1973. Left-to-right: Jalal, Jawhar, Mussin, Mawlud.

who were mentally disturbed were taken to the sheikh's house where they were tied up in a dark room and beaten with wooden sticks. Somehow, someone had decided that this would make them better. For years afterwards, Farouq could be seen roaming the streets for hours on end, barefoot no matter what the weather. In some ways, I was jealous of the freedom he had, even though the price for it was too high. The poor man ended up getting killed by the secret police in the 1980s when he failed to stop at a checkpoint during a curfew.

In the early 1970s, there was only one high-ranking Ba'ath official in Hawler, but it seemed he was busy building up a network of loyalists. During the ceasefire between the *peshmerga* and the Iraqi government, and throughout the period of peace, relations between the Kurds and the Iraqi government were tense. There were forever meetings and negotiations between leaders from both sides. Late in 1973, a group of men disguised as mullahs came to see Mustafa Barzani, a Kurdish leader and the son of Massoud Barzani. At the reception he was giving in their honour, the men blew themselves up, killing and wounding many. Miraculously, Barzani wasn't hurt. Rumour had it that the group that tried to kill Mustafa Barzani came from the network of loyalists gathered around the ' Party official in Hawler.

In 1974 war started again, and Hawler became deserted as large numbers of people, including many professionals, joined the *peshmerga* during what was known as the September Revolution. Among those who joined at the time was my brother, Jamal. During the revolution, anything with four tires was taken and driven up towards the mountains. Entire families would ride in these cars until they ran out of gas, after which they would proceed on foot.

The University of Suleimaniya, which at the time was the only university in Kurdistan, relocated its entire campus to the *peshmerga*-controlled town of Qat'al Diza in January 1974, little expecting that a massacre was soon to follow. On April 22, 1974, a squadron of bombers reduced the defenceless campus to rubble, killing and wounding hundreds.

During this time, the Iraqi Communist Party was a strong ally of the regime. Saddam's cordial relations with the Soviet Bloc and Cuba were the main reason why they were on the dictator's side. Many years later, my mother-in-law, Salama, had something interesting to say about how this alliance was playing out in the street: "In 1974, when the Iraqi warplanes came and devastated our city, Communists and their foes, instead of taking care of the dead and wounded, were busy trading accusations. One Communist woman was holding a piece of shrapnel and was swearing by Lenin that the bombs had come from the imperialist United States. The Communists were good with words. What was important was not the evidence but which side could shout down the other. In this respect, the Communists were second to none."

One evening, Zengena came for a visit. He was carrying about twenty loaves of bread. He said he was on his way to join the revolution in the mountains. I accompanied him to the outskirts of the city in the north. When the time came for us to take leave of each other, I felt compelled to explain myself. "I don't think I have the will to pick up weapons, nor do I have what it takes to become a *peshmerga*," I said. "If I come, I will become a burden to the cause. And besides, with Jamal already a *peshmerga* in the Zozik region, I don't want to make it any harder on my father. He's already worried that he may not see his other son again."

I could not find it in me to become a *peshmerga*. I did, however, take a big risk by joining the political wing of the Kurdistan Democratic Party, which operated clandestinely in Hawler to remind people in the city to support the revolution. This was all underground work, and I risked my life doing it. If I were caught, I would've been executed. I was on my guard all the time and thought to myself that it would have been safer for me to have joined the *peshmerga* with my friend that night.

News about the war in Kurdistan was hard to come by. The Iraqi regime did not allow any news of the revolution to be broadcast and the underground *peshmerga* radio was permanently jammed. Still, we tried to glean any bit of information we could from a brief mention of it on the Voice of America, Radio Israel, or Radio Monte Carlo, all of which broadcast in Arabic. We had to keep the volume turned right down so that there was no chance of anyone hearing the broadcast from outside. This meant that only one of us could listen at a time. Even though he did not understand Arabic, my father would not allow any of us to take on this responsibility.

The only thing my father could understand was the term "Kurdish rebels." Whenever he heard the phrase, he would raise his voice and announce, "They are talking about our situation on the international radio. The war must stop so that Jamal can come home and we can find him a wife." Even though my father didn't think it was fair for Kurdish freedom fighters to be called rebels, any mention of them made him feel that the Kurds were doing something right and that the world was not entirely indifferent to their cause.

On one occasion, the jamming of the *peshmerga* broadcasts made him so furious that he grabbed the radio and smashed it on the concrete floor. The next day, when he began to realize that it would be weeks before he could save enough money for a new radio, he regretted his rash action.

The war lasted little less than a year. On March 6, 1975, Saddam signed the so-called Algiers Agreement, which was brokered by the late Shah of Iran in Algeria, with American and Egyptian blessing. A key term of the agreement was that Iran would cease providing support to Iraqi Kurds. This dealt the Kurdish revolution a mortal blow.

Mustafa Barzani and some of his closest followers were given asylum in America. Some of his followers formed small splinter groups and vowed to fight on, but the vast majority accepted Saddam's offer of amnesty and went back to their homes after several months in detention. Barzani later died of cancer in America. After the war, he was a broken man. After his death, his body was temporarily buried in the Kurdish city of Shno in Iran but later, after the Kurdish uprising in 1991, his remains were reinterred during a large ceremony in his birthplace, the village of Barzan.

After the collapse of Kurdish revolution, Jamal, like thousands of other *peshmerga*, surrendered. He was imprisoned for months before being released and allowed to come home. We all had missed him very much. Jamal had come home, but he came home a broken man. We had not seen him or heard from him in a year. And then, within twenty-four hours, the revolution collapsed and there he was standing at our front door. Our happiness at seeing him again was darkened by the knowledge that he, like all the other *peshmerga* who had laid down arms, would be required to report to the military base in Hawler within twenty-four hours of his arrival in the city. We all knew what that meant, and so we made the most of the little time we had that evening. Jamal was saddened by the collapse of the revolution because the cause had not been lost on the battlefield.

The following day, Jamal reported to the military base, where he was kept in a barbed wire camp on the base for seven days before being moved to a prison on the base. He was released after a month, but others were sent to prisons throughout Iraq. The worst punishment was reserved for leaders, who were deported to Al-Ramadi and kept there in a concentration camp for an entire year.

It took Jamal a long time to recover from the ordeal of fighting and subsequent imprisonment. Before he joined the *peshmerga*, Jamal was well respected in the construction industry and so he started his job again. By 1980, Jamal had become quite successful and had dozens of people working for him. That summer, I went to work for him. But on the first day, which turned out to be my last day as well, I hurt myself badly when I stepped on a huge nail. I was in agony for days. The experience made me realize how ill-suited I was for this line of work, or for anything that required a practical bent. I didn't even make an effort to learn how to drive until Jamal talked me into doing so. For some reason I thought poets like me didn't have to worry about the mundane aspects of everyday life.

Following the collapse of the revolution in 1975, Jalal Talabani founded the Patriotic Union of Kurdistan. Massoud and Idris, Mustafa Barzani's sons, reorganized the Kurdistan Democratic Party and continued fighting for Kurdish people's basic rights. New Kurdish political parties were established. Slowly, little by little, the *peshmerga* regrouped. This time, it was a more politically diverse, agile and effective military outfit. Later, when Saddam turned against the Communists, many joined the *peshmerga*. It was quite ironic, since at that time, Saddam was still being supported militarily and politically by the Soviet Union. Indeed, the warplanes that attacked Kurdistan were all Soviet-made. This put the Communists in an awkward position and eventually caused the party to split. But for many, resigning from the party seemed to be the only way out.

A Teacher's Life

In the fall of 1976, I was hired to teach primary school in the village of Sktan. This was my first teaching post after completing my teacher training and I was delighted at the prospect of putting my education to good use. On the day of my departure, I checked my bag carefully before making my way to the taxi rank. Sktan was a tiny place that lay between Shaqlawa and Raniyah to the northeast of Hawler. I knew very little about the town where I was to teach, except that it was very remote and that I would have to spend my first night at the Hotel Safeen in Koya. From there, I planned to go to the terminal and find a taxi that could take me to Sktan.

I took the window seat in a Toyota car taxi from Hawler to Koya. As we passed my birthplace, Ashkaftsaqa, I felt an incredible sense of longing. I saw the *kapr* where Uncle Bapir stayed in the late fall. He had marked it by planting four trees in a square and building a fence around the site. I could also see the gravestones, including Zenden's, in the cemetery. Uncle Bapir had planted four tall slender trees and had built a wooden fence around the *kapr*. I wished the taxi driver would stop at Bapir's *kapr*, but he didn't.

I was the only customer at the hotel in Koya, and the lobby manager told me I was free to sleep in a room of my choice but that it would be wise to avoid windows because should the *peshmerga* attack the Iraqi regime's offices it would turn into a battle. I didn't sleep very well that night.

When I awoke, I went down to the lobby. "Where's the terminal for the taxi to Sktan?" I asked politely.

The manager gave me a quizzical look. Then, clearly noticing I was a city boy, he smiled and explained that I would have to go to the stable to find transport to Sktan. The minute I stepped outside and started walking, I knew I was going the right way because of the strength of the odour.

Koya had only one street running through it. The stores on the side were all small, and most were empty. In front of the open stores there were various vegetables and fruits. In the winter, though, there was no fruit to sell; they had to wait for next season to resupply.

I had scaled down my expectations from a taxi to a horse, but I still felt good about the journey. About halfway down the street, I found the local tea house. It was still early in the morning, but already a sizeable crowd had gathered to play dominoes and while away the hours of unemployment. I introduced myself. The villagers could tell right away I was from the city. When I told them I was going to Sktan one of the men looked down at my feet. He laughed when he saw my dress shoes.

"*Mamosta*," he cautioned me, "I don't think your shoes are suitable for the terrain." He then proceeded to tell me that the only way into Sktan was a seven-hour journey on foot. He finished by giving me one final word of warning: "It's rough and mountainous."

Just before lunch, I joined a caravan of donkeys and mules leaving for Sktan. The man at the tea house was correct: this was indeed a forbidding terrain. The torturous walk was not, however, without reward. The first two hours felt like the whole thing was unreal. The peaceful expanse of hills, mountains, gorges, and valleys made it seem like time had suddenly stopped just for me. At a shady spring, where we stopped for a little rest, I recall saying to myself, "Here you are, Jalal, in the midst of a heaven on earth. So try to enjoy it and don't complain." I began to write a poem. It was the first time since I had started writing that I had been surrounded by nature, and I found it inspiring.

By the time we passed the two mountain ranges of Bawaji and Awagird, I had absolutely no energy left. The men offered me a donkey to ride, but considering that everyone else was on foot and all the animals were carrying heavy loads, I declined the offer. I guess it was their way of showing pity for a city boy. We were still walking when it got dark. As the sun set, I turned to Bakir, the man who was walking just ahead of me, and asked the time.

"It is eight," said Bakir as he flashed his cigarette lighter to see the dials on his watch. Stars were everywhere, and the mountain ranges looked like giant shadows keeping watch over the foothills.

When we arrived at Sktan, the village seemed eerily quiet. I couldn't get a sense of the size of the village in the dark, but I could see a single light burning through one window. Bakir then told me it was the house where some of the other teachers in the village lived. At least it looked as if someone there was still awake. The caravan men offered to put me up for the night, but I chose to stay with the teachers. I knocked on the door and one of the men opened it for me. When I introduced myself as a new teacher at the school, they invited me in.

Realizing how hungry and tired I was, one of them promptly fried a couple of eggs. I sat down by the table and took my shoes off. By the time I had finished removing my shoes, he slid a plate of food in front of me. Even though I felt a little awkward eating by myself, I ate like a hunter. During our conversation over my meal, I discovered that the men who stayed in the house were all single like me. I could see by the looks on the men's faces that my socks were very smelly after the day's walk, but I didn't stop eating until every last crumb on my plate was gone. Only then did I remove my socks and take them outside.

It was rather strange being back in a small Kurdish village. This was the first time I had seen a kerosene lamp on the walls since my time in Ashkaftsaqa, where every evening my mother would have to clean the black glass and fill it up with more kerosene. I slept deeply that night and refused to wake even for a pee.

When I rose in the morning, the villagers were already in the midst of their daily routine. I cast my eyes around the village to get a better sense of where I would be working. The teachers' house was lower down the slope of the mountain than the rest of the settlement, and I had to look up to the mountain peak to get a good view of the village. There were some fifty houses scattered along the side of the mountain. A single road meandered through the town. I turned around again and looked out over the valley. Farther down in the valley there was a plateau, where the villagers were busy ploughing their lands. A little way off to my left, I noticed a solitary building just outside the town. This, I would learn, was the school building where I would be teaching. Behind me, the shepherds were already a good way up the mountainside with their flocks.

Even as the people were going about their daily tasks, there was an ominous atmosphere. In the distance, on a knoll just beyond the fields, an armoured military force appeared to be positioning itself for an attack on the village. Soon several others joined it. The villagers ran for cover. Those close to their homes ran inside to hide. Others found what shelter they could. I could not believe my eyes for it seemed that such a thing could not happen in such a remote place. Yet that's exactly what happened. On my very first day in Sktan the village was pounded with artillery and small arms fire for several minutes.

I sat inside the house with the other teachers. None of us spoke a word. As soon as the gunfire stopped, the soldiers came down into the village and started rounding up all the men. The officer in charge, a mean-looking man with a crooked moustache, looked us over contemptuously and then, pointing with his stick, randomly picked fifteen men to be taken away and thrown into the back of a military truck. I guess I was one of the lucky ones who escaped that day.

After the military force left, the villagers stood there crying. It was the first time I had ever seen a group of men crying together. After a short while, we went about the business of caring for the wounded and the dead. Scores of people were killed and wounded during the attack, including a man everyone called Crazy Omar. He was standing just outside his home when he was hit and was still alive when his parents dragged him inside. His mother said he didn't understand what had happened to him. He smiled as he was dying. The wounded had to be taken on horseback to the town of Raniyah, about five hours away.

We later learned that of the fifteen men who were taken away that day, five were executed at Abu Ghraib prison. The rest were given sentences ranging from three to fifteen years. I never saw them again. One of the local shepherds was among the people arrested, and for a week his animals were left in their stables and did not get to go to pasture.

At first, the villagers were not very excited about me being there as their new teacher. I suspect it may have been due to the number of times schools had been opened and burned down because of the war. By the time I arrived, they had lost hope of having a school permanently.

I spent two years in this village, teaching elementary school. There were about twenty-five children in the school. About a month after I arrived, the other three teachers were transferred out of the village. For a while, I was on my own. A month later, three female teachers arrived to take their place. They moved into the house where I had been staying since my arrival. I went and stayed in an empty room in the school building.

Shortly after the start of my third year in Sktan, I was transferred to a school in Smakshirin, where I would teach until my arrest in 1986. I returned to Hawler for the first time since leaving it and spent a week catching up with family and friends before heading off to my next assignment. Fortunately, Smakshirin was only about half an hour's drive out of Hawler, and I would commute every day.

I have never been able to get the small village of Sktan out of my mind. My biggest fear throughout my stay in the village was that what happened that first morning would happen again. Although I have forgotten much about my time in Sktan, I will always remember the sound of the fifteen men crying as they were being led away.

4 A World of Words

The Lure of Reading

I HAVE BEEN IN LIBRARIES during the darkest and happiest moments in my life. My fondness for writing and libraries goes back all the way to my school days in the late 1960s at the all-male Kurdistan High.

The home in which I grew up always seemed small and crowded. But then, so were all the homes in the Setaqan neighbourhood. Like most other kids in the neighbourhood, I would escape the confines of the home and go to the rooftop to study. Soon I would tire of this pastime and head back downstairs and outside to study under the streetlights. It would be bitterly cold in the winter and oven-hot in the summer, but we were teenage boys and we didn't seem to mind the weather as long as there were girls. Boys and girls would sit around pretending to be studying harder than anyone else. At least it made us feel good. I paid no attention to my mother's warning that the strong sun would make me lose my hair early. Or that I would get sunburned.

Every night, weather permitting, I would go and study by the street-light. I was not alone in my endeavours to become learned: by 10:00 PM there would be a crowd of young boys huddling around the streetlight. The more boys there were, the less studying we did. And so at the end of every evening, we would return to our homes having done very little studying but with a plethora of good stories rattling in our heads.

Eventually, I learned that I needed to go to the Hawler Public Library if I wanted to get any studying done. The library building was one of the most magnificent and most peaceful buildings in Hawler. Here, for the briefest of moments, I could escape from reality.

The library was built before the Ba'ath Party came into power. You would enter the building through a revolving glass door. At the time, it was the only revolving door in Hawler and people would come there just for the amusement of walking through the revolving door. Once inside, you would be engulfed by the silence of the reading hall. People would sit for hours at the beautiful oak desks, reading. Everywhere you could smell books. When I did not feel like reading, I would simply wander through the library shelves, skimming the titles of the books, or taking them out and fondling them lovingly.

It was in this room that I learned to be a quiet and silent reader. Time slipped by unnoticed, and every so often, the librarian would tap me on the shoulder to remind me that it was closing time, or that it was time to go to school. Time to go outside and face the reality of the world in which I lived.

Right opposite the Hawler Public Library stood Erbil High School. My school, the all-male Kurdistan High School, was about two miles away. Like all schools across the country, Kurdistan High had to share a building with another school. This arrangement cut the school day in half, but it was necessary because there were too many students and not enough buildings. The morning session started at eight and finished at noon. The afternoon session lasted from one to five. I liked the afternoon session better, because spending my mornings in the library seemed more rewarding than being at school. The library was also an escape from the hustle and bustle of our home, which was all the way across town on the east side of the city. It was a one-hour walk each way, but I didn't mind. From the library I would walk the two-mile stretch to school briskly, arriving in time to buy a boiled-egg sandwich from my favourite street vendor, who always threw in extra red pickles to keep me satisfied.

I wasn't all that interested in school. More often than not, I went unprepared. With so many interesting books in the library, I just couldn't bring myself to concentrate on schoolwork. Avoiding eye contact with the teacher was my way of trying not to be called upon. The technique worked in most classes, but not in *Mamosta* Mullah Hameed's class, in which we had to memorize verses from the Qu'ran. The punishment for not doing one's homework in his class was four strokes with a cane on the palm of the hand. It was intolerable. This class was supposed to be about religion, but in reality it was all about the glorification of Islam.

The last class in the afternoon session ended a little after five, but sometimes we would be let go early if the teacher happened to be absent. On such days, just before dinner, I would treat myself to a little sandwich of naan and scallions that my mother had planted in tin cans. It was always nice to see my father and brother Jamal returning home at the end of the day, but the person I was most eager to see every night was my grandmother. She was a superb storyteller. One of her stories would take four to five evenings to finish. I would think about the story all day, wondering how it was going to end. But the stories, being folktales, always ended the same way: the villain got punished and the hero got rewarded. It was predictable but satisfactory. Looking back, I can see that my grandmother's stories were a big influence on my imagination and my love for reading and writing.

As I grew older, I began to rely more and more on the library for reading material. The library's collection of Kurdish books was meagre in comparison to its Arabic and English holdings. I know for sure that the collection was much smaller than the Kurdish classics the famous printer and publisher Geew Mokryani had on display in his shop window. Whenever I went downtown, I always stopped in front of Geew Mokryani's shop window to look at his books. The display was like a magnet. There were many beautiful books, but the one book that always caught my eye, the one particular book that I really wanted,

was the complete poems of our national poet, Wefayî. I was crazy
about a love poem of his that the Iranian Kurdish singer Mazhari
Khaliqi had put to music. The song was beautiful, but I was eager to
see the poem in print. I started saving the first day I saw this book.
Every day I would make a detour on the way home to go and stare at it.
When I got home, I would count my money, but it was never enough.

Then one day I realized I didn't actually have to buy the book: I
could borrow it from the library, which had just acquired a copy. So I
spent the money on a kebab sandwich I had been craving for days.

By the end of the 1960s, reading had become my new passion. It had
replaced my fondness for soccer. Maybe it was because of the legends
and folktales Grandma had been telling me. Maybe it was because
I was born in the countryside, or maybe it was because I needed to
search for those things I had lost in life growing up in poverty in a
hostile environment. Maybe it was because of all of these things.

I was born in a house with no books or pens. My mother saw me
reading one day when my junior high school had just ended. It was a
collection of poems by Wefayî. She gave me a strange look but didn't
say anything. Later I heard her telling one of her woman friends:
"School is over. I don't understand why Jalal continues to read books!"

In December 2005, while on a visit to Kurdistan, I noticed how
eager my mother was to be around me. We had to share a room, and
on the first night, she insisted that I take the bed while she slept on
the floor beside me. I wasn't sick or anything, but she would get up
several times during the night to check up on me and make sure I was
covered. The following morning, I went and bought a second bed to
avoid my mother's protestations again.

The first few nights, because of the fifteen-hour time difference
between Edmonton and Hawler, I had difficulty sleeping. After tossing
and turning for a while, I would try to read by the light of the lantern.
Little had changed since I grew up in Hawler. The city, and the rest of
Kurdistan, still only had power for a few hours a day. And my reading
habits still bothered my mother. She thought all this reading was too
taxing on me. One morning after prayers, she said somewhat sadly,
"My son, you've spent a lifetime reading and writing. I feel I have lost

you to books. And then you went and left your homeland. I feel I have lost you twice. Your friends are better off than you. They're all here. None of them left."

And so that evening, to be nice to her, I turned the lantern down and pulled the blankets up over my head. Lying there in the dark, I reflected on her words. She would never lose her son, but I could also never give up reading. I lay there for a long time, but I still could not sleep. From time to time, I would hold up my blanket to see when the sun would rise and the smell of the fresh red tea my sister Ruqya made for breakfast would fill the house. At the first sound of her stirring, I tiptoed downstairs and read while drinking my tea.

At the time I went to high school, my Arabic was not good. Our education in primary school had been in Kurdish, but in junior high we had switch to Arabic. This sudden change, which came about without adequate preparation, forced many Kurdish students to give up school altogether. It was a tough struggle for me, and for some teachers, too, but I got used to it after the first year. What's more, I managed to learn enough Arabic to help plough my way through the works of such famous Arab poets as Al-Bayyati, Badr Shakir al-Sayyab, and Nazik al-Mala'ka, along with the translated works of international poets like Rimbaud and Baudelaire. If there was a motivation to learn Arabic at school, it was to gain access to more of what I really loved: poetry. And to feed that desire, I had to go to the library.

The library also fed other desires. Galawezh was the only woman employed in the library. Her dedication to her work was heartwarming and because she worked in a place that I loved and where I spent a great deal of time, I soon developed a youthful crush on her. I would make sure that I arrived at the library before she did in the mornings so that I could watch her arrive at work. As an excuse, I would stand outside and chat with the gardener, Said. He was very proud of how he took care of the library's flower garden. Every time I went to speak with him, I was afraid he would ask why I was at the library so early, but thankfully, he never did. He was an in-your-face type of a man who liked making fun of people. He never made fun of me, but I was always on guard when talking to him. Talking to him, however, was just an excuse to be where I could observe Galawezh. For some reason, observing her made me conclude that unmarried women walked differently than married women.

Come rain or shine, Galawezh always arrived on time, cloaked in her shiny aba. This outer garment concealed the European-style clothing she wore underneath. Like so many Kurdish women who worked in those days, she had to be careful to present an image of propriety to the world, but her European clothes underneath revealed her progressive views. In winter when it was raining, she would use her red umbrella until she arrived in front of the library. The raindrops created a tiny river on her umbrella. The stream of water would run to the edge of the umbrella and then drop to the ground softly. Once inside, she would shake the rain off her umbrella and walk towards her office. I would follow her so that I could savour the smell of her perfume that lingered in the entrance.

Galawezh had no trouble going up the wooden ladder dozens of time a day to take down books from the shelves. If the books had been up there for a long time, she dusted them by rubbing the covers against her chest. Galawezh was nice to all the patrons, but somehow I persuaded myself that she was extra nice to me.

It didn't take me long to recognize that Galawezh's hands were white and smooth while mine were rough and cracked. I felt embarrassed by them every time I needed to take a book from her. My mother would cover my hands with cream at night and then wrap them in a towel, saying by morning all the coarseness would disappear. But that never happened.

A Return to the Library

The day the Ba'ath Party came to power in a military coup in 1968, my seemingly idyllic world began to crumble. Shortly after coming to power, they took over the library and turned it into a prison. It was like a stab to my heart. Little did I know then that this would be the library in which I would eventually be imprisoned.

The Ba'ath Party didn't just take over the library. They also occupied houses, cafés, and parks. One particular café, the Baiz Tea Shop, was a city landmark. In winter, its giant kerosene heater kept people warm late into the night. Unlike our rundown house, the houses in the Baiz neighbourhood were built of stone and brick. They had balconies and open spaces and Mediterranean-style gardens. Their grandeur was truly a beautiful sight to behold. Now, the regime demolished some of these beautiful old buildings and in their place erected massive structures to house the party's and secret police's many branches. Seemingly overnight, what was once a beautiful city began to resemble a military garrison.

The library was moved to a temporary building—an ugly cinder-block structure—amidst government promises to build a new one to replace the magnificent building that I loved so much. During my return to Kurdistan in 2005 to visit family and friends, I visited the new Hawler Public Library. As we approached the building, I stopped, closed my eyes and stood there for a moment. My past and the image of the original library appeared right there before my eyes. Everything looked so real and beautiful. I recalled a time long, long before my arrest, before the place became my prison. I remembered the library that had had such a great impact on my life.

Sadly, the library was still housed that same ugly temporary building. More than thirty years later, this city of a million people was still without a decent library. The day I was there, the number of employees outnumbered the patrons two to one. Gone was the reading room that inspired me as a youth. Gone were the shelves of books that had graced the library walls, and gone was my teenage love, Galawezh.

Before I returned to Edmonton, I tried to track down Galawezh, but to no avail. By then, I calculated she must have been in her seventies. I was unable to find out if she was married or not, alive or dead. I hoped she wasn't a widow, for in Iraq life can be a lot harder for women than for men. Men can always linger around the mosque, knowing that they will be taken care of. Women don't have such an option. Galawezh had been a junior librarian at Hawler Public Library, but for me her name was synonymous with the library itself.

It was a sad moment to see it all relegated to memory. Yet, even though I did not know it at the time, my writing career had come full circle since it started in the Hawler library. Since leaving Kurdistan in

1996, I have lived in many places, but until then I had been unable to return full time to my professional as a writer. In 2007 I was appointed as the PEN Writer-in-Exile in Edmonton. I was given an office at the Edmonton Public Library. It was an opportunity to start over once again at a beloved library. From the moment I walked into the library to start my job as a full-time writer, I was embraced by the smell of books and coffee, because there was a coffee shop on the main floor. Linda Goyette, a local writer who was completing her time as the Edmonton Public Library writer-in-residence, was in the lobby waiting for me. For the first time in many years, I felt like I was home again.

My First Publication

In 1971 I was completing my second year at Kurdistan High. I remember that year well, for it was the year in which my name first appeared in print. It wasn't exactly my work, but it had my name attached to it. In a region desperately short of books, we would copy bits and pieces from books and magazines and display them on the school notice board. I had selected an excerpt from a poem by the writer Hanari, which I had come across in one of his books. But on the student poster, neatly framed and mounted on the school wall, it was presented as mine.

My first actual publication was a poem titled "The Ripped-out Cemetery" that appeared in a little magazine called *Rahela*, which a few friends of mine and I put together at Kurdistan High. Later we changed the name to *Beri Newe*, or *New Idea*. We were young and idealistic and totally fascinated by French poetry movements like Dadaism and Clericalism. We were determined to improve our writing and become part of this movement. It was an ambitious dream for a few young unknown school boys.

I read my first poem in public when I was eighteen. It was in the city of Koya during a national ceremony commemorating the life and work of the great Kurdish nationalist poet Haji Qadir Koyi. His work was an inspiration to many young Kurdish writers who wanted to use literature to promote an independent Kurdistan. The ceremony was hosted by the Kurdish Teachers' Association, and so all of us who were

Right: Jalal in Grade 10.
Below: Jalal's graduating
class, Kurdistan High School
in Hawler. Jalal is sixth
from the right in the third
row. His history teacher,
Polsyaqub, is ninth from the
right in the same row.

reading were at a loss as to why we had been invited, since none of us were teachers. On the evening of the poetry reading, I felt incredibly proud to share the stage with some of Kurdistan's most accomplished writers and poets, including Fareed Zamdar, Saadulla Parosh, and Jawhar Kurmanj. I felt even prouder when a friend played an audiotape of the reading as we drove back that night. We played the tape over and over, and we all agreed that a poet—me—had been born that night.

New books were hard to come by in Hawler. During the 1970s there were two bookstores in Hawler, Geew Mokryani and Razaq, which was also named after its owner. Mokryani's bookstore printed, published, and sold Kurdish classics, while the Razaq bookstore sold mostly left-wing books, and it was there that I saw for the first time a book by Karl Marx, translated into Kurdish. At that time it was fashionable to read left-wing books, and people enjoyed the ideas of social justice contained in those books. But the dream of a Communist utopia never came true. The Communist Party had been established in Iraq over sixty years before, and it had branches in Kurdistan but had never succeeded in taking power. The ideology never amounted to more than words.

But my friends and I were looking beyond Kurdistan in our reading at the time and wanted to pick up books by Western authors that were not available at either of our local bookstores. So Zengena, Tahseen, and I decided one day to make a trip to Baghdad to buy books. At the time, Baghdad was well known throughout the Middle East for its many bookstores. The trip was also an excuse for Zengena to visit a close friend, Hewa. Hewa's father held a senior position in the railway and after spending a year in Hawler, was transferred back to Baghdad.

For Tasheen and me, this would be our first visit to the capital, and we couldn't wait to get going. For many centuries, Baghdad was regarded as the intellectual centre of the Islamic world. The original city was founded in 762 CE by Abu Jafar-al-Mansour, the second Abbasid caliph. The old city is built in a circle around the grand mosque and the Golden Gate Palace, where the caliphs held court. Even from the earliest times, Baghdad developed along both banks of the Tigris River. The east bank settlement is known as Rusafah, while the west bank is called Al-Karkh.

Jalal and Zengena in Baghdad, 1976.

On the day of the trip, we arrived at the bus station early. We were clearly not the only passengers headed for the capital. Eighteen of us crammed into an old Mercedes minivan for the three-and-a-half-hour journey to Baghdad, but on this day, the trip took more than seven hours. The sun was barely up and already it was brutal. By midday, temperatures outside had soared to 40°c. The battered old van had no air conditioning and we were dying inside. Ice water, passed around in a bowl, provided blissful moments of relief, but this was a chore the passenger sitting next to the icebox performed only grudgingly. This was understandable, since people were shouting for water at all times.

Going up Mount Handrin, between Kirkuk and Baghdad, which marks in the Kurdish people's hearts the border between south Kurdistan and Iraq, proved to be too much of a struggle for the old van. We had to stop several times to let the engine cool off. From my window seat, I could see how desolate the rugged terrain was. Except for a few isolated military outposts, there was no other sign of life. Farther down, it was an endless stretch of desert. The air was hotter there, and there was virtually nothing to look at. But near Khalis, an hour's drive north of Baghdad, there was a marked change in the landscape: palm trees, which I had not seen before, stretched all the way to the horizon.

In the late afternoon I could see the high-rises of Baghdad looming in the distance. Hawler did not have any high-rise buildings and I was surprised to learn that we were still some twenty miles out of the city. The buildings looked so big and impressive, even from afar. At the bus terminal, Abdullah Zengena led the way. He had been to Baghdad before and knew which bus to take to the Maidan Bus Station, which was where we were headed. People were rushing everywhere, bags in hand, and I was glad I did not have to do this on my own. The double-decker buses in the city were another new experience, but I embraced it. As soon as we stepped onto the bus, I headed for the upstairs and a window seat. As we drove into the centre of Baghdad, the view from the top level of the bus was breathtaking, even though I was way too excited to take much of it in. The city streets were crowded. It was early evening and people were already heading out for the night.

We were so mesmerized by everything that we hardly noticed the bus driver pull up at the Maidan Station. We grabbed our bags and began to walk to the Hotel Erbil on Rashid Street, where we had booked our rooms. Rashid Street is the oldest and longest street in Baghdad and has become famous because it was on this street, not far from the Hotel Erbil, that Saddam Hussein tried to assassinate Abdul-Karim Qasim. Like many other visitors from Hawler, we chose this hotel because it bore the ancient name of our home city. As we walked into the lobby, we noticed several Kurds sitting in the chairs. It felt just like going into a tea house in Hawler. We were so keen to absorb as much as we could that it didn't even occur to us to take a shower or change before going out.

We ate as fast as we could (familiar stuff, rice and beans), and set out immediately to explore Baghdad on foot. At that time Baghdad wasn't the capital of fear, terror, imprisonment, and dictatorship it would become in a few years' time. We felt a sense of freedom that we hadn't felt before. In Hawler all the shops and restaurants and stores closed shortly after sundown. Baghdad, on the other hand, was big and it had an amazing array of shops, most of which remained open well into the night. People, cars, and women in short tight skirts were everywhere. We were too excited to be thinking about sleep.

When we finally got back to the hotel, another new experience was waiting for me. I had never slept on a bed before. Exhausted from the journey and our walk around the streets, I soon fell asleep. After breakfast the next day, we went to see Hewa. Zengena had the address and led the way. It did not take him long to get us thoroughly lost. By the time we found Hewa's house, it was lunchtime. Hewa's teenaged sister opened the door shyly and invited us in. We sat down in a row on the couch in the living room. I was extremely tired and shy and said nothing as Hewa introduced us to his parents. Hewa's dad asked us how we had come to their house, and we told him that we had walked. Hewa said, "It would have been only twenty minutes by the bus number 35." Tahseen and I cast a murderous look at Zengena.

Since it was already lunchtime, Hewa's family invited us to join them for a meal. They had roasted a huge fish in the oven, but because none of us had eaten fish before, we just nibbled. It would have been extremely rude not to eat. Hewa's father drove us back to our hotel late in the afternoon, but instead of going back to the hotel room to get some rest, we went to the closest restaurant and began eating rice and beans again.

Before settling in for the night, we decided to take in a ritual experience for anyone going to Baghdad: yoghurt. Even though it was late, the city was bustling with Arab traders who had brought their salt-laden camels to Baghdad to trade. We were looking for more local fare. Kurdish traders would bring their loads of cheese and yoghurt to the city, too, and we were headed to the most famous of all yoghurt stores in Baghdad: The Erbil Yoghurt Store, which was located on Rashid Street, not far from the Ministry of Defence. The owners brought their yoghurt straight from Hawler, and it was a much sought-after delicacy among the Arab traders. Their yoghurt had such a reputation that whenever people asked for directions to the Ministry of Defence, locals would say, "Oh, it's just up the street from Erbil Yoghurt..." and that would be enough to guide the visitors to the right place.

The next day we descended on the bookstores on the posh Sa'doun Street. We had never seen anything like it. Hundreds of books were spread out on the floor and shelves. I felt as if I had arrived in heaven, but soon a familiar problem brought me back to earth: I did not have enough money to buy all the books I wanted. Eventually, we all settled on a handful of books and paid for them. When we left the store, we headed straight for a bar, where we had tandoori chicken and a beer. We tried to get into the nearby Karvana Night Club, but we did not have enough money left over. So instead, we wandered the streets, enjoying the city and discussing our newly acquired copies of Baudelaire, Rilke, and Salinger.

It seemed appropriate to us young writers to find our way to Abi Nuwas Street, named after the famous Arabic poet. It is one of the most beautiful places in Baghdad. The street follows the banks of the Tigris River, and the many restaurants and bars and tea shops along the waterfront remain open until late in the night. We kept getting whiffs of fish, fresh from the Tigris, roasting on open fires. And alcohol, it seemed, flowed as freely as the river itself.

Baghdad in the early 1970s was very different than it is today. The city was alive, and no one feared kidnapping or beheading or car bombs exploding at all hours of the day. I felt no sense of discrimination among the people of Baghdad. It was too bad that we couldn't afford to stay more than three days. The following morning we took the same bus back home. On the way, in the darkening shadows, the solitary Mount Handrin looked mighty and foreboding. It was as if this ancient mountain that marked the southern tip of our Kurdish hearts knew something we hadn't even begun to suspect.

Writing in an Atmosphere of Fear

In 1979 Saddam Hussein forced his second cousin, Ahmed Hassan Bakr, to resign as president and the reign of terror began. Under

Saddam, the media, like everything else, was fully controlled by power and bloodshed. There was no room for free intellectual thought. That same year that Saddam came to power, I submitted my first collection of poems, *Dance of the Evening Snow*, to the censors for approval. The rule was simple: no permission, no publication. My request was rejected three times. There was no real reason for the rejection. My poems were non-political. They were an effort to create something different and beautiful. But that made little difference. Because the censors were so paranoid, they would reject whatever they were not familiar with or sure about. But on the fourth attempt I was granted conditional permission: anything they had marked in red had to be taken out.

After receiving the letter informing me that my collection had received partial approval, I had to go to the Ministry of Culture and Youth building in Baghdad to collect my manuscript. The building looked like a secret police office, and while I was in the building, I felt as if I could be arrested at any moment. By the time I left, I was a bundle of nerves.

Permission from the censors aside, I also had to find a publisher and pay for the publication myself, which wasn't easy, considering that as a teacher I was only making twenty-nine dinars a month. There was the famous Kurdish publisher, *Mam* Geew, in Hawler, but the books that lined the shelves of his store did not reflect what I was writing. He was advertising volumes of Kurdish classical poetry, and he didn't seem to be an appropriate publisher for my work, which was trying to bring something new to Kurdish literature.

I therefore approached another printer in Hawler, Saladin. Saladin's response was simple: "I don't have any idea about Kurdish or about books. We only print wedding invitations and business stationery."

I was frustrated. Then someone told me about Jamhour, a publisher in Mosul who would consider publishing my book. Mosul, situated about an hour by bus northwest of Hawler, is one of the three largest cities in Iraq. I had been to Mosul once before with two of my friends. We were still at school and had decided to go there to visit the prostitutes in the city's western Sahaji suburb. For me it was strange to be

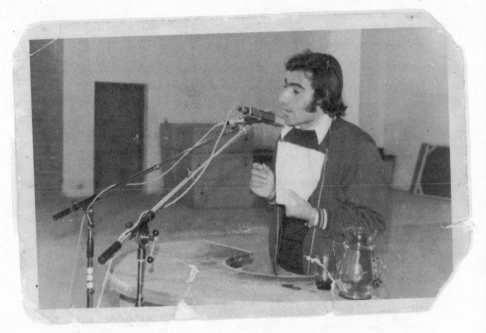

Jalal reading in Hawler, 1978. This reading was investigated by the Iraqi Secret Police.

shopping for sex among all those tired-looking women, some with their children standing by them, some with their husbands or pimps looking over their shoulders. Many of the people hanging around the houses looking to buy sex were from the high social classes, but looking for sex in these streets eliminated the social differences among us all. I hadn't had sex before, but even though the urge was strong, I just couldn't bring myself to do it. I felt so sorry for the children and the women. The two friends who accompanied me did find prostitutes; they both reported that they ejaculated as soon as they touched the women. One of them asked the prostitute to give him back half of the money, since penetration didn't occur. But the woman refused, saying it wasn't her fault.

At least this time my reason for going to Mosul was more memorable. I was extremely nervous as I walked into the office in the downtown area of Baptop. The manager spoke only Arabic and he tested my abilities in the language to its limits. Despite my nerves, it was all very exciting. By the time I left, we had agreed that I would pay six hundred dinars for him to publish my work.

Self-publishing had many problems and barriers, the most serious of which was distribution. It took six months and numerous visits to Jamhour Publishing to finally have the poems appear in print. I was ecstatic. When they called me to let me know that the books were ready to be picked up, I left for Mosul immediately. The books were stored at the local railway station, so I enlisted the help of a porter to transfer the boxes from the storage room onto the roof of the shared taxi that would take me and my books back to Hawler. While we were loading the boxes onto the taxi, one of the boxes broke and books spilled all over the street. Some of them landed in the open sewer. People came rushing to help. An old man among the helpers recognized my picture on the back cover—it must have been my long hair and shaved moustache, both of which weren't very acceptable. He looked up at me and said, "*Mamosta*, what did you do that for? Putting your picture on the cover of your notebook?" I responded with a smile.

There were other memorable moments distributing my book. I remember when I arrived at the Aso bookstore in Kirkuk. We were still busy opening the boxes when the first customers rushed in to buy copies. *Dance of the Evening Snow* was a well-received and critically acclaimed work. I had published 3,000 copies of the book and they were sold in a couple of months. Four years later, in 1983, two other writers, Abbas Yusuf and Dilshad Abdullah, and I submitted a joint collection of poetry to the censorship department. After three months, however, they replied with a rejection.

My problems with publishing did not arise only from my dealings with the government censors. During the Iran-Iraq war, a poet with similar first and last names to mine began publishing poems in praise of Saddam and his policies. Some people believed this person to be me, even though our styles and themes were totally different. Since I was on the editorial board of the journal *Hawdang*, a literary magazine that was concerned with modern writing, I felt compelled to write a clarification in the second edition of the magazine. I made it clear that I was not Sayyid Jalal Sayyid Hassan Barzanji, and that we were we not connected in any shape or form.

My note drew an immediate response. He complained to the government that I was writing unpatriotic poems. Fortunately, he delivered his report to a small neighbourhood police station and it did not come to the immediate attention of the authorities. This gave me time to arrange to have the report squashed.

The publication in 1985 of my collection of poems *No Warming Up*, proved to be even more burdensome. The Baghdad publisher, Al-Hawadith, apparently had no Kurdish-speaking employees. The result was a disaster: the book was riddled with errors. I spent days with my friends making corrections by hand. The changes ruined the look of the book, but there was nothing we could do about it. That book had no luck. In addition, three months after it was published I got arrested.

One Bright Moment

Books, writing poetry, reading, and politics weakened my appetite for everything else at this time in my life. I had little time to think about other things. Before I knew it, I was approaching thirty, and I thought to myself that I had better find myself a wife. The problem was where to start. I had never really been a social person and I did not know how to talk to women.

You see, the only way to talk to the opposite sex in those days was face-to-face. There was no e-mail or texting. You had to introduce yourself and speak to them. This is where the problem lay. For most of our lives, men and women lived separately. Men rarely mixed with women and couples could not display their affection openly. The most direct public communication couples had was to steal a quick chat through a cracked door as the other person passed through the neighbourhood. In summer, when people slept on the rooftops, you would scratch your head in a special way when the person you liked was looking. Sitting down and talking face-to-face was a new experience for me.

When I was a student at the Teachers' Institute, which was co-ed, I thought the easiest way to impress girls was to show them books and read poetry to them, but this didn't seem to work that well. Every night I would write a love letter to a classmate, Grail. I always planned on giving it to her in the morning, but I never did.

Later on, I had two experiences of falling in love. Both failed miserably.

Jalal's and Sabah's wedding celebration, 1982, with Sabah's aunts. Sabah is holding a baby as part of a Kurdish wedding tradition. Left-to-right: Nassrin, Sabah, Jalal, Sadia, Hero.

Sabah and Jalal on the first day of their honeymoon, in Masief, 1982.

Jalal and his daughter, Ewar, at home in Hawler, 1991.

The first time, my affections were one-sided and the girl did not care for me. The second time was with a teacher who worked with me in Sktan, and this time the relationship was serious and deep and lasted for three years. I proposed, but her father rejected my proposal, saying, "We don't want our daughter marrying a poet. Most of them are crazy or live in poverty." The rejection affected me greatly. I was depressed for a long time.

Then, in 1981, my friend Dawan had to have surgery. I went to visit him in the hospital every day. Another friend of Dilshad Abdullah's, Karwan Tahir, was also in the hospital at the time. While I was visiting one day, Karwan's sister came to visit him. Since she knew Dilshad, she popped her head into the room. Dilshad introduced us. Her name was Sabah. I could barely get a word out to return the greeting of this beautiful woman.

Fortunately, Sabah was more relaxed. She told me that she knew I was a poet because she had seen me reading in 1973 in Koya, which was where she lived. From then on, I would make sure I was at the hospital when she came to visit her brother. And every day Sabah and I talked. I soon learned that she was a writer as well, which I thought made her a perfect match for me. We could support each other when we wrote.

I started courting her. It took me several attempts, going from Hawler to Koya and back to muster up the courage to ask for her hand. In 1982 I finally asked for her hand in marriage. I went to Koya to visit her as I had done several times in the past. I could not say the words out loud, so I put my request in a letter. She accepted.

We got married that same year and spent our honeymoon in Masief, which at that time was Hawler's premier summer destination for newlyweds and holidaymakers. After a few wonderful days in the mountains, we left Masief and returned to the reality of life in Hawler.

We started a family right away and our eldest daughter, Ewar, was born in 1983.

5　Life in Prison

My First Visitor

IN PRISON NUMBER FIVE, there was one policeman who was
unlike the others: Sergeant Hassan, a Shi'a from southern Iraq, whose
people had also been treated very badly by the Saddam regime because
he believed that they supported Iran, and wanted to take over power
in Iraq. Sergeant Hassan tried to make our lives a little easier. He
would buy small items for prisoners and smuggle them into the cells.
Sometimes, he'd let us stay out a little longer in the afternoon, or make
sure we got medical assistance when needed. When family members
brought us food, he would make sure we got it—something other
guards never did. I sensed this was his prison as much as it was ours.

One morning, as we were being led out of the cell for our daily walk,
I happened to look up to the balcony that faced the hallway in front
of the cells. At first I could not believe my eyes. I blinked and looked
again. There was my younger brother, Kamaran, shuffling along, bent
over double with pain. Although we could not talk, I waved at him and
he nodded back at me. Later, I found out from Sergeant Hassan that

Kamaran had been held in a separate cell for juveniles but that on the day I saw him, he had been put into isolation because he had developed typhoid. That was the first time I knew that he, too, was in prison, and I worried for him.

Not long after that day, Sergeant Hassan created a stir among the prisoners when he said we were soon to be allowed to receive visitors. He announced the change on a Monday, and the first visits were to take place that coming Wednesday.

The news sent us all into a flurry of activity. We all longed to see our families and wanted to look good for them, and none more so than Shirzad, who had only been married for a week before the police arrested him. He was a tiny young man and was in the classroom in Rizgari High School when the secret police dragged him from his new life. The prospect of seeing his wife again, even from behind bars, and even for a short period of time, made him act like he had lost his mind. He couldn't sleep. He washed his hair under the cold tap and combed it over and over.

I, too, was looking forward to the visit, but in the end it was a little disappointing for me. When visiting time came, the guards led us out of our cell and into the passage just outside. The barred hallway curved around the perimeter of a large circular atrium. Solid iron gates about halfway around brought the area that was accessible to prisoners to an abrupt halt. Through the bars, we could see a crowd of visitors crammed into the hall beyond. There was no order to the proceedings. Prisoners jostled for a spot along the bars and the visitors tried to find their family members among the many faces. On the far side of the passage, I could see Kamaran being led to the bars. As the figure behind him straightened out, I realized with horror that it was my other young teenaged brother, Peshtewan. Until now, I had not known that he, too, had been in prison for as long as I had been. My heart felt heavy despite the joy of being about to see my family for the first time in many months.

I was expecting to see my wife and three-and-a-half-year-old Ewar, but when only my brother-in-law, Karwan, showed up, I knew something was amiss.

"Where's Sabah? Where's Ewar?" I shouted across the room.

"Sabah's in hospital. She's expecting to give birth to your second child any day now," he replied as he fought his way to the front of the crowd of people trying to get to the bars so they could touch their loved ones.

"But why is Ewar not with you?" I was desperate to see my little girl again.

"I wasn't really sure that the visit would take place at all," he replied somewhat apologetically. "I thought they would cancel the visit at the last minute just as they did previously. So I left her behind to spare her the disappointment."

When Karwan finally managed to hold on to the iron bars, he slipped a folded piece of paper into my hand. On the other side of the passage, I could see Jamal and his wife, Kafia, waving to one another from afar. There were so many people trying to get to the bars, she just couldn't make it all the way to the front. When it was time to go, children didn't want to go without their fathers. Many of them were crying and holding on tightly to the iron bars. The guards had to drag them away. Except for the guards, everyone was crying.

For once, I couldn't wait to get back to our cell. I hurried back to my square and opened the piece of paper. Not seeing Sabah and Ewar was a big disappointment, but I suspected what was on the paper Karwan had given me. I was right. It was a letter from Sabah, very similar to the ones Jamal would send my family in secret when he was with the *peshmerga* in 1975. It read:

Dear Jalal,

That evening when I went to the doctor, I could tell you were not yourself. I had never seen you so depressed. You got into your blue pyjamas so early. That wasn't you. I was hoping to be examined earlier so that I could come home sooner, but Dr. Attiya was adamant that everyone had to take her turn, including, as she put it, "members of her own family."

But, as it turned out, the wait was not a bad thing. Otherwise, Ewar and I, too, would have been taken, and your pain would've been far greater. When I got back, our neighbour, Zeen, came running to give us the news. She said they took you and your mother, locked the house, and

Sabah's letter to Jalal.

ⓒ

ئای ئەم نامە نووسینە نێوڕارام داینشتبوو ، مەکەی دەخوا و سەیرم دەکا ، وا ەقەی
دەر هێشنا دەێ دایە ئەو وەرتەی ئەیە دەرێم ێ ، ئارە کاوەبە ، ێ دەکە ۆ دەرێ
ئا ، ێ ، بابه ... مینکە دەمێت کایە ، ەکەی لەوەی لەجائ دەر مێبنام وەقت ، ێ ، ئەیە دەفتر
ی ، ئابیت ... دەرێ کا ، بۆم بۆ سی من کردوە

جەلوکەی رووح و گیانم / دەنیت ەەنجیە وەەقتە و کتاب و چەلەم بۆ نارد ناردوی نیشتی ؟
بۆم سبودسە کتابەکانیش عنوانم دای حوونت بۆ رئشادم وەرەقیصەرەوان کرد
بۆت بشنێ جاکە بویان چوڕ دشە ، ەاتەوە ، ەەوللا لێبیان دەیوەسم گەریۆیان
ەێنابە ، دەنا بێنج شەە بۆتدەشنێم ... جەبارک ، ۆخۆ ەەمووشتم نووسیوبە
خانـ بەخانـ

① مینۆن دەخەونت ؟ ەەوتکاێ دەکەوی ؟ ③ مینۆوەلی دەخۆن ...؟ ② ەۆت دەشوی
مینۆن ؟ ④ ئەو شتانەی بۆ تان دەبێنم گەرم دەگریتەوە .. ەاستە کە
ەاپناپ ، تاکەی دەمێنتەوە ⑤ ەەر ەینتە رەکچرەزاێ جوورک لەەدلێ
رادیۆ بۆتان بێنم ، استفادەی لێ دەکەت ؟ ⑥ ترمۆزک گەورە یان بچووکتان
بۆ بێنم ⑦ لێبوودیتان بەبوەرەەیە ؟ ⑧ داکیتو رۆتیە دەمبنی
ئەم شتانەم ەدە مۆە تە مەیلی بۆ بسرە

جەول ، گیان / لشتون و کامەوت ەاگیان باشە .... چیجایلا لوسە بیە .. ەوللا ، رو ، شۆو شوکر
نیە ... ەەرام جاوەلا ، شم بۆ دەمبنیان بۆ ، لا ، شۆو .. ەەنەق ئەوان بەخۆن

Jalal's letter to Sabah.

took the key with them. The shock was like a sudden blow to the head and I fainted. When I came back to consciousness, I was at my aunt Sa'diyya's. This is where Ewar and I had to hide for a while.

Your arrest was a terrible blow to me, but more so to Ewar, who obviously couldn't understand why her father was not with her. I was too afraid to go near our home, but one day when I heard that the government was planning to demolish it, I mustered the courage to go. Fortunately, it was just a rumour, but apparently the secret police had gone and ransacked the house. Your books and papers were all thrown out. No one dared to come near them except the children, who'd torn pages out to wrap their sunflower seeds in.

I was devastated by your arrest; I was even more devastated by the fact that there was nothing I could do to help. I wanted to be able to come and smash all the prison walls and free all the prisoners. Tell me: How do you sleep? What do you eat? Do you get to shower? Can you manage without reading and writing? I have hidden pen and paper for you in the rice dish Karwan brought you. They're wrapped in plastic. Oh, one more thing: Dr. Attiya helped me get admitted to the hospital under a false name, just in case the secret police were still looking for me.

Your Love,
Sabah

That night I found a piece of brown paper from a bag of sugar someone had brought to another prisoner. I cleaned it off nicely and wrote back to my wife:

My Love,

I don't have enough paper to tell you about all that happened to me since that fateful evening. But I know my being here must be very hard on you, especially with you being on the verge of having another baby. In a way, I'm glad you and Ewar weren't there to see me being blindfolded, handcuffed, humiliated, kicked and punched, and shoved into a military vehicle like a common criminal. It looks like so far we've managed to make it. When you come to think of it, this alone is a small victory. I'm

*not sure if this letter will make it to you or will remain here. I have only
room left to say I love you.*

A Shared Home

My mother always used to tell us about a couple of swallows that
built their nest in our home. Year after year they would return to their
nests around the same time, carrying grasses in their beaks. It was as
though they were telling us, "Spring is just around the corner." The
swallows would always start off by doing repairs on their mud-pellet
nests because they were not going to take any chances with their
chicks. They wanted the nest to be a safe place for them. So for us children, spring always meant sharing the house with the birds. I wonder
if we learned from them to make a home, or if they learned from us.
Standing in the cell and watching the sun rise the day after the visits,
my mother's words made me think of the English proverb: "East, West,
Home's Best."

Shortly after dawn, Aram said, "If they had put eighty-five animals
in our place, they all would probably have died the next day. Animals
don't forget what freedom is like, but we humans do. Just look at us:
we're slowly but surely getting used to being prisoners."

It hurt to think that here I was, in a prison only five kilometres
away from home.

Badran, who was thirty-two years old with a teaching background
and was arrested when he was standing in front of his class, said,
"Whoever said prison is like school, where one is constantly learning
new stuff, didn't know what he was talking about. I don't want to
have anything to do with schools like that. I want to be as far away as
possible from prisons. I want to live in peace with my family."

Rebwar said, "The kind of life you have in mind is not available
here. The dictatorship won't allow it."

Home seemed to be on everyone's mind since the visit. Even though
only a day had passed, some of the prisoners began to devise inno-
vative ways to support their families from inside the prison. Sadiq, a
light-skinned young man whose village had been destroyed and its
people forcibly relocated, was the only prisoner who knew how to knit.

From the wool his mother brought him during a visit, he made two pairs of socks. He offered to sell a pair for five dinars so that he could give the money to his penniless mother at the next visit. When Namiq offered to pay him seven dinars, Sadiq was very honest and insisted on five. A few of the other prisoners who could knit or sew began to follow his example and make socks or little sacks for the people who came to visit. I had neither the skill to make one nor the money to buy one.

Though the first visit had been brief, it had given us hope that more might be on the way. Every time he came to do his rounds, we would ask Sergeant Hassan when the next visit would be. By now, we knew that he understood our plight a little better than the other guards. Maybe it was because he was a Shi'a. Although Shi'as are the majority in Iraq, they lived in poverty under Saddam, just like most of the Kurds in the north. Just as they had done in Kurdistan, the Iraqi regime kept the south of the country underdeveloped. For many Shi'as, joining the military or the police was a way out of their situation. Yet even though some became high-ranking officials, the government didn't trust them and sensitive positions were off limits to them. After Saddam's fall, much to the dismay of the Sunnis, the 2004 election brought the Shi'as to power for the first time. The new situation, and the fact that Kurdistan is becoming increasingly independent, makes the idea of Iraq as a single state less likely.

Sergeant Hassan soon developed a standard reply to our questioning: "I'm just a guard here. This matter is beyond my authority. Once I know about it, believe me, I will bring you the news right away. You know, in a way, I'm like you: you're imprisoned, and I'm trapped. I am the key holder—the definition of my job is ugly and at the same time it makes me ugly, too. I'm from the south. I get to go home once every three months, and only for a few days. I spend two days on the road and only five with my folks. It is not enough. I feel terrible coming back here—I'm always, always homesick."

A few days after the first visit, I looked up from my thoughts to see the prisoners gathering around Sergeant Hassan. As he'd promised, he'd come to give us the good news: soon we'd be allowed a second visit. He seemed genuinely happy for us.

Kno said to me, "*Mamosta*, I miss smoking and drinking. I'll ask my wife Nasreen to bring us a whole bottle of arrack."

"And some cigarettes," I said. "But I don't think one bottle would be enough. Look, even the devout Muslims among us seem to have given up on Allah and are eager to drink."

He said, "You don't have to worry about them: they're beginners; they won't be able to drink much."

We were already getting excited for the second visit, even though we did not know when it would be. As is my nature, though, I worried about some of the prisoners. For some, like *Mam* Brahim, it had been an awful experience. I had just finished reading the letter from Sabah after coming back to the cell after visiting time and was still holding it in my hand when I saw people gathering around *Mam* Brahim. He was a devoted family man who, like so many other people, had moved to Hawler after the destruction of his village. He'd just gotten news that his *peshmerga* son had been killed in a government attack. *Mam* Brahim moaned softly. It was the second child he had lost to the war.

Mam Brahim had taken up singing after losing his first son. Sad folk melodies were his favourite and throughout the day, we could hear him singing. "They help me cope with my losses," he said. Sometimes it was hard to tell if he was singing or crying, since he always tried to put on a brave face. But at night it was a different story. Every night he would cry himself to sleep.

I worried a lot about him and I was always careful be sensitive. I let him know I was there to lend him a sympathetic ear. This approach encouraged him to open up to me. One day, shortly after breakfast, he said, "You know, I never got a chance to kiss my boys goodbye. Actually, I never got a chance to kiss either, alive or dead. You see, in our village it was unmanly for a man to kiss his children or just hold them. It was considered unmanly. A father couldn't even be present at his daughter's wedding. He actually had to leave the house on that day and not come back until the whole thing was over. When the children were little, many a time I had the urge to just pick them up and hold them, but I just didn't have the courage to do it. I didn't want people to go around calling me womanly. When we moved to the city, we were so poor I had to make them quit school and go to work. They did construction. They would come home in the evening exhausted. I felt sorry for them. And then they went and joined the *peshmerga*. I know it's too late for regrets but, unmanly or not, I wish I had a chance to kiss them just once."

Your Words Bring You Home to Me

About a month later we had our second visit. For days we talked about nothing else. I was walking towards the visiting room when Farouq, a forty-year-old man with five children, turned to me and said, "I have never kissed my children, but this time I'll try to kiss them on the cheek if possible."

"Do you really mean your children, or are you thinking of kissing someone else?" I asked with a wink.

Farouq smiled sheepishly. "Okay, you got me," he laughed. "I want to kiss my wife, and not just on the cheek, but deep down in her mouth. But even if this was possible, I'm just too shy to do so in public. But then, with my desire being so strong, I might just do it."

In the visiting room, I was full of thoughts about Ewar. About how whenever I went somewhere I would always get her something. About how she was going to react to seeing me behind bars. About what she was going to say. I was contemplating such thoughts when around 10:00 AM the visitors were allowed in. I could see Ewar in the crowd; my heart did a little jump. She was walking briskly ahead of her uncle Karwan. Amazingly, amid all these people, she came straight to me. She held onto the iron bars tightly as I tried to manoeuvre my mouth into the gap between the bars so that I could snatch a kiss. I got a little scratch on my face, but the effort paid off. I had drawn a picture of a tree in the prison courtyard the day before. I knew it wasn't suitable for a child of Ewar's age, but I just wanted to give her something. But I couldn't do it. Not with the guards watching. So I just held onto my daughter.

Ewar was very smart and learned to speak at a very early age. She seemed to understand what was going on, but it was too much for her. A torrent of words burst from her mouth: "Daddy, why can't I come in?

When are you coming home? Why won't they let you come home with me? Why all these metal bars? Daddy, Mom's in the hospital. They arrested Grandma Zerin and Aunt Ruqya. They also took Peshtewan and Kamaran. Daddy, I want to stay with you and Mommy."

I didn't want to lie to Ewar, but I just didn't know how to make her understand why I was there and why I couldn't go home with her. I couldn't think of anything better than to say: "Listen, sweetheart, in two or three days, we will all be released. I promise I'll take you to the shop where I used to take you, and then you can pick whatever toy you like."

People started getting ready to leave, and Karwan said they should be going, too. He said everyone was being watched, and that last time some of the visitors were detained. I slipped him my folded letter, and watched hopelessly as Ewar and the other children were dragged away by the guards. We were all crying. Ewar walked backwards all the way to the prison gate, waving constantly. I felt numb and weak. But what was hidden in the food Karwan had brought made me want to jump with joy—another letter from my wife.

Dear Jalal,

I love you now even more intensely. I suffer for you. You're like a sky I can never reach. It pains me that you're not with me. But in a way you're always with me. My only wish is to be able to hug you, to feel you.

As I told you before, the doctor is going for a C-section on Wednesday; don't worry about me. I hope we will have another beautiful child. I'm thinking about choosing a name you'd like. I haven't bought any clothes yet for the child. Yesterday I gave some money to my sister, Bafreen, to go and buy some fabric and have a few pieces made by the seamstress. My Love, I want you to realize that on Wednesday you'll be the father of our second child. You're not like most men—a boy or a girl for you makes no difference. I still remember what you said during that New Year party at Abd's. You objected to having a beauty pageant for the children. You said, "All children are beautiful. We shouldn't make them feel one is more beautiful than the other."

I'm so proud of having another baby with you. When I go to the operating room, I'll be thinking of you. I know the operation is a standard one, but just in case things go wrong and I can't make it, please come and visit my grave as frequently as you can. I was a child when I lost my father; I understand why the situation has been so hard on Ewar. She's constantly asking about you. Everyone has been so nice to us.

Dear Jalal, while in the hospital, I've heard some horrible stories from the women. They all seem to be under tremendous pressure from their husbands to produce boys. They're afraid that if they fail, their husbands would be forced to take a second wife or just divorce them. The woman on my right has nine daughters. Her only hope is that this time it's going to be a boy. This other woman, married for a little over two years, already has had two miscarriages. Her husband has threatened to take a second wife if she fails to give him a boy. Then there's this one, who appears to be from a well-off family. She's the only one who doesn't seem to be concerned one bit. She married late. She says, "My husband married me for my wealth, that's why I have managed to keep him under control. For these women, a boy is their ticket to a lasting marriage. It must be awful for them."

I'm sorry I'm telling you all these sad stories. Yours is the saddest. It is a crime you're not allowed to be with me when our child is born. But we must remain hopeful. In the meantime, please write to me. Your words bring you home to me.

Your love,
Sabah

A Poet Misses His Father

The Kurdish situation is very complicated. When the Iraqi regime perpetrated the chemical attacks on Kurdistan in 1988, many Kurdish leaders fled to Iran, where they were granted asylum. In turn, when Ayatollah Khomeini led the military campaign against the Kurds of Iran, some Kurdish leaders from Irani Kurdistan got asylum in Baghdad. And so it came about that while the Turkish and Iranian governments bombed Kurdish villages, they could still claim to have a good relationship with Iraqi Kurds. There was something decidedly strange about it all. Somehow Kurds anywhere in the region are never allowed to live in peace in a united Kurdistan. They always have to fight for survival.

I was fighting for survival here in prison, living for the day when I would be able to hold my little Ewar and her sister, whose name I did not yet know. It was late at night, and the thought of being away from my family made me think about my book-hunting visits to Baghdad. Once, when I had gone there on my own, I had the honour of meeting the great Kurdish-Iranian poet Hemin Mahabati. Many of his poems were put to music and sung as songs throughout Kurdistan. Mahabati was a very powerful romantic poet who was persecuted first by the Shah, then by the Islamic regime. Like many other Iranian Kurds, he'd sought refuge in Iraq. Strangely enough, he had been given asylum. I say strangely, because Iran had a similar policy with regard to Iraqi Kurds.

The first thing I noticed about Hemin was how hard life in exile had been on him; he seemed unable to survive without drink. Sadness was in his voice as he spoke: "I'm now forty-five. I was forced into exile at an early age. I've spent most of my life in exile. I never got a chance to spend enough time with my parents. I have never seen my child, who is a teenager now. I feel like their love was taken away from me. After all these years, that's why I still feel like an orphan."

I missed Ewar. I missed Sabah. And yes, like Hemin, I missed my mother and father.

I was dragged from my reverie by Sattar, who pushed his blankets away from himself and started shouting, "Help! Help! I'm going crazy! I can't take it anymore. I've been kept in this tiny place for nearly a year and a half, without charge, without trial. Oh, Allah, it looks like you're a prisoner, too! That's why you can't help me."

Sattar's shouting soon turned to weeping. It was as if this gave the other men permission to show their feelings, too. First Rafiq and Shamzeen broke down and started crying in support of Sattar. Then Hawez joined them.

The crying upset Hawraz. "I'm trying to sleep!" he shouted.

I told Hawraz to let the men cry. "It's all right," I said, holding his shoulder gently to calm him down. "It will make them feel better."

The crying grew more intense. Beside me, I could see how Hamza, whose *peshmerga* son had recently been killed, was shaking. Up to now, he had managed to remain strong, but now he, too, could no longer keep his emotions bottled up. *Mam* Brahim joined in with his sad songs of loss and separation. Tonight, it seemed fitting, and the other men joined in, singing or crying as their emotions took them. Little by little, sadness lulled the men to sleep.

When the cell room grew quiet again, I took out the piece of paper that Sabah had smuggled into the prison for me. On it I wrote:

Tell Ewar,
If I'm released
I'd come home running.
The next day I would take her out,
I'd buy her a doll.

Tell Ewar,
I need to have a small photograph of her
so that every now and then
I can take it out and kiss it.

Tell Ewar,
Your father sends his apologies
For not being able to be with her.

Tell Ewar,
Your father sends his apologies
For not being able to let her in:
The keys are with the police.

The Worst Deprivation

It seemed as if I was the confidant other prisoners could come to if they needed to talk. One morning, as we were being let out for our daily trip to the bathroom, I was approached by a young inmate named Antar. Something, apparently, had been troubling him.

"I've been very depressed these past two weeks, *Mamosta*," he said as he edged his way in next to me. "No, it's not the imprisonment. It's something rather personal. You know, I used to wake up with a monstrous erection every morning. I'd be too embarrassed to get up; I'd wait until the erection was over. Sometimes I even had to masturbate under the blanket. I'd try to bring my wife's image during lovemaking before my eyes, but my wicked desire always made me think of another woman—a neighbour whom I'd seen just once and purely by accident. I was on the rooftop studying, and she happened to be walking naked from one room to another in her house. It was just a fleeting moment, but it doesn't seem to go away. It's her body, not my wife's, that my mind's eye is so obsessed with.

"*Mamosta*, I've been told that the regime puts a certain drug in soldiers' food during war in order to make them not think about sex or to make them impotent. Could it be that the regime is doing the same thing to prisoners like us?"

I was desperate to go to the bathroom, so I kept my response brief as I shuffled my way down the passage. "I've heard about them doing that in the military," I said, "but I don't know if the regime is doing the same thing to prisoners."

Antar shook his head disconsolately, "I hope you're right, *Mamosta*."

I thought we were done after that revelation, but no, Antar hung in there. "You know, I'd been married only three months when I got arrested. Like you and all other prisoners, I committed no crime, and no one in our family agreed to our father becoming a *peshmerga*. It took my wife and me a whole week just to feel a little comfortable around one another. Then her period came. I don't think we were together more than five times in total. That's why I miss her so. I cannot live my life without her. I know it is *haraam* to commit suicide, but I still contemplate it.

"During the last visit, as I was talking to her, my erection was as hard as a rock. Well, *Mamosta*, that's the way it is with the monster we've got: it follows its own desires. It doesn't care about where and when. What scares me, though, is the change I've been noticing in myself: these days when I wake up, the energy is not there. I don't think I'd be of much use to my wife if I continue to be like that. I've been told women's sexual drive is seventy times stronger than men's. That's why they do female circumcision—it's to bring their sexual desire under control."

I still don't know whether the guards were to blame for his condition, but I knew Antar was onto something: prison did leave you feeling like you were of no use to your family. It did take away your manhood.

There was just enough time left for me to rush to the toilet before Sergeant Hassan locked us back in.

Nature's Ways

I was fifteen years old when my father bought me my first umbrella. It brought me great joy. Before that, when going to school or shopping, my only protection against the rain was a basic plastic bag, which covered only my head and left my whole body exposed to the rain. I hated coming home and having to sit near the stove and watch the steam rise from my body as I warmed up. Now, with my new umbrella in my hand, rather than being annoyed by the rain, I welcomed it.

One night when I was a teacher in Sktan school, there was an exceptionally heavy rainstorm. As my mother used to say, it was the type of raindrops that were sure to lead to flooding. The rain continued for hours and with such ferocity that in several places water began to seep through the mud roof. I put out whatever pots and pans I had to collect the water and prevent the dirt floor from becoming wet, but the water seemed to have the upper hand. In just a short while, miniature creeks were forming everywhere. I had never been annoyed by water like that. I moved my bed to the only dry corner left in the room and strung the umbrella my father had given me over it, just in case.

The intrusion of the storm into the room had forced me into a narrow dry space, and I resented being enclosed like that. It was terrifying and I couldn't fall asleep. However, something beautiful resulted from the rain: when I ventured out in the morning, the fog had transformed the landscape into a work of art, with the main mountain peak looking like a graceful woman just waking up. It was hard to believe that nature could produce such extremes.

The night when I saw lightning through the tiny hole in the ceiling in prison number four, I realized that to be a prisoner was also to be cut off from nature. I wished then that I might hear one more time the sound of rain attacking the roof of a house so hard I could feel it. Like that night in Sktan.

It was the narrowness of my personal space in prison number five and the inability to even hear or see nature from where I was that made me think of storms and of being closed in. I was trying to think how I would describe that feeling to Sabah when I saw her again when suddenly I remembered the time when my close friend Sa'doun's body was pulled out from the river in Kalak. He had gone to spend the day in the tiny hamlet with his family when tragedy struck; he drowned while learning to swim.

I followed the crowd as the men carried his body to the mosque in preparation for burial. I mustered the courage to take a peek and watch as they washed the yellowish body. They wrapped it in a white shroud and a blanket, and then placed it in a wooden coffin. The men took turns carrying the body to the cemetery on their shoulders amid shouts of *"Allah u Akbar."*

I have never been fond of graves. At the cemetery, I peered timidly from behind the men as the body was lowered into the freshly dug, narrow grave. I felt a pang of sadness coupled with horror.

And as I stood thinking about it, I realized that the space they'd put Sa'doun into was still bigger than the space I had in prison. Sometimes in prison the two men beside me would fall asleep on their backs, forcing me to crouch until one of them turned over or awoke. Being in prison was worse than being in a narrow grave.

Ghareeb's Disappearance

One day, the door of our prison cell was opened unexpectedly. It was Sergeant Hassan, accompanied by two secret policemen. One of them called out, "Ghareeb Karim! Come forward!" We all looked at one another.

The policeman repeated the call, somewhat angrily, but Ghareeb didn't seem to be among us. A new prisoner perhaps, I thought. He ordered Sergeant Hassan to go and get the prisoner name list, which he did promptly. The two secret policemen stayed behind, their eyes scanning the prisoners huddled together in the room.

When Sergeant Hassan returned, the secret policeman grabbed the list and began reading out names. There were fifty of us.

"Jalal Barzanji!" I raised my hand.

"Stand over here." I rushed to where the policeman pointed.

"Jamal Barzanji!" Jamal hurriedly joined me.

There were fifty of us. The secret policeman read out forty-nine names, telling each of us in turn to stand to one side. We huddled together tightly, terrified.

That left one lonely prisoner on the other side of the room. The policeman turned to the fiftieth inmate and screamed, "You animal! You dog! You're Ghareeb Karim! Why don't you answer?" Ghareeb's body cringed as he tried to make himself invisible before the onslaught.

Right there before us, the policeman kicked Ghareeb a couple of times, calling him more names. Ghareeb, who had been with us for just two days, said, "Sir, believe me, until this moment I couldn't recall my name. Yes, I'm Ghareeb, and our home is in Koran district."

The policemen led Ghareeb away. We never saw him again.

The Third Visit

Sabah, who was still recovering from her recent operation, was unable to come for our third visit. Karwan and Ewar, however, along with several relatives, did come for the thirty-minute visit. No sooner had the visitors been let in than I saw Ewar hurriedly pushing her way through the noisy and unruly crowd of mostly women and children. She came straight to me, clutching the iron bars and trying to climb as high as she could go. I put her little hands in my hands, kissed them over and over, and even managed to snatch a few awkward kisses to her face through the metal barrier. I was imagining how this inter-view gave her hope and happiness.

Ewar was eager to talk. "Daddy," she said, "Mommy has a new baby. She's so small! She's with Mom in the hospital."

We talked a little more before the rest of the family joined us and we spoke of other things. We joined in some of the other conversa-tions with people around us. In the course of the visit, we learned that four men, whose fathers and brothers were in jail with us, had been killed: two in clashes among rival Kurdish parties, and two had been executed by Saddam. Everyone remarked on how stupid and pointless it was for Kurds to fight each other.

Back in the cells afterwards, we all sat down and mourned the dead like a family, despite our political differences. Later that evening, Jameel turned to me and said, "I think just the two of us are awake."

I was in no mood for talking, so I simply said, "Not everyone under their blanket is asleep."

That night I wrote:

In the morning I'm in prison,
At noon I'm in prison,
In the evening I'm in prison,
At night I'm in prison.
One wing of my sleep
falls down into an empty world.

Before the visit was over, my mother-in-law snuck me a letter, which she had folded neatly and concealed in her hand. "It's from Sabah," she whispered as she put it in my hand.

The goodbyes, like the time before, were especially hard on the children and the parents. What kept me composed was my eagerness to go and read the letter. The food and the pyjamas they brought me, the warmer white ones with red stripes, could wait.

Back in the cell, I quickly unfolded the letter and began reading:

Dear Jalal,

I still feel we're together, every moment. I see you all the time. The operation had to be put off for a few days. There were some complications with regard to the baby's position. You taught me how to be brave. The operating room looked like a spaceship to me. When the operation was over and I returned to consciousness, I didn't have the slightest idea what had happened. I was disoriented and dizzy, and in a lot of pain. At first I

thought perhaps the baby didn't make it, but I felt relieved when I heard
the baby crying, and the doctor, with a hand on my forehead, was telling
me, "Ewar now has a beautiful little sister."

Dear Jalal, this time around, with you not being with me during the
delivery, the experience was totally different. I felt the whole thing was
unreal. Anyway, I'm glad it's all over and I hope our children will never
grow up fatherless the way I did. My sister, Nowruz, named the child
Niga. I hope you like it. I have also to tell you this: late at night when I
opened your book of poems, Dance of the Evening Snow, *randomly, I*
saw these lines:

I love you more than ever before.
Don't go,
Take me for what I am,
For it's too late now:
Nothing can take you away from this love.

Your poetry makes me appreciate the beauty and power of words. They
give me a piece of you. They take me to a beautiful world.

Dear Jalal, there's been some talk about some of your writer friends
trying to put in a good word for you with the government. I was told that
most of them had good things to say about you, but that two of them did
their best to prolong your ordeal. They spoke against you.

It's getting late; the children are asleep. I know you don't want to talk
about what it's like to be there, but from what Karwan has told me, the
place must be dreadful.

Dear Jalal, you know, the first thing Ewar says in the morning is,
"Mom, why is Father not coming home?"

Your Love,
Sabah

Health Issues

Diarrhea was common among the prisoners. The soup they gave us
seemed to be the culprit. Sometimes, some of the inmates just couldn't

wait until toilet time. They would soil their sherwals and be forced to stand in their dirty clothes until the guards let us out again. Then they would hurry to the bathroom and rinse their clothes out in cold water before putting the dripping clothing back on their bodies and returning to the cell.

Back and muscle pain from all the standing and lack of movement was also common. I had to try really hard to hide my back pain from Ewar when she visited. I did not want my daughter to see her father in such pain.

One evening when we were ordered back into our cell room, I felt dizzy and disoriented. I couldn't concentrate. I had to be helped to walk the little distance to our room. I never did get medical help for my problem while I was in prison, even though the condition persisted. When I was finally released, a doctor diagnosed me with high blood pressure and gave me pills that stopped the dizziness.

I also developed an eye infection, for which Sergeant Hassan was kind enough to get me a cream, although it didn't seem to help much. The infection lasted several days.

My eye infection was followed by another problem: a lump was forming on my neck. I didn't know what it was, but it scared me. I did not want to die in prison without seeing my family one more time, without having a proper burial. I didn't tell anyone about it, not even Jamal. I took to holding my hand on my neck to cover the lump from view until I could get some help.

The only health care available to us was in the form of an occasional visit by a nurse. Not that it was much help. Without examination, he gave us only pills for every health issue, whether it was a skin rash or some other ailment. Even so, on the nurse's next visit, I went forward and asked him if there was anything he could do about the lump. Stretching his hand through the iron bars, he squeezed it gently several times. Then he said he wasn't sure what it was, but that he'd take a second look in a fortnight. He said the swelling didn't seem to have any roots yet. This was a bit of good news, but I was still terrified and remained so until he returned after about ten days and we received permission from Sergeant Hassan for me to come out from behind the bars so that the nurse could take a closer look.

The nurse had been a student at the same high school I attended, but even though we recognized each other, we spoke very little, as he feared reprisal for appearing too friendly towards the prisoners. He wasted no time setting about his work. He cut out the growth very quickly, right then and there on the concrete floor and without anaesthesia. It was painful, but I felt so relieved afterwards.

As I was instructed, I removed the bandage after five days and Jamal assured me it was healing nicely.

Cancelling the Visit

Shortly after my eye infection cleared, Sergeant Hassan came to do his evening rounds and he told us that another visit had been scheduled. We were all looking forward to it, especially me, since this time I was expecting my wife to come. I had even prepared a little present for Ewar—a bead purse one of the prisoners, Fatih, made for me. But the evening before the visit was to occur, Sergeant Hassan came and dashed my hopes. He said word had come from the higher-ups in Baghdad that only male visitors were to be allowed for this visit, and that from now on the visits would alternate monthly: one month for men, one month for women. I would have to wait another month before I could see my wife and child.

When Sergeant Hassan had left, Haider said, "What about little girls?"

I replied, "They probably consider four-year-old girls as adult women."

Being told on such short notice that women would not be allowed to visit us the next day was a huge disappointment indeed. It put all of us in a sour mood. Our bad moods lasted until we were let out for our daily walk. As the door opened we could hear a commotion in the hallway. We could see the guards shouting and shoving some people. The men seemed to be in agony. Some of them were throwing up. They all had difficulty breathing. They couldn't talk. Worst of all, they seemed to have lost their eyesight.

At this point I had no idea what chemical weapons were, but after my release, I found out who these men were and why they were in such awful shape: they were villagers from the Balesan and Wasan regions, and Saddam had bombed their villages with chemical weapons. These were some of the victims. That night I just couldn't sleep. It was my worst night since my arrest.

The next day, as we were getting ready to receive our male visitors, Sergeant Hassan came with even more disappointing news: the visit had been cancelled altogether. I put the little purse away, and when Sergeant Hassan came by, I asked him quietly what had become of the wounded men from the night before. He said that late at night they came and took them away. He knew no more than that.

That evening, for the first time, I failed to observe my daily routine: I failed to look at the prison's only tree before getting locked up for the night.

6 Fear in a Different Form

The Release

AT THE TIME OF MY ARREST IN 1986, my mother and sister were
also detained in the same prison in which I was held. Their prison cell
ended up being right beside mine, and all the time they were there,
I wished for their release more than my own. Sergeant Hassan would
give us weekly updates on how they were doing, and on one occasion
he brought me a sweater that Ruqya had knitted for me in prison.
Fortunately, my eleven-year-old sister, Hero, had been playing with
friends outside when the police arrested us, and as a result they did
not take her. That night, she went and stayed with Sabah's family
until my mother was released.

The government militia tried hard to make life uncomfortable for
the families of those people they detained. But it was not only the
family of detainees that suffered. Anyone could be a victim of their
abuse. Sometimes, they would raid Kurdish cities and throw women

and children into the back of their military trucks and release them in the middle of nowhere with the words, "Go to your rebels in the mountains." The women and children were left there to fend for themselves.

After eight months, Sergeant Hassan brought Jamal and me the joyous news that they had released my mother and Ruqya. The militia took them to an area some fifty kilometres away from Hawler, in the area near Gomaspan Police Station, where the *peshmerga* had attacked a police station when we still lived in Ashkaftsaqa. They left the two women there in the bitter November cold, with no food or water, wearing only the thin clothes they had been wearing when they were arrested in springtime. As they drove off, the officials warned them never to come near Hawler again; they were not Iraqi citizens and Hawler was an Iraqi city.

Fortunately, my mother had grown up in the area and as soon as the militia left, they began to walk towards the Koya highway. Eventually, someone took pity on them and gave them a ride to my mother-in-law's house in Koya, where they stayed for a couple of days. But my mother and sister could not bear to be so far away from us. They wanted to be close to our prison, so that they could be at home in case we were released soon. They also felt that being close to us in Hawler was better than being far away, where news about us would be even more difficult to come by. So they secretly returned to Hawler and hid at the houses of relatives, keeping a low profile, moving from one house to another frequently so as not to draw attention to themselves.

My mother and my uncle also began to make plans to get me released. In Kurdistan, bribes sometimes made things happen. In a meeting, a member of the secret police had indicated he might be able to secure our release for a sum of 5,000 Iraqi dinars, which at the time was equal to about $15,000. It was a lot of money. As a teacher, I earned 150 dinars a month at the time of my arrest. With both me and Jamal not earning money and with having to send money to support Kamal, who was still with the *peshmerga*, 5,000 dinars was equal to more than two years' earnings. My mother and my uncle began to speak with relatives to see if they could borrow the money. After a long time, they managed to collect the money and handed it over to the secret policeman. He took the money but didn't do a thing.

With their efforts to secure my release with a bribe coming to
nothing, and with plenty of money owing to family members, they
could do nothing more than wait on the mercy of the Iraqi regime for
our release.

I knew nothing of their efforts to secure my release. I had settled
into the daily routine of the prison and was focused on surviving so
that one day I could see my family again. Every morning was the same.
Sergeant Hassan would unlock the door of our cell so that we could
go to the bathroom. He was in the habit of knocking before opening
the door in the morning to warn us of his entrance. When he opened
the door, he was ever so careful not to hit Salah, whose spot was just
behind the door. As soon as he walked in, he would greet us with a
"Salaam!" But this particular morning was different. The door was
opened too suddenly and too fast for Salah to be able to move and the
door hit him, leaving a little bruise on his head.

Two secret policemen entered right behind Sergeant Hassan. One
of them started addressing us in Arabic, which more than half of the
inmates couldn't understand. We were ordered to stand in single file
in the hallway. Visits like this from the secret police seldom meant
good news, but we knew better than to drag our feet. We grabbed our
belongings and shuffled into the passage as quickly as we could. Once
we had settled there, we were told we were to be addressed shortly
by none other than the governor of Hawler, Ibrahim Zengena, and a
senior military official, Major Hamoud.

We were all searching for an explanation for this surprise visit
when security details began pouring into the place. Soon the highly
placed duo appeared. We were able to recognize the governor because
we'd seen him on television numerous times when we were still free.
He was a Kurd who had sold himself to Saddam. In our eyes he was a
traitor. He spoke first: "The Leader-President Saddam Hussein, may
Allah bless him with His protection, has decided on his birthday to
issue a general amnesty for prisoners. You are all included in the
amnesty. He has pardoned you for your crimes against the revolution.
I want you from now on to devote yourselves to our beloved leader.
Keep him in your prayers and ask Allah to keep him safe and well.
Empty your heads of everything not compatible with the goals and

ideals of our revolution. Be loyal to the Ba'ath Party and its pan-Arab aspirations. When you are outside, you'll see how much progress our revolution has made."

We stood there in shocked disbelief. While we were letting the governor's words sink in, Major Hamoud stepped forward. His message to us was more chilling: "We have files on each one of you. You have been disloyal citizens. We were planning to make you suffer much longer. But you were lucky this time: our Leader-President pardoned you. However, you will be under our surveillance: if you get out of line again, this time there will be no mercy. We won't even take the trouble to arrest you. We will just shoot you dead right in front of your homes."

Ako, who had been married for thirty years but still missed his wife terribly, responded to this wonderful news by singing and dancing. The good news had elated us all, but we were still wondering if Saddam would keep his word, for we had seen him on television saying, "What's the law? The law is what Saddam Hussein says." Suddenly changing his mind would not have been out of the ordinary for him.

Hajo didn't allow himself to be bothered by what might or might not happen. When the dignitaries had left, he called Sergeant Hassan over to his side. "I want you and your family to come to Shaqlawa and be my guest for the summer," he said. "It's only a half-hour drive from here— a great summer resort. People come from all over the country." Hajo's gesture touched us: we all wanted to do something nice for Hassan.

Antar, whose erectile problems turned out to be the side-effects of depression, was thinking about something else altogether. "I'm glad I didn't commit suicide," he said.

"You sound better already," I told him. We both laughed.

And just like that, my ordeal in prison came to an end. Without any further ceremony, we were told to stand in single file and leave one by one in an orderly fashion. At the door I stopped, and when I saw Jamal, Kamaran, and Peshtewan just behind me, I realized our release was for real.

As I walked through the second door of the prison, fear began to leave me. At the third door, thoughts of freedom rushed into my head. It was all still very new and unreal to me. At the last door, I was forced to slow down and wait for Kamaran, who could not move properly because his legs had been damaged during his bout with typhoid.

It was strange to be able walk outside again without restriction. It was as if I was just learning to walk. It was even stranger to open my eyes in the sun after being cooped up inside for so long. I breathed in the fresh air for the first time in years. The sun on my face felt heavenly and hotter than I remembered it. It was just before noon, but it felt more like late evening to me. The perpetual neon light that burned in our cell had thrown my sense of time completely. As I stood there, I could not help wondering how that light had never once gone out in all the time I was in prison, yet the lights in my own house needed to be replaced every few months. And then it struck me: tonight, I would be able to watch the sun set and feel darkness envelop me once more. I would experience darkness again.

Those who had money with them left in cabs, but neither my brothers nor I had any, so we had to walk home. Jamal, Kamaran, Peshtewan, and I hugged each other and then set off along the road. I was wearing the pyjamas Uncle Mamad had brought me on one of the visits. I had lost so much weight that I constantly had to pull up the pants. I was dirty, my hair was messy, and I was wearing some flimsy beach-style flip-flops. On the way home, some boys thought we were a bunch of crazy homeless men and started calling us names.

"Hoi ha!" they shouted. "Shame on you!" When we ignored them, they quickly lost interest.

We had walked some way before we realized that we did not know where we were going. After a brief discussion, we decided to go to Uncle Mamad's house, which was about half an hour's walk away. I was still feeling very scared and worried that the police may come and pick us up again, that the release was nothing more than a cruel game, so I suggested that we get off the highway and take the back alleys home.

As we made our way through the Baiz district, I could see how civilian life had been forced out of sight and how landmark buildings had been taken over by the military. The people on the streets looked poorer and even more stressed than before. And yet, despite the hardship I could see all around me, I was filled with a sense of great joy at being free at last.

We had no idea what to expect when we got back home. Would our houses still be there? Would our families still be there?

Jamal and I were walking in front when we arrived at Uncle Mamad's house. We knocked. We could hear people moving about inside and we wondered who was there. When Uncle Mamad's son, Khalid, opened the door, he was flabbergasted. "Jamal and Jalal have been released," he shouted at the top of his voice. He had not seen the others yet.

My mother, Ruqya, and Jamal's children were all there. They all came running towards us barefoot. Everyone cried. My mother didn't know which one of us to hug and kiss more. Then she saw the two younger boys.

"Only now I feel I'm not a prisoner," she said over and over as she hugged us and held her sons to her.

Through all the commotion and emotion of our welcome, I kept looking around for the three people I wanted to hug more than anyone else in the world at that time.

"Where are Sabah and the children?" I asked as soon as I could get a word in.

"They've gone to stay with her family in Koya," my mother replied.

"Let's get you cleaned up and fed and then we can take you there," Uncle Mamad suggested.

Uncle Amin called his barber friend, Fakir, to come over to my uncle's house to cut my hair. I had had my hair cut only twice during my time in prison, and by the time of my release, it was long and dirty. In prison, we were given a can of water—but no soap—every few months. This is what we could use to wash ourselves with. As my hair fell to the ground, I could feel the weight of the prison lift off my shoulders.

When Fakir had finished cutting my hair, I took a shower. As I undressed, I dropped the old pyjamas into the bin. Feeling the soap glide over my body felt wonderful, and at the end of it, I enjoyed the luxury of a towel! Over the freshness of the air that surrounded me, I could smell food cooking. How my mouth watered for the taste of chicken and rice! I had borrowed some clothes from Uncle Mamad and I was grateful to have clean clothes to wear, even if they were a bit big for me. I was still a little cold, so I pulled on the one item of clothing I had kept—the sweater that Ruqya had knitted for me while she was in prison.

When we were ready, Uncle Amin and I climbed into his beat-up 1974 Lada and drove off to Koya. Because of the state of the car's engine, we drove far slower than I wanted. The road was quiet. There were no people standing by the side of the road asking for rides. No children playing. No livestock, either. The abandoned picnic places and rundown buildings reflected the tangible sense of fear that surrounded us.

When we got close to Ashkaftsaqa, I looked through the window on my right. All I could see was grey ground. The tombstones in the cemetery were the only thing left standing. It took us forever to get to my sister-in-law Bafreen's house. Bafreen answered the door. "*Kak* Jalal has been released!" she announced excitedly.

Even now, decades later, it is impossible for me to find words to describe properly what happened next. Sabah leapt from her chair. There are no words to capture the look on her face. I simply can't find the words. Happiness doesn't come close. She ran to me, screaming with joy as she leapt into my arms to hug me. Life washed back into my soul in that moment. Little Ewar pushed her way in between us and clung to my legs. Tears flowed.

"Thank God you've come back to us!" Sabah muttered over and over again.

There was just one thing that upset me dreadfully. My dear little two-year-old Niga wanted nothing to do with me. Even though Sabah had shown her photographs of me, she did not want to know this stranger she had never seen in her life. It was painful. It would take a long time for her to get used to me.

As soon as she got a chance, my mother-in-law sat me down and spoke to me earnestly. "Listen to me carefully. From now on you need to stay away from books and poetry and other such stuff. They got you into trouble. I don't want that to happen again."

Fear Didn't Leave Me Alone

After three days in Koya, we all returned to Hawler. Walking onto the street where my mother stayed and where our house stood was an emotional moment. Our house had been standing empty while I was in prison. The day after my arrest, the police had ransacked my house and taken away everything they thought was valuable. Our furniture and my books were tossed carelessly into the street. Then they locked up the house and left. People were scared to take my stuff, since they feared reprisal. And no one would come near my books, for clearly reading was a dangerous pastime. Eventually, the bravest among the young children tore out the pages and rolled them into makeshift cups in which to dole out the sunflower seeds they sold for pocket money.

Sabah and I had nothing left. For the second time in my life, my family would have to start all over. The first time, in 1963, I was a child and restarting our home wasn't my concern. It was my parents'. I remember my father rented a house after he was released. He had to start from scratch. With Bawakir, Khazal's husband, he would try to purchase a few housewares every day, buying just the basics: things to sleep in and cook with, or a tea set. I thought how hard it must have been for my father and mother to furnish a home when they had just moved to the city.

We moved in with my mother so that we could start rebuilding our lives. With little hope and empty pockets, I didn't know where to start again. My mother had only moved back into her house the day before we returned from Koya to Hawler, and everything was still in disarray. They had only a rug in the living room and for a while I sat on it when I wanted to look out of the window. From the window, I could see a steady stream of relatives and friends coming to welcome me back home after my release, as was customary. My only regret was that they could not come to *my* home, for my home stood empty and abandoned.

Sabah returned to our old home once to collect some stray items the secret police had missed, but no one had been there since then. Despite everything I had lost, the fact that my bookshelves had all been emptied and destroyed affected me the most. I didn't have any money to buy books, so I was forced to borrow from friends.

I continued to wear the clothes I had borrowed from my uncle because we did not have the money to buy me a new set of clothing. For the first week or so after my release, I stayed at home to recover. When I did go back to the school where I had been teaching, I was told that I had been fired and that they had received a letter from the police informing them that I was no longer allowed to teach.

For the next six months, I was unemployed and I stayed home as if under house arrest. I spent most of my time reading and writing. I hid my writing underground, or in other safe places because I was expecting to be arrested again. But I simply could not do what my mother-in-law had suggested on my release: stop writing. That is not the way of a writer.

Before my arrest, Sabah had been the director of the Department of Electricity in Hawler. After my release, she was demoted to an entry-level position as a junior bookkeeper. After six months I was given a job at the personnel office in the Department of Education. The job didn't require much skill. All I did was file papers for the pensions of the retired or dead teachers and their families. I didn't enjoy the job, but I had to stay on as I had no other means of income. In some ways, it was nice working with dead people because they were always quiet and never had problems.

We managed to survive by getting rid of the few things we still owned. The night I was arrested, I had parked my vw sedan on the street outside our house. The police didn't know it was my car, because if they had known, they would have taken it. That same night Uncle Bawakir had his son, Siyamand, move the car to his house, where it stayed until my release.

Sabah and I are writers. We have always cared more about books and reading than about material things. We have never been good at saving our possessions, which is why, after we got married, we left our wedding jewellery with Sabah's mother for safekeeping. Now we had to sell the jewellery as well.

With the money I bought some clothes and a few things for our house. I couldn't furnish our home the way we had furnished it right after our marriage. The loss of our belongings was terrible, but the worst thing for me was that the poems from *Dance of the Evening Snow* and *No Warming Up* that the censor had refused to let me publish were lost forever because of the raid on my house. I had hoped to get them published someday after my release and after censorship had been lifted in Iraq.

My experiences in prison affected me tremendously, and at first I was unable to trust those around me. Our life was becoming harder by the day. It was clear that genocide and the elimination of Kurdish culture was the regime's ultimate goal. At night I felt I was in a giant prison. I couldn't write without thinking of censorship, but it didn't stop me. I was living in constant fear. I was out of prison, but I wasn't free yet.

An Anfal Story

I walked out of prison and into the thick of the Anfal genocide campaign. Suddenly, the anguished cries we had heard in the passage one morning while still in prison began to make more immediate sense. At the time, I had struggled to understand the concept of chemical warfare; now I saw its horrifying effects first-hand.

For two years while I had been in prison, since March 1986, Saddam Hussein's cousin and leader of the Iraqi forces in Kurdistan, Ali-Hassan al-Majid, better known to the rest of the world as "Chemical Ali," had led a campaign of horror known as Anfal against Iraqi Kurds. The name of this campaign was taken from the title of the eighth sura in the Qu'ran. The title of the sura, Al-Anfal, literally means "the spoils of war" and refers to the Battle of Badr in 624 CE, when 319 followers of Islam managed to triumph over 900 non-believers. Under Ali's command, soldiers attacked every village in Kurdistan, and according to his orders, it was legal for the soldiers to loot and take cattle, sheep, goats, money, and even women as spoils of war.

I was released two months after the infamous attack on Halabja, the largest chemical weapons attack in human history. More than 5,000 people died that day, and more than double that number were injured. Everywhere you went in Hawler, the stress of living under Saddam's rule was evident. It was awful. People were afraid the regime might once again resort to chemical weapons. They covered their doors and windows with plastic and placed buckets of water by the entrance in the mistaken belief that the water wouldn't allow the chemical gases to get through. Sabah and Ewar, then five years old, wanted me to do the same thing in our house. I went to the Sheikh Allah Bazaar and bought some plastic sheets, nails, and a hammer. At the Bazaar, I also saw some gas masks for sale. I suspect they had been smuggled out of the military stores.

At home, I set about the task of covering our doors and windows. Alas, I am a poet, not a handyman, and I did a lousy job. The nails were all crooked and the sheets were askew. Sabah wasn't satisfied with the job. She and Ewar remarked that they were worried that I didn't do the work properly and that the chemicals would spew through the windows.

By the beginning of 1989, barely a village was left standing in rural Kurdistan. Kurdish resistance was weak and most of the *peshmerga* had withdrawn to the safety of faraway mountains. Some had gone to Iran and others had become refugees in Europe. Saddam's regime seemed poised to crush Kurdistan forever. Saddam had built himself a villa atop Mount Hassan Beg in the heart of Kurdistan. This was a deliberate show of his control over the region. He stationed military units on most of the hills and mountaintops. The regime was more determined than ever to impose its vision of Ba'athism and Arabization on Kurdistan, even if it meant forcibly removing the entire population.

The Anfal campaign has haunted me ever since my release from prison. On the twentieth anniversary of this crime, in 2008, I saw on a Kurdish satellite television channel an interview with a woman whose family had been victims of Anfal. She said, "We didn't know what Anfal was until we were told it was a campaign against non-Muslims. So I said, 'It looks like we're not accepted as Muslims.'"

That is true. To Saddam and his regime, we were Kurds first and foremost. And that was enough to incur his wrath. The Anfal campaign was carried out in stages over three years between 1986 and the end of 1989. During Anfal, ground soldiers systematically destroyed settlements and assisted in the mass deportation of Kurds from their homes. People were executed by firing squads and chemical warfare. At the end of the three years, the mass graves, the piles of rubble strewn

In Koya, the outcome of Anfala. An orphan trades sweets while her grandmother watches, 1991. (Photo by Kamran Tahir.)

around the countryside, and the widespread famine said more than the numbers: 180,000 men, women, and children disappeared without a trace; 570 tons of grain were burned; 45,777 families remain unaccounted for; 39,178 homes were destroyed; 381 schools, 657 mosques and hospitals, and 781 villages were burned down; 1,430 orchards were decimated. Hundreds of freshwater springs were shut with concrete. Fifty-two water tanks and forty-seven mills were demolished. The looting included 472,770 livestock and 15,000 mules.

Anfal was devastating in other ways as well. It led to the spread of many diseases and the return to the wild of hundreds of domesticated animals. The Anfal victims were people whose villages had been protected by mountain ranges for hundreds of years. Because these people had grown up in a natural environment, they learned early on to be truthful and trusting. Before building themselves a home, they would first build a mosque. When one of them became ill, instead of being taken to the doctor, a sacrifice would be offered in his name.

There were many stories about Anfal on the streets of Hawler when I came out of prison. Each one was more horrific than the next. One of the many stories that stuck in my mind was the one a stranger told me one morning at a tea house near our home.

"I'm from the Germian area near Suleimaniya, towards Kirkuk," he said. "That's where the Anfal campaign started. One morning, a column of military trucks and tanks approached from the west, trailing dust behind. The villagers didn't have the slightest idea what was awaiting them. Their lives did not revolve around these things. For cash, the villagers took their tobacco, sunflower seeds, pomegranates, and goats on horseback to the city to sell. Those in need of better transportation would load their stuff into Mala's Land Rover, which came once or twice a year. Each time the vehicle would be surrounded by children. For them this was just another adventure. I understood their inquisitiveness, as I, too, had the same inquiring bent as a child. As usual, the children gathered around the tanks and military trucks. They were filled with wonderment, even as the soldiers were forcing them into the trucks, because they had never been in a truck before. Not knowing what was going on, their excitement knew no bounds.

"The soldiers then went from door to door collecting the men and women. Those who couldn't climb into the backs of the trucks were lifted by two soldiers and thrown inside. When each truck was filled to capacity, its canvas door was pulled down and shut tight; the villagers could no longer see their village. After a while, the villagers began hearing explosions. Before long, they could smell smoke. Some could even tell if the smell of the burning came from their own homes. Before, when people looked up, they saw a big sky; now they saw only the canvas they were under.

"After our village was burnt down completely, the military withdrew a little. They took those survivors they had rounded up during their attack with them. The infants among the prisoners were constantly crying. The mothers were not sure if it was because they were hungry or because they missed their cradles. The elderly prayed that they be allowed back to their villages soon. The military trucks stopped in an open area, where the soldiers lifted the back flap of the truck for a short while. Hundreds of trucks were parked there.

"They separated men, women, and children and took them into military convoys, and they tied the underwear and clothes of the women onto a pole hanging from the women's convoy so that the men could see.

"A child was crying, 'Please return me to my village, I want to be with my friends.' He didn't know that all his friends were in the trucks nearby. The trucks then, back doors pulled down and closed, drove off; they continued driving for a night and day. The people were without food or water. Many children and old people died.

"The men in the convoys became hungry and thirsty, and given no water or food, they urinated in their own shoes and drank it to quench their thirst.

"The mountainous landscape gave way to the light yellow sand of the Tobzawa Desert, and the trucks kept going until they reached an area that was completely barren. There they stopped. The people were ordered out. Meanwhile, mechanized shovels were busy digging huge trenches. The people stood in groups; they didn't know what was happening. The children stared silently at the monster machines. The shovels turned around and went behind the people and then started pushing them into the trenches. Even then the villagers didn't seem to know they were moments away from being buried alive. Amid the cries of the young and the old, the villagers soon disappeared beneath the desert sand.

"I was a shepherd and I was not in the village at the time. That is the only reason why I am here today. For a long time we wondered where our families were and why our village lay in ruins. When I discovered what had happened, I turned my back on the place and came to the city."

We may never know everything that happened during that awful time. In July and August 1983, Iraqi security troops rounded up 8,000 people in Barzanja and took them to resettlement in camps near Erbil. They never returned home. The strategies used in this attack were refined and used to even more deadly effect in the Anfal campaign of 1986 to 1988. Of late, according to news reports, some of the Kurdish women taken during the Anfal campaign ended up being sold to nightclubs in Egypt. The facts about Anfal were not fully known until after Saddam's regime was overthrown; hundreds of mass graves and secret prisons were uncovered.

Rapareen, or the Uprising

About two years after my release in May 1988, on August 2, 1990, Saddam decided to invade Kuwait—an act of aggression that ultimately led to the first Gulf War. The Iraqi regime soon found itself in big trouble and Kurdistan received a reprieve.

In Iraq, every eighteen-year-old male had to serve eighteen months in the military. Everyone, that is, except Saddam's family and close friends. College students did their service following graduation, and so, once I had finished my teacher training, I was drafted into the Army. In all my life, I have never used a weapon. Fortunately, because of poor eyesight, I was exempted from using a gun. I was given clerical work instead, but when they found out I had no desire to join the Ba'ath Party, they transferred me to a military store. I hated shaving and polishing my boots every day and several times I was punished for being lax about these tasks. By the end of my term in the army, I hated black boots and camouflage clothing altogether.

Compulsory military service provided Saddam with permanent access to trained soldiers for his many wars, such as the invasion of Kuwait. The invasion did not go well for the Iraqi forces. Despite overrunning Kuwait and declaring it Iraq's nineteenth province, the initial victory was bittersweet. The invasion met with universal condemnation, and after a series of failed negotiations, on February 24, 1991, the U.S. led an international coalition in a massive assault on Iraqi forces. By the end of the month, Iraqi forces had been expelled from Kuwait and a ceasefire was in place.

The following day, on March 1, unrest began in the southern Iraqi port of Basra. The uprising spread quickly, and by March 4 people in Raniyah, a city to the northwest of Suleimaniya, were launching attacks against Saddam's forces in the region. In the year since Saddam had turned his attention away from Kurdistan, the *peshmerga* had managed to regroup under the armies of Kurdistan Democratic Party and Patriotic Union of Kurdistan, and they were ready to seize

A Kurdish dance in 1994 in Halwer, with Jalal second from the right and Ruqya fourth from the right.

Nowzad Rafad, Jalal, Dilshad Abdullah, and Karwan (Sabah's brother) discussing writing under censorship in Iraq, September 10, 1984, eighteen months before Jalal's arrest.

the moment. Within a matter of days, the Kurds managed to turn the tables on the regime, forcing the government to flee and abandon basically everything. The authorities had no time to cover up their tracks. As the Kurdish forces swept through the cities of Kurdistan, they freed prisoners and set fire to the known prisons. In every city, they uncovered secret underground prisons.

By March 10 the *peshmerga* and the uprisers controlled every city in Kurdistan except for Mosul and Kirkuk. In Hawler, the fighting continued throughout the night. By that time, all the Iraqi military leaders had fled to Mosul, leaving the rank and file to fend for themselves. Civilians armed with sticks and other makeshift implements joined the *peshmerga* in chasing the Iraqi forces out of the city. On the morning of March 11, they gained complete control of the city and from our home we could hear the sound of patriotic anthems resounding in the streets of Hawler. I had not heard this type of music and songs for fifteen years because all these songs had been banned and people had been arrested simply for possessing a recording of them. People were shouting slogans amid intermittent bursts of gunfire. I felt patriotic.

I rushed out to see what had happened: the *peshmerga* had liberated Hawler! As they swept through the city, I was filled with a mixture of pride and fear. Pride at what we had achieved; fear at how we would keep this freedom. I could see the rescued prisoners emerging, weak and malnourished. Many were practically naked. The women among them had cigarette burns all over their chests. The prisoners were in a daze and had no idea where they were or where their homes were. The situation quickly galvanized people into action. Women rushed to clothe the women prisoners. They took them into cars and homes and alleyways, where they were given some privacy while they waited for clothes.

A huge crowd of men and women and children quickly gathered. Seeing the *peshmerga* in Hawler's downtown boosted everyone's morale. Men armed with shovels, clubs, some with Kalashnikovs, called for a march on Baghdad to rid Iraq of Saddam. A man, jumping up and down on the roof of the secret police building, shouted, "I can't believe I'm doing this! I have never done this before!"

Following the Kurdish uprising of 1991 and the Shi'a revolt in the south, a lot came to light about the regime's prisons. At a public inquiry led by the Kurdish authorities, a man called Taho, who was a night guard at the government-owned and-operated asphalt factory, told his story. He said he'd seen, more than once late at night, the secret police coming in their special SUVs to the cemetery behind the plant. There, they dug mass graves using a giant shovel that they kept there for that purpose. Into these holes, the Iraqi forces dumped the bodies of Kurds killed during torture sessions in Saddam's prisons.

They did their gruesome deeds at night because they didn't want people to know about the graves. They did not want the families to be able to come one day and dig them up. Hiding the casualties was also Saddam's way of keeping the national morale high. In that sense, you could say that the regime saw both the living and the dead as the enemy.

People with sticks, stones, shovels, and guns were attacking the places from where the regime ruled. There was complete unity among the fighters; it made no difference whether they were from the city or from the mountains. Even the *Jash*, the mercenary Kurds who had fought on the side of the Iraqi forces during the revolution, turned their guns against the regime. All the offices of the military intelligence, security, and Ba'ath Party were taken over and, after being picked clean, they were set on fire. The empty shells of burned cars and spent bullets could be seen on the road. There were bullet holes on the roofs and the walls of the buildings.

The victory also led to much looting. The windows and walls of many buildings had been destroyed during the fighting, and now people could be seen taking big sacks of rice, bed frames, curtains, television sets, telephones, guns and ammunition, even an execution chair. I recognized Bakir and his brother. They each had a Persian carpet under one arm and were shouting, "Saddam's fallen!"

Taho, who I knew from my neighbourhood, used a military truck to haul all the stuff he had taken. He said, "Nothing gives me more pleasure than free stuff." The looters had no problem selling their wares, since most of the things were not available in the local market. We bought a sack of rice and a case of tomato paste off one of them.

Among the many stories that came to light after the uprising, none affected the nation more profoundly than the execution of a group of Kurdish men by firing squad in Mosul in the 1980s. Their families had been forced to pay for the bullets and burial ground.

The collapse of Saddam's dictatorship in 2003 brought to light many more mass graves. When they were digging the mass graves, the pieces of bones were put in a white bag to be put in a coffin. Pieces of clothing or dates of execution helped people discover where the bodies had come from. As the coffins filled up, they were loaded onto the roofs of cars and sent back home. Many of the coffins were almost empty, but the mothers pretended that they contained the bodies of their beloved sons. The coffins helped them find closure.

Following the uprising in 1991, various elections were held in Kurdistan. Every organization wanted to elect new representatives to replace Saddam's puppets. The Kurdistan Writers' Union, Hawler Branch, held their elections at the ugly library that had replaced the one Saddam had turned into a prison. I was elected president. Our mission was to promote Kurdish literature through magazine, book, and newspaper publications. We often held gatherings, such as presentations and seminars, and also helped writers establish their careers.

For several days people were in a festive mood, dancing anywhere they could. During one dance, Yahya's wife, Hasima Kuristani, without even consulting her husband, offered her daughter in marriage to a Kurdish official, but because the man had two wives already, he in turn offered the girl to one of his bodyguards. Enraged, Yahya divorced his wife.

It was a strange, happy time for Kurds as they celebrated their moment of freedom.

A Twist of Fate

On the evening of March 31, 1991, Sabah and I went out for a poetry reading at the Cultural Centre Hall. When we got there, I could tell something was not right. Even though it was close to the starting time, the hall's doors remained shut. As I drove back through downtown, I saw truckloads of *peshmerga* on the move. Big guns had been placed on the city squares and fortifications had been built around them. An attack on the city seemed imminent. Some people gathered at the local Kurdish political parties' offices in the hopes of finding out what was happening. Inside, however, they found that the leaders were also listening to the radio, just like everyone else. They, too, did not know what was happening.

Since the uprising, Hawler had been without power, and running water had to be brought in by tankers. The water had not been sanitized and we had to boil it thoroughly before we were able to use it. At nighttime people would huddle around kerosene lamps until it was time to go to bed. But that night we got power and water back. Our neighbour, Gulizar, was washing her front porch. She said, "I'm glad I didn't die before I had a chance to enjoy this precious gift—running water—from the uprising."

That night no one slept. Everyone was anxious for news. By early morning artillery shells could be heard landing near the city. Instead of the white smoke from the bakeries, we saw the black smoke of the bombs rise above the city. People started running. Some people were already leaving for the border areas. There was a severe shortage of gasoline because the regular supplies were cut off after the uprising and fresh supplies had to be smuggled from Baghdad or Mosul. Many couldn't afford to pay the bootleg prices, but they fled the city in their cars anyway.

Fortunately, I had stored forty litres of gasoline at my home for an emergency. Without it, we would not have been able to leave. While Sabah hurriedly dressed the children and got as much bread as she could lay her hands on, Jamal and I siphoned the stored gas into our cars and prepared for the journey. He and my mother stayed within a few doors of each other, so we loaded everyone in our family into our two vehicles. We crammed eight people—me, Sabah, Niga, and Ewar, Sabah's mother and grandmother, Sabah's brother, Karwan, and his mother-in-law—into my small vw sedan and slowly made our way through the crush of people fleeing the city. People were leaving in any way they could: on foot, on bicycles, motorcycles, in cars; everyone was heading towards the border. It was a similar story in the cities of Kirkuk, Duhok, and Suleimaniya. It was estimated that over the next few days, three million Kurds fled their country. As we headed north along the Hamilton Highway leading to Iran, we could see abandoned cars littering the side of the road.

When warplanes suddenly appeared, people started to panic. I stopped the car. We all scrambled out of the car and stretched out on the ground, face down, until the planes were gone. This was the third time that I had hidden myself from a plane. The first time was when my family fled Ashkaftsaqa; the second time was during the Iran-Iraq war, when the planes bombed Hawler. On that occasion, Aunt Goly was killed by a bomb that landed on her home.

When we resumed the journey, we got separated from my mother and brothers. A little way farther down the road, we ran into a young boy from our neighbourhood, Hashmand, who was heading in the opposite direction with a companion. They each had a Kalashnikov in their hands. He was part of a young radical movement called *shurakan*, which had been established after the uprising. When we asked them where they were going, they shouted back that they were going to defend the city. I looked at the magazine taped onto his rifle and shook my head. They were young and naïve, but I remember when I, too, believed I could change the world.

Sabah's mother was trying to stop them, but I held her back, saying, "Let them do what they must do. They are young. They will come back." I knew their folly could not last. I was right. They returned to Hawler, but on seeing that it would do them no good to fight, they found their way to Iran through Raniyah. We met up with them again in exile.

There were eight of us in the car, even though it could only seat five. By nightfall we had reached the town of Harir. We pulled over and started a little fire off the road. It was hard to enjoy ourselves because we were so frightened. So we took off again. I drove again to reach the border quickly.

In the village of Hawdiyan, where the road splits into two, one leading to Turkey, the other to Iran, people had traded their cars for donkeys because their cars couldn't go up the mountains to the Turkish border. As a result, most villagers now had a few cars parked outside their homes, without anyone knowing how to drive. We still had some gasoline, but we bought some more from an Iranian vendor who had crossed the border to sell gas by the side of the road and then we continued on our journey. I was the only driver among us, and I would drive until I could no longer keep my eyes open. After a short nap, I would open my eyes and start driving again. I could sleep properly once we were safely in Iran.

At least there was a road leading to the border with Iran. The people who had chosen to go to Turkey had to travel on foot through the mountains. With old women and young children to think of, Iran was the better option for us. Besides, it was early April and there was still plenty of snow on the mountains. At least being huddled in the car would give us some protection from the elements. It was very slow going. At one point, it took us two days just to go five kilometres. We kept heading north towards the Iranian border. By now, we had run out of the supplies we had brought with us from Hawler. We tried to get more food from locals, but the refugees who were ahead of us had already traded or bought anything that was available. We were tired, cold, hungry, and very, very frightened. The two little ones, Ewar and Niga, complained and fought all the time. We tried to give them food, but by now dry bread could no longer console them.

As we drove up the narrow mountain pass, we heard a woman moaning behind a rock. My mother-in-law said she was about to have a baby. We could not see her, but we did see a man holding a sharp piece of stone, perhaps playing the role of a midwife. Whether it was the woman's husband or father we couldn't tell.

During the exodus, some 20,000 children and hundreds of men and women died. Sabah's grandmother, Rahna, who was sixty-three, was concerned about all the prayers she had missed. When we crossed the Iranian border, we met up with Sabah's brother, Kawa. Nana Rahna wanted to change cars and so she travelled with them as they went off in search of a place to stay. After their arrival in Mahabad, they all went to eat, leaving Grandma in the car as she had requested. When they came back with a dish of kebab and tea for her, they found her dead. A local by the name of Agha Hijazi helped them with the burial. The unmarked graves of hundreds of Kurdish refugees dot cemeteries in Iranian Kurdistan. Nana Rahna's is one of them.

Among the many people fleeing the cities throughout Kurdistan were some of the very same soldiers who had earlier had a hand in carrying out the Anfal campaign. Amazingly, no one was thinking about revenge. As we fled, news about the fighting travelled with us. We heard how Iraqi forces advanced through Kurdistan, routing the *peshmerga* troops. The advance ended just north of Hawler, in the village of Kore. The *peshmerga* finally managed to blunt the advance and rout the government forces. They even destroyed seven tanks. But still, Saddam's air strikes instilled fear in our hearts and people continued their journeys into exile.

It took us seven days to make it to the Iranian city of Khana, 250 kilometres away from Hawler. As we approached, we heard airplanes. The children were frightened, but we managed to calm them down by explaining that these were United Nations planes dropping water bottles and cakes. They were there to help us, not harm us like the planes they had seen on the first day of our flight. The packages fell all over the place and refugees rushed to get to the supplies. We didn't get anything, and so I resorted to buying food and water from those who had managed to pick up two or three ration packs.

We had arrived in Khana in the early evening, and as we walked through the city, darkness was falling fast. People were returning home and I realized with a growing sense of desperation that we needed to find a place to stay for the night. Ewar and Niga were exhausted. I had not slept for more than ten minutes at a time for an entire week. The other adults in our group could not face another night of trying to sleep in a crowded vehicle.

I was thinking about buying some nylon at a local bazaar so we could set up a tent on the street when we were approached by a man. He introduced himself as Sayyid Niya and asked if we were refugees. When I said yes, he invited us to his home. I had to leave the car on the main road as his home was in an alley.

Sayyid Niya looked over fifty. His wife, Sayyid Zada, looked younger than him and was sitting on the floor by a warm stove on which something seemed to be cooking. There was a teapot on a samovar. The house smelled of burning spirits and tea. As we settled down,

Sayyid Zada remarked loudly, "Iraqi refugees are here again. Every ten years they make problems for themselves. And for us, when they come. The price of everything goes higher. The mosques and streets are filled with refugees. This is the worst! I have never seen anything like it."

I wasn't in a mood to respond or to argue with what she said. Sayyid Niya felt embarrassed by what his wife said, but there was little he could do. In her own way, she was right. The refugees from Hawler outnumbered the town's people. Wherever you went, it was like walking in Hawler—you always ran into people you knew. On the road in, I saw a friend who was also a member of the Kurdistan Writers' Union. He was standing in front of a tent that was only fifty centimetres high. It seemed to me that was his home. There was a pot of soup in front of him, and he said, "It's been two days since I bought this soup to sell, but no one has bought any, so now I have to take it back into the tent to eat it with my family."

The locals were very kind to us. Each family was hosting at least three refugee families. This was the first time I realized money couldn't solve all problems, and so I said nothing when Sayyid Zada spoke.

It was Ramadan and Sayyid Zada was fasting, but after breaking her fast with a date, her mood changed for the better, and she invited us all to eat with them, saying it was our home, too. We added extra sugar to the children's tea to make them less hungry. I didn't know whether Sayyid Niya was fasting or not; his personality reminded me of my father's: he always had a healthy scepticism of religion.

As we ate, Sayyid Zada told us a story about her daughter's relationship with a Kurdish refugee from Iraq in 1974. It was the first time I had heard a Kurdish woman talk about a love affair between her daughter and a boy. After supper, we got ready to go to sleep for the night. We were excited, because for the first time in a week we were able to sleep in clean beds.

In the morning, I went with Sayyid Niya and did some grocery shopping. When we arrived home, Sayyid Zada smiled for the first time since we had arrived. "Agha," she said in a voice filled with emotion, "we live on cob corn. You've bought us more stuff than the monthly ration we get from the Iranian government."

Sayyid Zada's house had three rooms. We slept in one of the rooms, and the couple and their daughter slept in the other two. The basement of their house was filled with chickens, and one could hardly take a step without encountering chicken droppings.

One day, Sayyid Niya brought another refugee back to his house. It seemed to us that he did not have any duties other than to bring refugees into his home. That refugee turned out to be a friend of Sabah's who used to live in a luxury home in Koya. Now he would have to stay in the basement. As we had seen the basement and knew how dirty it was, we were embarrassed to bring him down there. But he had been sleeping under a nylon tent for two days, so his reaction to the basement was, "Wow! What a beautiful place!"

Returning Home

When the news of this tragic exodus reached the West, the late president of France, François Mitterrand, fought to create a safe haven for the refugees. It did not happen overnight. Diplomacy seldom does. But in the end, his efforts succeeded and a no-fly zone was created. Iraqi aircraft and military were ordered not go beyond the 36th parallel, which meant that it was safe to return to areas north of that. International humanitarian relief aid kept being dropped from the air, but after a while their operations were expanded significantly on land.

The creation of the safe haven in Iraq at the end of April 1991 by enforcing a strict no-fly zone was intended to protect Kurds in the north and Shi'as in the south of Iraq. The resolution brought a special joy to the Kurds who had fled the country after Saddam's reprisal. Now they could return to their homes without fear. It took a while to get our affairs straightened out, but after two months in Iran, we were finally going to be reunited with my mother and brothers. We joined the convoys of cars loaded with everything from blankets to cradles, heading home. People had tied mattresses and rugs to the roofs of their cars. Some had managed to obtain large trucks to transport goods back to Kurdistan. From time to time, the convoys would pull over to the side of the road and people would dance on the streets in an effort to express their joy at being able to go home.

When we reached the town of Rawanduz just inside the Kurdish border with Iran, some members of the Kurdish Writers' Union and I decided to remain there while we re-established the union and prepared for an upcoming conference in Shaqlawa. Rawanduz was known as a seat of resistance against Saddam's regime, and we wanted to talk to some of the Kurdish leaders there about what we as writers could contribute to the Kurdish cause. Sabah and the children continued travelling home to Hawler, where she would stay with her mother and her brother until my return.

We were shown the town's famous gorge, and one day we were taken to the top of Mount Hassan Beg where Saddam had built himself a summer home. The road zig-zagged its way all the way to the top. It was scary to drive up. For the army, or for himself, Saddam would build roads to the highest mountains, but for the people in towns twenty minutes outside of major cities, there were no roads. On the first day of the uprising, villagers in the area had looted the villa and picked it clean. Later, it was burnt down. By the time we arrived at the mansion, there was nothing left except for broken pieces of wood. But still the view was impressive.

After Mount Kandil, Mount Hassan Beg is the highest point in Kurdistan. It is about thirty kilometres north of Hamilton Road and about 120 kilometres out of Hawler. On a clear day, you can see the shadow of Hawler from the top of the mountain. Standing up there on the mountain, I could see why Saddam had chosen this spot for his villa. It was strategically placed near the borders with both Iran and Turkey, and the view was breathtaking. He always chose the most desirable locations to build his villas. He had many such places all over Iraq, and they were all surrounded by stone fences and guards. I looked around at the remains of the fence and the guard posts. Although Saddam was defeated and his villa had been destroyed, you could smell and feel fear and blood coming through the concrete casement on which we stood.

I looked out over the valley at the trees and the snow that covered the tops of the mountains all year round. It was late spring, and the snow along the slopes was beginning to melt, slowly turning the tiny streams into rivers that would bring life to the valleys of Kurdistan.

Hama Sadiq, Jalal, and Aziz Akrey at a lecture in Hawler, 1992. The lecture was about the genocide in Kurdistan.

Jalal in his office in 1996, as Executive Director of Hawler Culture and Art.

Shepherds had raised their tents and were herding their animals. People were celebrating their presence in the beautiful land, because never before had they been allowed to come to the mountain where their ancestors had been allowed to roam free.

The air had a meditative quality about it, but I could not forget that this was where a dictator had built his home.

Back in Rawanduz after our sightseeing tour, we settled down and set to work. With writer Nazhad Aziz Surme, the Kurdistan Writers' Union organized a literary conference. We recorded the proceedings on audiotape, and afterwards I drove to the nearby KDP radio station on Mount Shirin and delivered a copy to them so that they could broadcast it. I took another copy to the PUK radio station in Galala.

A month later we moved the office of the Kurdistan Writers' Union to Shaqlawa. There, for the first time since the uprising, we drank bootleg arrack. In Shaqlawa, the Kurdistan Writers' Union held its annual conference, which was named after the uprising. I was elected a member of the governing board and the editorial board of the union's journal *Nuseri Kurd*, or *The Kurdish Writer*. For two to three years I worked as a journalist. For a while I edited the journal *Rebazi Newe*, or the *New Path* and worked in the Kurdistan Regional Government.

After four months travelling and working for the Kurdistan Writers' Union, I returned to Hawler. When I got there, I discovered that our home had been looted. We had to furnish it again. About a year after our return from Iran, our son, Jwamer, was born. Life was hard for us in Hawler, but at least we had three beautiful children.

The creation of the no-fly zone made the Kurds feel safe again. The U.S. warplanes patrolling the skies over Kurdistan were a daily reassurance that we were being protected. Sabah became the director of a carpet factory that specialized in making hand-made rugs. In 1992 the KDP and the PUK held elections in Kurdistan and many Kurdish people went out to cast their votes. Voters were dressed in colourful dresses and danced and sang outside the polling stations. In 1992 a parliament and government were formed, and power was divided equally between the leading parties. Dr. Fouad Ma'soum became the first prime minister, and Jawhar Namiq the first speaker. It was the first Kurdish parliamentary election to happen on the soil of Kurdistan.

7 Searching for a New Beginning

Crossing Borders

THREE YEARS AFTER THE FORMATION of the Kurdistan Regional Government in 1992, war broke out between the PUK and the KDP. The fighting was essentially over who should have more power and how to distribute revenue. At the same time, a short but ferocious fight broke out between the PUK and the Islamist Revolutionary Guard Corps. The struggle ended with the routing of the Islamists. In 1995, Robert Baer, a CIA case officer, managed to negotiate a truce between the warring parties, but it did not last long. By August 1996, the fighting between the PUK and the KDP worsened. After a bloody battle, the PUK gained control of Hawler, the capital of the Kurdistan region. Some regions around Hawler, as well as Duhok, remained under the control of the KDP.

About the same time, Iranian forces penetrated deep into the area that was controlled by Iraqi PUK and attacked the Iranian PDK, which had its office in Koya. Fortunately, there were no casualties among people; but as is always the case, birds and animals become victims of war. News reports mentioned only that "a few chickens were killed in the attack."

On August 31, 1996, Massoud Barzani, president of the KDP received some assistance from the Iraqi Forces and drove the PUK out of Hawler and Suleimaniya to the Iranian border, where they regrouped after a few months when Jalal Talabani, the secretary-general of the PUK, received war supplies from the Iranian government.

Receiving help must have been hard for both sides, because both countries that were backing them in this ugly war had suppressed Kurdish nationalism in their individual countries. However, this was the only means by which political parties could survive in this suicidal war.

The KDP and the PUK each set up a government and parliament— the PUK in Suleimaniya, close to Iranian border, and the KDP in Hawler, close to the red-line border of the Iraqi forces. The Baghdad regime also created its own administration for the region in the town of Makhmour, half an hour's drive from Hawler. The village of Takawir on the highway between Hawler and Koya marked the border.

Another ceasefire agreement between the PUK and the KDP was signed on September 25. Despite the ceasefire, fighting continued and another, more permanent, peace agreement came in to effect on November 24. A year later, the leaders of the two parties signed a power-sharing agreement. In terms of the agreement, Jalal Talabani would become the first Kurdish president of Iraq, while Massoud Barzani was the president of Kurdistan province.

In 2010, when the majority of Kurdish people voted for Massoud Barzani and he was elected president of Kurdistan province for four more years, Barzani apologized for all the lives lost in the war.

For those Kurds who were not involved in the fighting, the situation was awful. In an effort to raise awareness about the importance of peace in the region, the renowned Kurdish artist, Ismail Khayat, painted a series of murals on the rocks overlooking a major highway. Writers, artists, politicians, and others, both at home and abroad, did their best to bring the fighting to an end, but to no avail. Some writers, including the critic Shazad, planned a different kind of protest: they wanted to set themselves on fire in front of the governor's office in Hawler. But when the planned protest generated little interest and was largely ignored, they scrapped their plans. After the failure of the group's plan, Shazad went and picked up the bag of groceries he had left in a tailor shop and went home, disappointed but relieved. Life in Kurdistan carried on.

I don't believe in suicide; life is better than death. I don't want to rush to die. That's why I chose not to set myself on fire or perform any other kinds of heroics. Instead, I let my words do the talking. The painter Namiq Ali and I protested against the war through poetry and painting.

Early one evening in October 1996, Ewar came running up to me where I was sitting in the lounge. "*Baba*," she said as she tried to catch her breath, "there are two vehicles full of armed men in front of our home." I glanced through the window and saw some armed men getting out of two olive-coloured vehicles with no licence plates.

I did not hesitate. This time I was wearing flannel pyjamas. Cream, not blue. I walked calmly out of the back door of our house and made my way to the house next door, where my mother and Jamal lived. I didn't want anyone to be suspicious. From their home, I walked straight to Uncle Mamad's house. Better safe than sorry, I thought. I did not want to end up in prison again.

Later that night I learned from Sabah that they had indeed come for me. At that point, I realized that I could not remain in Hawler and began making plans to leave the country for good. Sabah and my mother both tried to convince me to go to Suleimaniya rather than leave the country.

"You can't leave our country, my son," my mother urged me. "It's too far away. Go to Suleimaniya. At least there you know you will make good money."

My mother was right, I would be financially successful if I went to Suleimaniya. The war between the PUK and the KDP had caused a split in the media and since I worked through the PUK media, I would not have struggled to find a job there. However, if I did go to Suleimaniya, I would clearly be identifying myself with the PUK.

I did not wish to be tied down to any political party, and I wished to keep my freedom. I also did not agree with the war. I even had a poem published about my opposition to the war. For me, moving to Suleimaniya was not an option.

"You can take the car to Baghdad and then drive up there through Kirkuk," Sabah persisted.

"You know I can't do that," I said. "I am opposed to this war and I have to go to a place where I can continue to be an independent writer. I do not want to take sides in this civil war."

I turned to my mother. "With the war going on, we cannot make telephone calls between Hawler and Suleimaniya. But if I were in a European country, I would be able to call you."

This seemed to sway my mother, whose main fear was that she would never hear from me if I was not in the country.

Eventually they gave in. The next day, I made a trip to the Sheikh Allah Bazaar, where you could buy almost anything if you knew where to look. The Bazaar lay a few blocks east of downtown Hawler. As I approached the Bazaar, the crowds became unbearable. There was hardly any room to squeeze through between the people and the stalls. Everyone knew that smugglers were a dime-a-dozen in the Bazaar. I made my way though the crowds to a particular smuggler who had been recommended to me. He took out a box full of fake passports. Together, we flipped through the box to see whether any of the faces in these passports could be me. Unfortunately, not one did. This meant that the smugglers had to take a few days to get their contacts in the Passports Office in Kirkuk to help them make one for me.

About a week later, I went back and collected my passport. The smuggler gave me the address of a man in the border town of Zakho who could get me a visa for Turkey and then help me get across the border to Silopi in southern Turkey. He also gave me an address for Karzan, a sea smuggler in Istambul who moved people between Turkey and Greece.

When I planned to leave, I slowly began to sell everything in the home. It was hard for me to sell the things that held special memories for me. The only things I kept were a select few books that I gave to my mother to keep for me. At least this gave her some hope that I would return one day. Jwamer and Niga were still little at the time and didn't understand the significance of their father's departure as much as Sabah and Ewar did. They understood perfectly and were fearful of the future.

On the morning of my arranged departure, I said goodbye to Sabah, Ewar, Niga, and Jwamer and to my mother and brothers and sisters. My mother-in-law was also there to say goodbye. I did not know when I would see them again and it was hard to let go of my children. Everyone pleaded with me to allow them to come to the terminal with them, or at least to let my brother come with me, but I refused. I wanted to draw as little attention to my departure as possible. Everyone cried as I left.

Whenever the bus stopped along the way, the passengers would get out and buy something to eat at the kebab shops. Usually I enjoyed trying the food along the way, but the stress of the journey had destroyed my appetite. All I could manage was some tea.

The border crossing at Ibrahim Khalil lay right on the border with Turkey, not far from Zakho in an area controlled by the KDP. Some people who wanted to get out of the country paid the smugglers and did not bother to get visas. They took their passports and went to Zakho, from where the smugglers would take them across the dangerous mountain passes into Turkey. I knew that would not work for me, which is why I chose to get a visa.

When we arrived in Zakho, I went straight to the Iraqi Turkmen Movement offices and bought a visa. At the offices, they said it would take three days to process. While I waited, I stayed in a hotel in Zakho and attended to some last-minute details for my trip. During the civil war, no one was allowed to make long-distance phone calls in Kurdistan. In Zakho, however, some people who had cell phones would take people to the tops of the surrounding hills and charge them to use their phones to make international calls. I found someone who rented out his phone and made a call to another smuggler I'd been told to contact. At least I knew him. His name was Faro and he was from Hawler. His father was the muezzin who called the faithful to prayer five times every day. Faro lived in Kiev, and he assured me he would meet me at the airport when I arrived.

Three days later, I collected my passport from the smugglers. Inside was a stamp: I was holding a brand new visa. From the smugglers' offices, I went to the border post at Ibrahim Khalil, where people could cross over into Turkey. Turkish drivers had lined up on the side of the road to take people across by the carload. Four passengers shared a taxi.

As we drove towards the checkpoint, I was terrified. I could see from the landscape outside that we were going through the north of Kurdistan, but I did not recognize the roads at all. It was also the first time that I saw wooden houses close to the highway. This novel sight made me forget my troubles a little bit.

When we got to the border crossing, the driver took our passports and handed them to the customs officer. We got out of the car. He walked over to us, stopping in front of each one of us to check our passport. The name in my passport said "Jalal Abbas," and I kept repeating the name in my head in case he asked me my name.

After checking our passports, the guard walked to the back of the car and checked through all our luggage. My heart sank. I had put a copy of each one of my published books, *Dance of the Evening Snow* and *No Warming Up*, into the inside pockets of my coat, along with notes I had written in prison. As he checked our luggage carefully, I became worried that he would do a body search on us and find the books. That would get me into big trouble. Fortunately, he did not. Fifteen minutes after arriving at the border post, we were allowed to pass through and drive to Silopi.

I felt very sad and my heart pounded with fear as we crossed the bridge. Taking the books and notes with me had been a risk, but I had wanted to have my writing with me wherever I went. In the end, my decision turned out to be a good one because these books would help me when I applied for refugee status.

From Silopi, I took the bus to Ankara. It was the first time I had travelled on a bus where they served tea and coffee and hand sanitizers. I sat down and waited nervously for the bus to leave. I was in a hurry to get to Ankara so that I could make my arrangements and get to Ukraine as quickly as possible. The farther I was from Iraq, the better at this point. We travelled through many cities, and each time we approached the lights, I thought, *This must be Ankara.* But no, we just travelled straight through the city. Eventually the high-rises looming in the distance caught my eye. This was Ankara; there was no doubt about that.

We arrived at the bus station around 9:00 A M. As the passengers were leaving the bus, I was thinking about my next step. I had arranged for another smuggler to get me through Turkey to Ukraine. Could I trust this smuggler? I didn't speak any Turkish and I felt vulnerable. At that moment, I realized that I did not have a visa to enter Ukraine!

I looked around me. The bus station in Ankara was clean and huge. This was the first bus station I had been to where there were no pools of urine by the outside wall, as was usual in Iraq. I held onto my suitcase tightly. In it I had a suit and tie, two shirts, two boxer shorts, and a few other basic necessities. My plan was to wear the suit while travelling to Ukraine. But I soon realized this would be a mistake, since tourists never wear suits when they travel. I took a deep breath and set out on the next step of my journey. Since I could not speak any Turkish, I showed the taxi driver a piece of paper on which I had written the address of the Hotel Farah in the Olus district. This is where the smuggler had told me to go.

Ankara was the first foreign city I had seen. I'd been in Baghdad, but that isn't like Ankara. Ankara is a tourist city, and it shows. It was the most beautiful city I had seen, with various gardens and fountains everywhere. There were more Western visitors than I had ever seen. I could see how hard Ankara was trying to become Western so that Turkey could join the European Union. And maybe Turkey will one day if they focus on resolving the human rights issues concerning the Kurds in their country. The style of clothes, houses, and shops was completely different here. However, I was too concerned with the journey ahead of me to fully enjoy the city.

I wore the clothes I told the smuggler I would be wearing: black slacks, a jacket and a blue shirt. At the hotel, the smuggler walked over to me and gave me a warm welcome. We chatted for a while so that he would not look suspicious. During our conversation, the smuggler told me that he would have my plane ticket and a visa for Ukraine ready for me in the morning. As we parted ways, I gave him my fake passport along with $1,300.

That evening, I ate dinner in a nearby restaurant. I went for something familiar: roasted chicken.

As he had promised, the smuggler got me the visa and the plane ticket. He also arranged for a taxi to take me to the Ankara airport at four in the morning. I was to fly to Istanbul, and from there, after a change of planes, to Ukraine. I wore the suit for the occasion. The taxi arrived late, at 5:00 A M . I was waiting at the door, and we drove off without delay. I was very nervous and confused. I had never travelled by air before. When Saddam was in power, no one was allowed to leave Iraq except his high-profile followers. Along the way, I kept looking at my passport and the visas. These were the first official documents I had owned, and they were fake.

At the airport, I stood at the entrance to the terminal. I had no idea where to go or what to do. I couldn't even ask for help because I didn't speak any Turkish. I showed my ticket to some employees and they directed me to the right gate. I showed the officials my ticket and my passport. I tried very hard not to look too nervous. Everything went well and I got through the customs.

As we boarded the plane, I thought I would be able to get myself a window seat, just like a passenger in a car. It was my first time on an airplane and I did not know that airplane seats are numbered and that you get assigned specific seat. I marvelled at the nice entertainers who showed me to my seat and helped me buckle my seat belt. They showed me how to loosen it so that I could go to the bathroom. When it came time for food, I was worried because I did not know what to order, but they give me chicken, which I enjoy. I wondered how they knew I enjoyed it.

At first, I was a little disappointed to discover that I had been given a seat in the middle row, but I soon realized that there was really nothing to look at up there and that made me feel a bit better. Outside the plane, I was surrounded by an endless expanse of milky void. Seeing clouds here, clouds there, clouds everywhere, made me wonder how the clouds stored all the rain and whether they remained calm or became violent during a storm, and whether it was all true where I was, far, far away from all the injustices committed daily below in so many parts of the world.

From Ankara, I flew to Istanbul, where I changed planes and flew to Kiev. When the plane landed in Kiev, I followed the passengers timidly. I was the last person in line for passport control. While we waited, I slipped $200 into my passport, just as the smuggler had told me to do. It felt as if the line was not moving at all and everyone was watching me. I grew more and more nervous with every second that went by. At last I reached the front of the line. I handed the passport to the officer. He opened it, glanced up at me, and put it aside. Then he asked me to go and wait by the wall.

I waited for a long time. Outside, it grew dark. The officer who had taken my passport was replaced by another. By midnight, the airport crowd was thinning out, and before long the passport control closed for the night. I was left sitting in the terminal. I tried to rest a little on a bench across from the toilet, but a woman custodian rudely asked me to leave. I gathered some discarded newspapers to use as a blanket and stretched out on the floor. From where I lay, I could see that the bench remained empty all night. I couldn't understand why she had kicked me off.

Throughout the night, I kept thinking about Faro and how he might be able to smuggle me into Holland or Germany, or even Sweden, and how later I would arrange for my family to come and join me in our new homeland. When I opened my eyes it was daybreak. The control officer on duty asked me to come forward. I walked over cautiously. I had had many hours to think about all the awful things that could happen to me. He gave my passport to another officer who took me to a private room. The officer asked for more money. Before I left Hawler, Sabah had sewn a little pocket inside my underwear to keep my money in. I did not want the officer to see where I kept my money, so I asked to go to the toilet. Hidden from view, I took the money out and returned to the room.

The officer took $300 and told me that my passport and visa were fake and that he would have to deport me. Dejected and tired, I picked up my bag and was soon on a flight to Istanbul.

I had spent plenty of money in my attempt to get out of Kurdistan, only to have my passport confiscated and then put on a flight back to where I had come from when freedom seemed within my reach. The officer in the little room had kept my passport and my biggest fear was that the Turkish government would send me back to Iraq.

Ankara 1997

At Istanbul airport, I was relieved when the airport officials returned my passport. It gave me another chance to try to go into exile. Now I had two options: either register as a refugee with the UN in Ankara or try the perilous smuggling route over the Aegean Sea to Greece. I sat in the airport lounge considering my options.

"If I take the smuggler's route, I'll be in Greece in a few hours—if the police don't catch us and if the boat doesn't sink. Then I'll no longer have to worry about being deported," I said to myself.

But, when we had talked about it in Hawler, no one in my family wanted me to take the boat. Besides, ever since Sa'doun had drowned in the Kalak River, I had been afraid of water. "But going back to Ankara to claim refugee status will take too long," I told myself. I could feel the paper with the address of a sea smuggler, Karzan, in my pocket.

In the end, I decided to try to cross the Aegean. I knew crossing the rough waters in a small boat would be risky, but I decided it was a risk worth taking. I took a long-distance taxi to Karzan's house. Along the way, I was too focused on getting out of Turkey as soon as possible and I saw nothing of the beauty of this ancient city. When the driver dropped me off, I walked up to the door and knocked. A tall skinny man with a moustache opened the door a crack and said, "May I help you?"

I introduced myself and he opened the door and let me in. Inside, the room was already full of other refugees looking for a way out of Turkey. As we waited for Karzan to tell us more about the trip, the conversation was all about who made it to Sweden or Germany, who was caught, who was swept away by the sea, who got accepted, and who got rejected. I was troubled by the risk I was thinking of taking, and I could feel my dream of freedom sinking with every tick of the clock on Karzan's wall.

Eventually Karzan felt that there were enough of us in the room. He began by advising those of us who wanted to be taken to Greece by boat to wear jeans and T-shirts so that we wouldn't draw attention to ourselves. "Anatoly is a tourist city," he said. "You will stay there until tonight, and then we will take you to the Adriatic Sea. When we get there, you will get on a boat that will take you to Greece. But the boat will only leave the Turkish coastline if the wind stops and the waves become calm. My role in the business is over as soon as the boat gets you to Greece. When you arrive in Greece, you have to claim refugee status at the nearest police station. In Greece there are many smugglers who will take you to any European country you like for a fee."

After his little talk, he brought us all supper. I thought this was such a nice man to do this for us. After supper at Karzan's house, people who had already decided to take the boat to Greece began to line up at the washroom so that they could shave their facial hair. They wanted to look more like tourists. A man of about fifty paced in and out of the washroom a few times, and appeared to be second guessing the decision to shave his facial hair.

After a while he spoke. "Is shaving my moustache *haraam*?" he asked. "Should I talk to a mullah about this?"

"The interpretation of Islam is little different here," I replied. "A mullah here may believe its fine to shave your moustache, but do you really have time to ask at this point?"

"What do you mean it is a little different?" he asked me.

"I think they are more open-minded about such things," I said.

Finally, the man went into the washroom and shaved, but when he came out, he put his hands on his face to cover the areas that no longer held facial hair.

I was still thinking about going on the boat, so I asked Karzan, "How much did you say the trip cost?"

"It's $1,200 for adults and $800 for those under eighteen," he rattled off the amounts.

Because I didn't have that kind of money, I decided to leave Istanbul and go back to Ankara. As I prepared to leave, Karzan asked me to pay him $50 for the food. So much for the niceties.

From Karzan's house, I went straight back to the bus terminal. I took a bus headed to Jazeera and Silopi in the south of Turkey. My spirits were down and I had very little hope of ever getting my

freedom. I worried about military checkpoints along the way. I had
managed to get myself a window seat and, as I always did in hard
times, I looked out the window for consolation. I could see many
houses with lights in them. They reminded me of my family back in
Kurdistan. I remembered the evenings I spent with my family and
how after work or an event, I'd hurry to get home as I passed the
houses with lights on. The view through the window did not bring me
peace as I had hoped it would. Around me, most of passengers were
asleep and the bus was driving through the mountains in the dark, so
I retreated into myself and got caught up in my own thoughts.

Because I was the only passenger who wanted to get off in Ankara,
the bus did not bother going to the bus terminal. When we passed
through the city at 2:00 AM, the driver simply pulled up at the side
of the road and let me get off. I threw my bag over my shoulder
and nervously began to walk towards the terminal. I did not have a
permit to stay in Turkey and if any policeman stopped me, I would be
deported back to Iraq immediately. I shuddered at the thought.

I lingered at the station until daybreak. When the sun came up
I decided to find Hashim, an acquaintance who had been living in
the city illegally for six months. I had been given his address by my
brother-in-law Karwan. Because I couldn't give the taxi driver directions in Turkish, I simply showed him the address I had written on
a piece of paper. He dropped me at the foot of a hill and pointed to
the top. I began to climb the hill, counting the steps as I went along.
A place with so many steps leading up to it had to be very fancy,
I thought as I pulled myself up yet another step. After 122 steps, I
reached the address on the paper. I was looking for a fancy building,
but there was none nearby. I asked a passerby where it was, and he led
me through the door to the right. It was not fancy at all. Clearly, not
every house built on a hill is a castle. The old building was rundown.
As I walked in, I noticed that the doors to all four rooms in the house
were shut tight.

I knocked on the second door on the left down the passage. It took
a while for Hashim to open. Once inside, he apologized. "I thought it
was the police," he explained. Things were different here in Turkey,
I discovered. Sometimes when the police came to a house to capture

Above: Jalal and a fellow refugee, Abdurahman, in Madame Teza's house, Ankara, 1997.
Left: Jalal and Hashim in Ankara, 1997.

refugees to deport them, they did not break down the door to get in. If no one answered the door, they would return on another day.

After giving me a little rest to recover from climbing the stairs, Hashim mentioned that I was lucky because there was an empty room in the house. He took me to Madame Teza, the landlady. The old woman's room was clean and cozy and fully carpeted. Framed passages from the Qu'ran hung on the walls. As we left, Hashim whispered, "She is obsessed with reading the Qu'ran in Arabic." He was right. She cared little for us, but she was jealous of the fact that we were able to read Arabic.

Madame Teza had a refrigerator and stove in her living quarters, but the room I could rent was bare and cold. It had one small window and there were a stained mattress and blankets laid out on the floor. A few dishes lay about, but not much else. She asked me to pay her 4 million Turkish lira, or about $40, for rent up front and 5 million lira damage deposit.

I looked around the room. I noticed a small hole near the top of my door. I soon learned to check through that hole to see whether it was safe to open the door when someone knocked. Because I am short, I had trouble reaching the hole, and standing on things to do so reminded me of trying to see through the hole in the roof in prison number four. Shortly after I had been given the keys to my room, Madame Teza brought me an electric heater and a small bottle of gas for the stove.

The building was crowded and there were hardly any amenities. My room had a small table in the corner that I could use for cooking or washing up. However, I had to go outside to get water to do anything. There was also only one toilet for all the residents, and it was infested with rats. To make matters worse, the house didn't have a shower so we had to go down the 122 steps to the *hammam*. The situation reminded me of Mto, a childhood friend of mine. He lived in a small house with ten other large families and one washroom. One of his neighbours, Ramadan, would stay in the washroom for half an hour or more, so Mto would walk to the nearest mosque and use one of the eight or so washrooms there. The mosque back then was a place of relaxation, where less privileged people who could not afford to have fans in their homes went to escape the heat and have a nap. Now, mosques are open only at prayer time.

Hashim helped me do some shopping. I bought a propane tank for the heater and the stove, some dishes, and groceries. Groceries were very expensive and very few people could afford to buy meat. Signs of poverty were all around me. Throughout the fourteen months I lived in Turkey, people always complained about high taxes and the lack of employment. Everywhere you went, people talked about health care and the expense of medication.

Turkey clearly was caught between copying the Western lifestyle in order to be accepted as member of European Union and maintaining the traditional way of life, which was much more Eastern. People in the cities wore Western clothes and men and women mixed freely. You could see lovers kissing on the street. There was a sense of liberalism in the cities that certainly did not reflect what I saw in the rural areas. And yet, underneath this openness, an Islamic mentality pervaded the society. There were mosques everywhere and they were always filled with people attending to their daily prayers. The older political figures in the country also held fast to a stricter, more conservative line of thinking. When I returned again in 2005 on my way to Kurdistan, I spent two nights in Istanbul. Much of the liberalism I had encountered on my first visit to the city was gone. There were more women wearing headdresses than I had seen seven years earlier. The political double standards were also more evident. When Kamal Ataturk introduced a secular constitution to Turkey after the First World War, he brought in many positive changes, but he also missed a few important things, such as not recognizing the twenty-five million Kurdish people in Turkey as full citizens. Their plight had been ignored over the years, and by the time I arrived in Turkey, their situation was desperate.

Hashim informed me that the *karkhana*, the red light district, was situated at the bottom of the hill on which we lived. The semi-nude women, he told me, could be seen through a display window. The place even had a cashier. He was convinced Madame Teza's daughter worked there and suspected that she gave most of the money she made to Mullah Khoja at the local mosque to buy her forgiveness from Allah.

All refugees were required to register with the police no later than five days after their arrival in Turkey. However, because I had not planned to stay in Turkey when I first arrived and because I had travelled from Istanbul to Ankara, I had not had an opportunity to do so within the allotted time period. Now I was an illegal resident and in violation of the law. Living in constant fear of being deported was very stressful, and I pitied those people who had lived like this for years. Meanwhile, my writer friends, Mussin Omer, Nazand Bagikany and Farhad Shakali, were trying to get me asylum through the International Parliament of Writers, which was passionate in its defence of freedom of expression and supported writers who had been imprisoned. The Parliament fought for writers' release and then helped them resettle in safe countries. Since Mussin and Nazand were living in Paris, they registered my application with the PEN offices in Paris. Farhad was a student in Sweden at the time and tried to find me asylum through student channels there.

Nights in Ankara were cold. The stove couldn't warm up my room and I barely recovered from one cold before the next struck. As I lay in my bed one day, I thought of what my mother once said: "For a sick person, nights are much harder than days."

One morning on my way out to get a cup of coffee, I ran into a young girl trying to manoeuvre her way down the stairs while carrying a bucket of water. I introduced myself and offered to help her. She smiled and said her name was Sungul. Her family were Kurds from southern Turkey. Her father was in jail and her mother never seemed to do much as far as I could see, so it fell on ten-year-old Sungul's shoulders to fend for the family. Sungul and I soon became daily companions along the road as she went down the steps that would take her to the bus stop, where she would try to sell her water. It was sad to look at this little Kurdish girl trying to make a living in the city. Compared to her situation, I thought mine no longer looked all that bad.

Seeking Asylum

One morning after I had been in Ankara for three or four days, Hashim and I went to the office of the UN High Commissioner for Refugees (UNHCR) to see whether we could apply for refugee status. The offices were in the wealthy Çankaya district of Ankara, where all the embassies and diplomatic offices were. We had met some refugees who had gone to the UNHCR and had got them to protect and support them and assist in their resettlement in a new country. Just seeing the office building with the blue flag bearing the UNHCR banner on the roof made me feel safe.

We joined the long line of people already waiting in front of the building. I could see UN staff going inside with swipe-card keys, and I wished that I could just tag along with them and tell them my story. Half a block away from the offices a man was lying on a very dirty mattress, complaining about his destiny. "My case has been rejected and I refuse to leave until the UN reconsiders and approves it." I didn't know why his case had been rejected, but the more I listened to him, the more frustrated I became. The next time I came to the building, I noticed that he was no longer there. When I asked about him the guards at the entrance told me the Turkish police had arrested and deported him.

There were dozens of Kurds, Afghans, and Arabs seeking asylum. As soon as the High Commission's doors opened, a police officer came and collected our passports. A feeling of safety rushed over me as soon as I entered the building.

Inside, we were led to a waiting area, where we waited as they called us forward one by one. When they called my name, I followed the woman into a private room. A Kurdish interpreter introduced herself to me and then introduced the UN lawyer who would conduct my interview. I was very excited that I could finally tell my story to someone who would listen. The lawyer asked me many questions about my family and my life in Kurdistan. She asked me about Saddam Hussein and about being in prison. Many more questions followed. When it got to the part about being smuggled out of the country, she asked me why I had not gone to Suleimaniya. I explained about the civil war and about not taking sides. I showed her my poem, "War." I told her about my writing and how I did not have freedom of expression. I showed her my two books and the scraps of prison notes. The lawyer took these and made copies. The risk I had taken to smuggle the books and some photos of me reading at events across the border at Ibrahim Khalil now paid off because they proved I was a writer.

After three hours, the lawyer asked me to come back the next day. Again, she spent three hours asking me questions. When she had finished the interview, she said, "We will let you know the result of your interview."

I learned from other refugees that it could take up to eight months to get a response from the UN, which was very frustrating for the people whose freedom depended on the result. I learned, too, that the mailman always delivered our mail around eleven in the morning, so I made sure that I was at home at the time. Just in case. If no letter arrived, I would go to the UN offices twice a week to chat to some of the other refugees. It was a great way to stay in touch with what was happening back home and to gather snippets of news from newly arrived people.

It was during one of my visits to the UN High Commission that I met Shwan, another refugee from Hawler. He lived in a house in the Olus neighbourhood. We soon became good friends and I visited at his house often just to get out of Madame Teza's dreadful hovel.

Shwan's dream to build an airplane in which he could fly over Hawler's ancient citadel was dashed when the civil war started. His father was killed in the fighting, leaving Shwan to fend for the family on his own. Still, Shwan continued working on his plans for his dream airplane. It took him a year to build the body. It was put on display in the municipal hall of the town of Diyana. The hall's back wall had to be pulled down to get the plane in. Later, he moved it on a flatbed truck to Ankawa, where he pitched a tent, got himself what he needed to eat and cook with, and devoted his time fully to the project. It was a big curiosity for the people. Some thought it was perhaps one of those airplanes that were used for patrolling the no-fly zones. He wrote out elaborate plans, which he burned onto two CDs, but these had to be put on hold when he became a refugee. Shwan's hope now was to get a European country to offer him asylum through the UN office in Ankara.

When people in Ankara found out that Shwan was an electrician, they would call on him for any repairs that they needed doing. Often, Shwan would tell me, "You know, I really liked it when people called me *wasta* Shwan. To be called a master technician means a lot to me."

There was another reason why Shwan wanted to get to a European country. Once there, his plan was to become naturalized and then return to Ankara and declare his love for Afshar, a slender and handsome Kurdish brunette from Agri. Her father was very homesick. He couldn't find a job in Turkey, but fortunately both Afshar and her brother had jobs. Shwan would look for opportunities to go to Afshar's house, and he constantly hoped the oven or some other electrical device would break down so he could go and visit her. Once there, he would prolong the job as long as possible.

I remember Shwan telling me one evening, "I've never felt this way before. I am madly in love with Afshar, and I know she loves me, too. I don't want to declare my love to her yet, because I'm a refugee now. I want to go to Greece by boat. But what if I don't make it and drown? I want to get accepted in a European country first, and then I'll tell her everything. I want to visit my mother, too. I miss her terribly. As soon as I arrive in Europe, I'll call Khoja, Afshar's neighbour. It would be great if Afshar herself came to the phone. I'll then declare my love to her. I can do that better over the phone than in person.

"Afshar is eager to be close to me, too," he continued. "I know she wants her thighs to be felt by my thighs, her beautiful slender hands to be caressed by my thick masculine hands. I know she wants me to hug her, to kiss her. One time she told me, 'At home we speak *Kurmanji*, but at school everything is in Turkish. When they hear me speak Turkish with an accent, some of the Turkish students call me a terrorist. What's that?' I didn't know what to say, because at that time I had no idea what the term meant. If we were in a European country, we would not have to worry about such things."

Sadly, the UN rejected his application, so Shwan began to make plans to leave Ankara and go to Istanbul, where he hoped to find a way to get to Greece. I tried to warn him about the dangers of taking a boat across the Aegean, but he refused to be dissuaded from his plan. The day before he left for Istanbul, the two of us went shopping at the Kizilay Market in Ankara, where he bought himself a suit. I understood his desire to own a suit. In the early 1970s Kurdish people still wore their traditional clothes, except for those who worked in government offices. Western-style pants were not worn casually and were forbidden. That morning at the market, Shwan told me, "When I wore Western trousers for the first time, I waited until no one was outside before mustering the courage to venture out. I was terribly shy. But as soon I got out, this naughty boy, Khalil, saw me. He jeered at me as I took off at full speed. I didn't come back until it was pitch black." I had been lucky, I thought. The first time I wore pants was on a rainy day, and there were not many people about to mock me.

After our shopping was done, I said goodbye to Shwan and returned to Madame Teza's. Shwan went to Istanbul and found a smuggler there to take him across the Aegean. News spreads fast among the refugee community. A few weeks after Shwan had left, we heard about a group of refugees who had tried to make it across the Aegean in storm. Among the passengers was a little girl named Sava. Sava's father had been living in Germany for three years, working as a dishwasher. Because he didn't have the papers to bring his family over legally, he tried the smuggling route, spending most of what he had saved on the venture. He had prepared a room, complete with toys, for his daughter and was very excited about them finally coming to join him. He'd told his friends in Germany: "My father was dead poor when I was a child; he could never afford to get me what I liked. Now I consider myself lucky to be able to get for my daughter everything she wants."

He arranged with a smuggler to get his wife and daughter out of Hawler to Turkey and then got them on a boat. That night on the Aegean Sea, as the mother was trying desperately to prevent her daughter from being swept away by the raging sea, little did she realize her fate, too, was about to be sealed. One by one they disappeared into the deep and unforgiving waters. It took fifteen days before the Turkish and Greek coast guards were able to recover the bodies of some of the people who were drowned that night.

Sava's father had been in constant contact with the smuggler, and the night he was told his wife and daughter were to be in the Greece-bound boat, he stayed up all night, worrying. In the morning, as he was flipping through the channels, the TV remote fell out of his hand when he heard the news: overnight a boat had gone down in the Aegean. Around noon, his friends called to inquire about his family. They called and called, but there was no answer. The friends rushed to his place, but no one came to the door. Alarmed, they informed the police. They found him on the floor—dead.

The Kurdish community raised money for his body to be taken back to Kurdistan, and after considerable delay and bureaucratic hassle in Turkey, the body finally arrived in Hawler, ten days after his wife's body was recovered. Everyone wanted his grave to be next to his wife's, but because space was not available, he was buried some twenty metres away. As for Sava, her body was never found.

Shwan, too, was in the same boat. He ended up drowning that night. The CDs with all his hopes and dreams were lost with him, including the one about being a refugee in a Western country, which floated with his body across the Aegean Sea.

Shwan's death was a big shock for me. I cried and cried. He was a good friend, and a good cook. I couldn't cook anything but fried eggs, and he cooked for us. I could only wash the dishes after the food had been eaten. After he left Istanbul, I felt very lonely. Living without friends, and with only a few words of Turkish at my command, was very challenging.

As I had no legal status in the country, I was unable to travel to the scene of the disaster. I called my friends in Istanbul daily for news. They did find Shwan's body and sent it back to Hawler, where it was buried in Tayrawa Cemetery not too far from his home. For a while his mother visited his grave every day. At home, she would often sit in a room all by herself, crying her eyes out while clutching an enlarged photograph of Shwan. She didn't want her other son and daughter becoming more upset than they were already. The doctor warned her that if the crying did not stop, she might eventually go blind. At one point her eyesight became so weak her daughter had to take her by the hand to the cemetery. The daughter stopped doing that when she turned sixteen because she was too shy to be seen with her mother in the cemetery. In the end, Shwan's mother did go blind. Whether it was from crying too much nor not, I don't know.

Two men in that boat survived, thanks to the inflated tubes they had with them. After a couple days in the hospital, they were deported back to Ibrahim Khalil. It was their third attempt at escape. They said to the media, "We were no more than a hundred or so metres away from the shore when the boatman started to panic. He said he felt dizzy and cold and was terrified of the waves. He had difficulty controlling the boat. We tried to help, but it was no use. The man was gripped by fear. The boat lost its balance, and the passengers began falling into the sea one by one. The tubes turned out to be our lifesavers."

The smugglers went into hiding for a while. One of them was reported to have said, "These people died because that was Allah's will. We've so far helped hundreds of people get to Greece. Many have been granted asylum, and have become successful, buying homes and businesses and helping their families back home. When you come to think of it, we have played an important role in helping Kurdistan's economy develop. This kind of loss was to be expected. A lot more Kurds had been killed in the civil war." He sounded just like a politician.

Twenty days later, I got a letter from the UN, asking me to come for another interview. This time I was taken to a private room and told my application for political asylum had been approved. They took my photograph and made me fill out some forms.

Walking back to Madame Teza's house I didn't know how to express my happiness, or how to share this great news with Sabah. She was still in Hawler, and I had no way of contacting her directly. I finally managed. Although I was very excited, I knew I had to downplay my news when I got back to Madame Teza's, because a few days earlier we had heard that Hashim's application had been denied.

After a while, a letter came from the Canadian Consulate in Ankara, asking me to come for another interview. I was excited, but also worried because I had heard that the Canadian Embassy only accepted labourers. If that was true, I was sure my application would fail. And I would be miserable. I was forty-five and a writer. I did not see how

I would be able to be a janitor and still write poems. It would be hard for a writer to become a janitor. I also knew what had happened the last time I applied for a manual labour position. In 1972 Dilshad and I needed jobs for the summer and so we registered with the Labour Union for a job as mosquito killers. We would be required to spray houses with bug spray that would kill the mosquitoes. After one month of waiting, the Labour Union finally put out the list of people who had been hired. We rushed to the offices to see whether our names were on the list of successful applicants. We looked from top to bottom, and one more time from bottom to top, but our names were not there. Looking around, it seemed that all those who came to see the list were not hired. Later, I realized that the employers must have told the successful applicants in advance that they were hired. I was very disappointed. Clearly, I was not meant to be a labourer. If Canada was only accepting labourers, I was in deep trouble.

Even though I was not cut out for manual labour, I was prepared to work. I wondered, too, what they paid people in Canada. When I was a student, I had a job teaching illiterate people at a school for five dinars a month. The job lasted for about three months before the school was closed. Later in life I would teach again, this time receiving eleven dinars a month. I would give half to my parents, and the other half I'd spend on myself. When I became a fully qualified teacher my monthly salary was twenty-nine dinars.

At the time, I was very excited about getting so much money and felt independent for the first time. My colleague and best friend, Faiq, and I both bought suits, which we would pay for monthly. I don't remember exactly why, but we did not pay the tailor for two months. The tailor was beside our favourite tea shop, so for those two months we would enter the tea shop through the entrance in the back alley. To our great shame, the tailor caught us and asked why we hadn't been paying. We promised to pay double for the next two months to make up for it out of embarrassment. To this day I have not defaulted on a payment again.

Fortunately, my interviewers told me they were also looking for journalists, which excited me. I was very relieved when I saw that on my visa application that was what it said. When I arrived in Canada though, I realized quickly it would be too difficult to master the English language well enough for me to be a journalist.

A few days after hearing that I had been accepted in Canada, I went to Shwan's house. It was fortunate, indeed, for not long after I had left, the police arrived at Madame Teza's place. If I had been there, I would have been deported. I decided to move out of Madame Teza's and went and stayed in Shwan's house. I slept in a small alcove in the passage. It was at the foot of the stairs leading to the bathroom. At night, I would wake up and see rats as large as cats watching me from the top of the stairs. Some days, Shwan would tell me how he had to fight with the rats to use the bathroom. I carried on going to the *hammam*. It was not a great place to stay, but it got me away from Madame Teza's and the 122 steps I had to climb up and down several times a day.

My move turned out to be very well timed, too. Not long after I had moved out, the Turkish police arrested Hashim near the UN office, and he was promptly deported.

Exile in Sivas

Through an acquaintance, I managed to pass on the good news about our acceptance in Canada to Sabah. I also gave her a number where she could contact me. It was for Khoja, our next door neighbour. He had a little office beside his house, which he opened for business every afternoon. Long before opening time, people would already be lined up in front of his door. This success was based on a solid idea: Khoja would sell prayers to people in search of good luck, and wealth. Among his clients were lovers, prostitutes, businessmen, women, men, and students. Khoja's business plan had only one flaw: he did not know how to write prayers in Arabic, even though most of his clients were refugees who spoke only Arabic. The ever-resourceful Khoja soon found a solution. Every night he would bring a bottle of scented ink, a pen, and some paper to Shwan. In exchange for a million Turkish lira, Shwan would then spend his evening copying out Qu'ranic verses. A week before Shawn was to leave Istanbul, Khoja asked him to write down as many verses as he could recall. I stood watching this operation. Whenever Shwan couldn't remember the chapter or verse of a sura, he simply asked me to repeat the title of one of my poems and he copied that down. Khoja knew no better, and his clients certainly would never know. In this racket, accuracy was not always the first concern. I am not sure what happened to Khoja's business when Shwan left, but I am sure that if I stayed in Shwan's house, he would have asked me to become his partner in crime.

Sabah was still in Hawler with our two daughters and Jwamer. I knew they planned to join me, but I was not sure how they were going to manage it. Not being able to speak with Sabah regularly nearly killed me. One morning, Khoja said I was wanted on the telephone. I knew immediately it had to be Sabah. I was eager to talk to them since we hadn't talked since I had left home four months ago. Sabah said she and the children were in the border town of Zakho. She explained that a woman smuggler had obtained Turkish visas for them, and that in two days they would all be arriving in Ankara. My daughter, Niga, who was now nine years old, wanted to know if I was with Ibrahim Tatlises, the famous Turkish singer, as Uncle Karwan had told her I was. I replied, "When you come, we'll go and see him together."

On the evening of their expected arrival, I got a ride to the bus station with Zaki Abi, a Kurd from Mardin in southeastern Turkey. I had met Zaki before when he had come to visit us at Shwan's home. On those occasions, Shwan would translate poems from *Dance of the Evening Snow* to Zaki. Zaki always felt extremely sad that a writer who wrote poems that affected people's lives was living in such harsh conditions. Zaki Abi was nice man but he was busy. After Shwan's death, he visited me twice a month.

As we waited at the bus station, I wondered whether Sabah and the children would recognize me. I had lost some weight since my arrival in Turkey. I had also shaved my moustache to blend in better so that I would not be recognized as a Middle Eastern man by the Turkish police. Even though I had been granted refugee status, I still remained on guard for the Turkish police, who didn't seem to care too much about what the UN had said. It turned out that the bus carrying my family was delayed. I felt embarrassed that Zaki had to wait such a long time with me at the bus station.

When the bus finally arrived, I rushed forward to hug Sabah and the children. The girls flew into my arms, but my son Jwamer, who was just three at the time, didn't seem to recognize me. He didn't want to come near me at first. Instead he ran to Zaki. He had never seen me in casual clothes, only in my smart clothes that I wore to work. Maybe it was because Zaki was well dressed while I had casual clothes on. I don't know. But I did know that this was the second time that one of my children didn't recognize me and it hurt as much as it had done the first time.

On the evening of my family's arrival, Zaki invited us all for dinner at his home. He and his mother stayed in an apartment on the fourth floor of a high-rise building. His mother welcomed us in Kurdish. After having some tea, Zaki made a short speech. Zaki's mother offered to let Sabah and the children have a bath. Sabah was shy, but I encouraged her and she accepted the offer. Among the many delicious dishes we were served was some kind of bread stuffed with minced meat. Niga told her older sister Ewar, "This is the Ibrahim Tatlises *lahm hajon*." For besides being a famous singer, Tatlises also owned several restaurants and Niga had seen the signs for them.

I had not been able to find a place where we could all stay together, but Zaki and his mother insisted that we spend the night at their house. We accepted the offer graciously. We were given a nice bed and a comfortable room. I was very happy to be with my family again and relieved that they had escaped from the hell in Iraq. But I was also concerned about what would happen the next day. I did not know what we would do. I felt guilty because my family had suffered because of my writing and I was afraid they would ask me why I returned to the same work after I was released.

The room in Shwan's building was too small for all of us, so the following day, I went back to Madame Teza's. I did not want to, but it was the only thing I could think of. She did have a room for rent and so we stayed there for about a month while I looked for a better place. When I did find a place, we moved immediately. However, it never felt like a home, and we weren't there a lot. We wanted to be outside, away from the living conditions as much as possible. One day we stumbled on a park by accident and saw people there having a picnic. So Sabah began to cook and we brought the food to the park every day. That way, we could get away from our house.

As soon as we had a chance, I told Sabah to register herself and the children as refugees so that they would not be illegal like me. On the way to the UNHCR offices, the taxi driver was taking the long way so he could increase the cab fare. I didn't care because I knew now that I was going to Canada with my family.

We stayed in Ankara for three months. Every morning Sabah had to go and report to the police. I would walk with her, but I always waited at a safe distance. One day she was told she had to leave Ankara within two days, but that she would be allowed to stay in Sivas, which was a city east of Ankara, in central Turkey. We went straight to the post office to see what we could learn about Sivas. There were always a few Kurdish refugees at the post office, trying to call friends and family in Europe or North America, or asking for help with their asylum applications. We hoped there would be someone who knew Sivas. We did meet some Kurds there and one of them promised to get us some information and the address of a Kurdish woman by the name of Chro who was living there. I was glad the man had given us her name, for Chro helped us a lot when we finally got to Sivas.

Two days was not a long time to sort out our affairs in Ankara. Fortunately, we did not have many things to pack. Everything we owned could fit into two bags. We left by bus early in the morning but didn't get to Sivas until after sundown. It rained most of the way there, but the rain stopped as soon as we arrived. As we stepped off the bus, it was cold and breezy. The sky was filled with wood smoke. Everywhere, we saw people heading home for the night. We were the only people at terminal who didn't have a home to go to. It was hard to arrive somewhere after seven hours on the bus only to know you had no place to go. I knew we couldn't check into a hotel because I didn't have papers. Chro's was our only option.

From the taxi, I could see that most men were bearded and most women wore headscarves. We seemed to see a mosque everywhere we looked. Later I learned that it was in this city that the famed Turkish writer Aziz Nesin came close to being killed when the hotel he was staying in was firebombed.

When we arrived at Chro's house, I was too shy to go in, but Sabah said, "Look, they're refugees, too, just like us." She walked right up to

the door and knocked. Chro opened the door and Sabah introduced us.
Chro smiled and invited us in. The family turned out to be very nice.
They were refugees from Suleimaniya and had been in Turkey for
about six months. They, too, had been accepted into Canada. We ate
dinner with them, and they did everything they could to make us feel
at home. They had a son and daughter close to Ewar's and Niga's ages
and the children hit it off nicely.

Over dinner we learned the Islamists were running the city. To
blend in, Sabah and Ewar, who was older now, got themselves headscarves the next day. After a few days, we found a house to rent about
fifteen minutes' walk away from Chro's house.

We spent the first night in our new house without power. I went
to the store to buy candles, but not knowing how to say "candle" in
Turkish didn't help. I finally came across a store where the store owner
understood what I meant when I said *"mom,"* which is the Kurdish
word for candle. We spent the night huddled around the candles. The
children were scared, and Sabah and I did not sleep because we had to
look after them when they woke up looking for daylight.

In the morning the owner came and asked us to leave. We never
did get a reason for being kicked out. We went back to Chro's house
until we found another house. Rental properties were plentiful, but the
perception was that refugees couldn't afford the rent. That was why I
made it a habit to pay the rent at least two days in advance. This time
we found a place in the north of Sivas. Shortly after we moved into our
new place, I went to the store to buy a cake and some more candles.
This time for Jwamer's birthday. Sabah cooked dolma and we had a
little family celebration.

Winter was harsh in Sivas and quite unlike anything I had
experienced before in Hawler. Sabah had lived in Koya, where you
did get snow, so it was not strange for her. It was something new for
the children, though, and they loved playing in it. I was the only one
who suffered. In Hawler, snow fell a few times during the winter
and seldom stayed on the ground for more than a day or two. In Sivas,
snow would remain on the ground for three months. The heating
system worked on coal, which was neither efficient nor clean. On

*Left: Jalal and family
in Ankara, 1997. Left-
to-right: Ewar, Sabah,
Niga, Jalal, Jwamer.
Below: Even as refugees,
living with fear and
poverty, there were
bright moments. A
snow-covered play-
ground in Sivas, 1997.
Left-to-right: Ewar,
Jwamer, Niga, Jalal.*

Birthday celebration at Chro's house in Sivas, 1997. Chro is third from the left.

winter nights the city looked like a smokehouse. I had a lot of difficulty getting used to the heating system.

Because we were not Turkish citizens, our children were not
allowed to go to school. This meant that we had to teach them
ourselves and look after them all day. Sabah and I would find empty
playgrounds, and we would take the children there for hours at a time.
At night, we visited other refugees. We always talked about our dream
of travelling farther and finding a safe home.

In November 1997, a letter came from the Canadian Consulate
telling us that our visas had arrived. The final destination given on the
papers was Edmonton, a place we had never heard of before. This was
the news we had been waiting eleven months for and it was exciting,
but also quite frightening. After that, my perception of Turkey
changed, and I felt my fear slowly slip away.

Chro's family also heard from the Canadian Consulate around
the same time as we did. Their visas had also arrived and they were

destined to leave on the same day as us. Their final destination was
Toronto.

A few days before leaving Sivas, we all went shopping. Sabah and
Chro got themselves long winter overcoats and hats. Sabah chose a
short black coat. Chro, who always seemed to favour left-wing political
views, decided on a red coat. I teased them about it, saying that they
had only bought the coats so that they could look like Western women
when they boarded the plane.

We also bought new clothes for children, and a shirt for me. I was
wearing the suit I had thought I would be wearing to Ukraine. Sabah
kept hoping we could settle in Toronto, too, even though our papers
said Edmonton was our final destination. We had some arguments
about asking to have the city changed, but again I would not compro-
mise. I said, "We need to follow our destiny and go where we are
supposed to be."

8 Another Attempt at Starting Over

Flying to a New Home

WHEN OUR BUS LEFT SIVAS EARLY in the morning on February 28, 1998, it was snowing. We arrived at the Istanbul International Airport in the early evening. At the airport, we met another family of refugees heading for Canada. We waited twelve hours until the plane finally took off at 6:00 AM. Throughout the night, I feared one last effort by the police to find me and deport me back to Kurdistan because I didn't have a residence permit.

Before leaving Sivas, I had to pay an $800 fine for staying in the country illegally without a residence permit. I borrowed the money from three refugee friends in the city. Even though I had paid the fine, I was still very nervous about being picked up by the Turkish police and deported to Kurdistan. There were several refugee families in the airport, some of them from Iraq. We all put our stuff on the floor and waited for our departure. Some of the people attempted to learn English using dictionaries. Others were changing their clothes to make them more suitable for Canada. Everyone was going to Ontario except us. We were going to Alberta. Sabah pleaded with me to go to Ontario, but I kept telling her that our destiny was in Edmonton.

We had been waiting to leave for eleven months, and now here we were finally waiting to leave. It was an exciting evening, our last in Turkey. I could not wait to get into the air where I would be free from the fear of being arrested by Turkish police. I had no idea what would happen to us in Canada, but going to a country that had opened its doors for us was a blessing.

Sabah and Chro had made us some chicken sandwiches to eat along the way to Istanbul. At the airport, we found a place to sit down and we all had the last of the sandwiches. Jwamer was crying a lot, but we all knew it was probably just because he was still small and very, very tired.

In the morning, a UNHCR officer helped us with the paperwork we needed in order to board the plane. When everything was done, he gave us all blue bags that had IOM (International Organization of Immigration) written on it in huge letters. The IOM is another department of the UN that helps people board the plane to the countries they have been accepted in.

We had a six-hour delay at the Amsterdam airport, which was amazingly crowded and busy. Everything around me was new. It was almost too much to take in at once. The airport's noise was almost deafening, and the bustling of people rushing to make their flights and rushing to their terminals and baggage pickup was incredible and unnerving. The one thing that kept me calm throughout the six hours was that I no longer felt any fear of being deported. Back in Hawler, we knew a writer who had lived in Amsterdam. When he came back to Kurdistan, he told us, "It was a country of flowers." We deeply wished to go outside and experience this, but we dared not venture away from our gate. We were down to our last $20. We spent five on a phone card, which enabled us to tell the people back home we were safely on our way to Canada. The rest of the money I spent on some chicken sandwiches for the children. The Chinese employees in the store were also a new experience and we assumed that they, too, were immigrants.

Finally, we boarded the plane for the last leg of our journey. The plane flew over the Atlantic Ocean for hours. It was a little scarier than

Jalal and family at Amsterdam's Schiphol airport, on the way to Canada, 1998.

flying overland. We did not know how long it would take to cross the Atlantic or what to expect on our arrival. For a long time, the screen on the plane showed our plane hovering over the ocean. The only thing I had learned from some refugees who had friends in Canada was that it was very cold in winter. Now that we were finally on the plane headed to safety, the excitement of the moment made us forget about the weather. Our pockets were empty, but our minds and hearts were filled with dreams and hopes.

When we landed in Toronto, we initially thought it was Edmonton. We didn't understand the fact that we would be landing in Toronto and from there we would go to Edmonton, so it came as a surprise to us when we were told we had to change planes for another flight of four hours to Edmonton. In the Toronto airport we grabbed the kids' hands because we were scared they would go missing. We were all carrying our IOM bags, which made it easy for an immigration officer to spot us. He led us to a place where many other people with the same bags had gathered. They seemed to come from over the world, and it looked like they were all immigrants. From there, we were taken to customs to do all our immigration paperwork. Two officers approached us. They were both Middle Eastern, and because our papers identified us as Iraqi, the man began to speak to us in Arabic, which impressed us. We were surprised that an Iraqi would be welcome in such a high position of employment. We wanted to ask him numerous questions about Canada and get many of our questions answered, but it was clear he was trying to get his job done, so we began to quiet down. In Iraq there were no lineups for things, just a rush, so the orderly lineups at Immigration impressed me.

At the Immigration Desk, we were each given a thick green newcomer's uniform winter coat and heavy rubber boots and gloves. Sabah's new black coat looked thin and summery compared to this. It slowly began to dawn on us that winter in Sivas was nothing compared to what it would be like in Canada. After we had cleared Customs and Immigration, we went to look for our luggage. Bag after bag emerged from the carousel. We got all our bags, except for mine. It was difficult to explain our problem in English. The few English phrases I had learned on the plane to Toronto only made things worse. People assumed that I could speak English. Everyone was very helpful and did their best to help me find my luggage, but to no avail.

Eventually, we gave up. By that time, we had missed our connecting flight to Edmonton. We were tired, hungry, and very concerned about our luggage. Again, we tried to find help. In the end, an immigration official took us to a hotel in Toronto where we spent the night. At the hotel, we checked in and went straight to bed. In the morning, we were taken straight back to the airport. It was only when we were all in the plane and Ewar had started writing up her diary, that we realized that with all the commotion, no one had made note of the name of the hotel.

Losing My Luggage

The luggage incident at Toronto Pearson International Airport was the third time I had lost my luggage. Both the previous times had happened while I was travelling by train or by bus. It did feel good to know that this time it was not my fault.

Once a month, I had to go from Sivas to Kayseri to get our monthly stipend from the United Nations. On the first trip, I took the train with two other refugees, Khosrow and Herish. I did not know where to go in Kayseri, and I wanted someone with me in case I got arrested and deported for not having a valid residence permit. Having witnesses with me meant that someone could tell Sabah and the children what had happened. After that first train trip, I always made the trip by bus. That made me feel a whole lot safer.

The seats in the train were hard and it was freezing cold. The train was depressingly slow and made the six-hour journey feel twice as long. When I was child I dreamed of travelling by train, but this train ride made me feel incredibly frustrated. Khosrow and Herish had taken pillows and blankets along so they could sleep and stay warm, but since I had no experience, I had not taken anything with me. I couldn't get to sleep, so instead I sat looking out of the window. The strange wind coming through the window disturbed my thoughts and dreams, however, and after a while, I could do little more than pray we'd arrive in Kayseri soon.

By the time we arrived at our destination, it was around noon. I was tired and hungry because I had not eaten since the night before. We hurried off the train and my companions immediately started walking. We'd been walking along at a fast pace for about an hour and a half when I asked, "Isn't there a taxi or a bus that we could have taken to the bank?" By now, I was forcing my tired feet to keep up with them.

They laughed at my city feet that were so unused to walking. "*Mamosta*, it seems you have not been a *peshmerga*. If you had been, you would have learned to walk," said Herish. Then he added, "But don't worry, we're almost there."

That "almost" turned out to be more than half an hour.

"We're here," said Khosrow as we approached a very ordinary-looking building in the city centre.

"Are you sure this is it?" Herish asked.

"Wow, this is your fourth time you've come here to get your salary, Herish! And you still are not familiar with where the bank is?" Khosrow responded.

"Don't blame me, it's the houses. They all look the same to me," replied Herish.

A policeman was standing in front of the bank. My heart began beating faster and faster. But nothing untoward happened, and after we got our stipends, we all went and ate kebab sandwiches. Later we went and did some shopping in the city's famed carpet bazaar.

I couldn't wait to get to the bazaar, because our trip to Canada was approaching and I was going to get some things to take with us. The mall was very long, and there were incredible carpets of numerous colours hanging everywhere. Tucked away between the rows and rows of carpets were some tea shops. I have been fascinated by carpets ever since I was a child. My aunt made them, and I loved watching her work. She would swipe her fingers through the threads quickly and effortlessly and I was amazed that she could make things so beautiful with what looked like so little effort.

When Sabah and I were engaged, she was manager of a carpet-making company in Koya. Whenever I visited her, she would take me into the hall where they made the carpets. She said they were attempting to compete with the Iranian carpet makers, who were world-renowned. It worried me that all the workers seemed to be between nine and fifteen years old and that they were spending five hours a day making carpets rather than being in school. But I also knew it could not be helped. They came from very poor families that relied on any extra income that came in.

After wandering through the different carpet shops, I picked a few and paid for them. We returned to the station just in time to take the overnight train back home. I was already dead on my feet after a day of walking and the extra weight of the bag of shopping on the way back made it worse. Once more, I was cold and uncomfortable and could not sleep. This time, the darkness hid the scenery from me and I could not even look out the window. I let my thoughts wander to my past and my future with my family in a new country.

We arrived at 6:00 AM and I went straight home and slept. It was only after I woke up and wanted to show Sabah and the children the carpets I had bought at the bazaar that I realized I had left my bag on the train.

"I don't know when you will face reality and stop living in your imagination," Sabah said, shaking her head.

The second time I lost my luggage was in 1998, right after we were informed by the United Nations that our visas had arrived. I left in a great hurry and caught a bus to Ankara so that I could go and collect the documents. As I got onto the bus, Sabah reminded me to buy four curtains and two blankets to take with us to Canada, because we had learned from a friend that such things were terribly expensive over there.

Once back at the bus station, I kept the documents with me in a small carry-on bag but put the curtains and blankets in the luggage compartment of the bus bound for Sivas. Then, looking at my ticket, I noticed that there was still half an hour before the bus departed. So I went for a little walk, got myself a sandwich, and then returned to the bus and embarked just as the bus was leaving. By now, I had become somewhat familiar with the road between Sivas and Ankara and slowly it dawned on me that I was on the wrong bus.

"Where is this bus going?" I asked the bus attendant nervously.

"Bursa," he said.

I began to panic. I told him I was going to Sivas.

He replied calmly, "It seems you're on the wrong bus."

He suggested I get off the bus immediately and try to get a ride back to Ankara. The bus driver stopped at the side of the road and let me off. In the rush to get out, I left behind my jacket and suitcase with the carpets and curtains. I realized what had happened almost immediately and started running after the bus. Fortunately, the bus attendant saw me and realized what had happened. He stopped the bus and gave me my hand luggage. I was very grateful because our immigration papers were in the bag. I do not know what I would have done if I had lost them!

I cursed myself for my carelessness.

I stood at the side of the road and waved at passing vehicles but to no avail. Cars were zooming by, but no one seemed to care about my situation. It was beginning to get dark when a truck finally stopped. He knew from my Turkish that I was an outsider.

"Where're you from?" he asked.

"I am a Kurd from Iraq," I replied in Turkish.

"Are you a *Kurmanj*?" he asked.

"Yes, I am," I replied.

"I, too, am *Kurmanj*," he said in Kurdish.

On the way, he talked about all the cargo he had taken to Kurdistan and his experiences travelling in Iraq. Soon we settled down in silence. I was too tired to talk about politics. In Ankara, he dropped me off near the terminal. I went to the place where I had purchased my ticket. The man said, "What happened to you? The bus waited for you for more than fifteen minutes, but there was no sign of you so it left. Now you will have to wait for the bus leaving at midnight." At seven in the morning, I arrived at the terminal in Sivas terminal without my stowed luggage.

Sabah simply shook her head. I could say nothing to redeem myself.

And now I had lost my luggage in Toronto. Sabah insisted it was because I had put a string of spices in my suitcase. Three weeks later we got a phone call in Edmonton. I picked up the phone, but I could not understand the man's English. He spoke too fast. I handed the phone to Sabah, whose English was a little better than mine. She did understand. When they had finished talking, she said, "They found your bag." Three hours later, someone from the airport brought the bag right to our door. The bag of spices was still inside.

The next day Sabah made delicious dolma.

Our Final Destination

We left Toronto early in the morning on February 28, 1998. During the plane ride, the captains allowed all the kids, including Jwamer, to walk up to the front of the plane and look at the world through the front windows. Sabah and I were very impressed at this kind gesture. In fact, the generosity of all the people we had met so far was overwhelming. We arrived at the Edmonton International Airport just before noon. An immigration official spotted the IOM logo on the bag I was carrying and hurried over to us. She gave us a warm welcome. As it happened, the woman was an Iranian Turk who had moved to Edmonton. She knew few Kurdish words, but we were able to communicate in Turkish, thanks to the Turkish we had picked up during our stay in Turkey.

When we drove away from the airport, it was snowing. I was amazed by the piles of snow by the side of the road. I asked the people who were taking us into the city if it would ever melt, and they told us that the snow in Edmonton usually stayed on the ground until April or May. It was only March now, and I did not look forward to the long winter. Already, my toes were frozen solid despite the warm boots I was wearing. When we got out of the car, we all felt a new kind of cold—a cold that our bodies had not experienced before. Inside any building, however, it was warm.

We were given keys to a two-bedroom apartment at Welcome House. For our first dinner that evening we were served macaroni and meat, which we hardly ate, because it looked so unfamiliar. But we helped ourselves to bananas, which in Kurdistan most people couldn't afford.

We were eager for the snow to stop so that we could go for a walk and enjoy our newfound freedom. But the snow did not stop for three or four days. None of us had ever experienced anything quite like this and we stayed inside. It took us a long time before we began to go out in the snow.

On the second day after our arrival, another immigration official came to see us. She gave us two cheques—one for the purchase of household items, the other our salary for the month. That was when we learned that the Immigration Office would help us every month for our first year in Edmonton. We were very grateful indeed because we were still learning to speak English and we had already realized it was going to be very difficult to find jobs here. When I received my second cheque from Citizenship and Immigration Canada, I transferred $800 to my friends in Turkey to pay for my fine.

We stayed at Welcome House for two weeks. After that, we moved into a three-bedroom apartment that the Immigration people helped us find. For the fourth time in our lives, Sabah and I had to furnish our home from scratch, but this time we were getting tremendous support from Immigration Canada. This made such a difference.

We had moved into in a mixed neighbourhood and we still felt very new and strange. But everyone was very nice to us and tried to make us feel welcome. I remember how stunned we were when our neighbours came to wish us a happy Eid. In fact, we had forgotten about Ramadan because we were so busy adjusting and we were still struggling to communicate with people. There were so many new things to learn—street names, how and where to shop, how the legal system worked, how to fit in, how to look for a job. One of the biggest problems was transportation. All the shops where we could buy groceries were far away from where we lived. Getting around was very difficult because we did not know how to call a taxi or take a bus. After a while we got to know some members of the Kurdish community who had cars and they would take us shopping from time to time.

The knowledge I had acquired from reading many books over the years proved helpful in understanding some of the customs. Soon Sabah and I found ourselves attending English language school. The student body was diverse. Our class looked like a microcosm of the world. Before they asked us where we were from, they taught us how to say, "We are glad to see you." But for me learning a new language at forty-five proved to be difficult. Sometimes I was afraid of what lay ahead, and I worried that my bright future may not happen because of all the trouble I had learning the language.

The Immigration people also gave us two bicycles to help us move around the city more easily. I had not ridden a bicycle since I was a child and had rented one from Ibo's bike stall in Hawler. It took me a long while and a fair amount of bruises and falls to learn then, but now it came back easily. I taught Sabah how to ride hers, and soon we were making good use of them, going for rides together in the evenings.

The children began to go to school very soon after we arrived. It was nice to have them learning again. Sabah and Jwamer took the bus to school while I rode my bike around town. After school, we would leave Jwamer at the school's daycare centre. Ewar and Niga walked the short distance to school, but it was difficult for them to make friends and get used to the educational system. The move from Kurdistan to Turkey was a shock for the kids. We lived a good life in Kurdistan and we had worked hard for the privileges we'd earned for our kids. It was traumatizing for them to go from a life of relative luxury to living and sleeping in one bedroom.

When we arrived in Canada, our living conditions improved. Due to our lack of English education and the fact that we struggled to speak the language, Sabah and I couldn't help the kids. Jwamer was young and learned the language and way of life quickly. Ewar, although having troubles of her own, went to school in an older grade with more mature children. But Niga struggled. She had a more difficult time integrating than the other two. In her diary, Niga, describes these early days as "daily battles" she had to wage. Children picked on her and made her feel frustrated about our family's financial situation. It did not help that when we eventually got a car, she was taken to school in a tiny Toyota that barely worked. Day after day she was picked on, yet she still managed to grow. As our time in Canada wore on, Niga integrated more and more. By the time she reached high school, she was fluent in English and her ability to engage with other people had improved to a point where it was one of the strong suits of her personality. I think her story in our family is one of the most impressive ones, because she dealt with the most severe problems and overcame them.

Four months after our arrival, a lady named Kelly MacKean, who volunteered with the Catholic Social Services in Edmonton, became a regular visitor on weekends. She would help us with our English. Sabah's English was better than mine. After some improvement in my English, Kelly found me a job at the Centre for Multicultural Awareness as an advisor to newcomers and immigrants. With the help of a reference from Yvonne Chiu, another friend we had made, I also found myself a part-time job at the Edmonton Mennonite Centre for Newcomers. The Mennonite Centre also helped people who had immigrated to Canada to adjust. Working with other immigrants really helped me to adjust quickly, and I was thankful that I was able to help other people settle in, even though I was also still very new to the country. Sabah got a job as a community worker at another local organization, the Changing Together Centre.

These were all big changes in our lives. After about eight months, I got myself a driver's license and bought a car. Learning to drive in

Edmonton was very different. There were more cars here and the rules and road signs were all different than those in Iraq. For a while, I always made sure the tank was full, just in case I got lost. But I soon got used to it and we all enjoyed the freedom of having a car to get around in. Now we could explore more parts of the city.

During our stay in Turkey, life was a daily struggle for survival and I was afraid that a lack of freedom and the difficulty of my situation might eventually pull me away from the pen. But as soon as I came to Canada I began to realize that this would not be the case here. Here, I would no longer suffer a lack of freedom and my situation wasn't ever going to be too hard to handle. In Canada, I found out early on that writing was not subjected to censorship, and that writers did not have to fear going to prison for expressing their views freely. This was incredible, as I had come from a country where every aspect of our lives had been controlled through blood and force.

However, because of family responsibilities and language difficulties, I could devote little time to writing. But then luck seemed to be on my side. During my first year in Edmonton, I attended a cultural conference at the University of Alberta. There a Kurdish student named Soran introduced me to the well-known Canadian writer and journalist, Linda Goyette. She, in turn, introduced me to many other journalists and writers, including Satya Das, Shirley Serviss, and Alice Major, all of whom were active in the writing community in Edmonton.

Linda soon became a good friend to us. One cold evening, she took me and Sabah to a book launch. I tried my best to follow her in our 1986 Toyota because I wasn't familiar with the address to which we were going. The heater in our car wasn't working, and I could not see clearly through my windshield. Sabah tried to clean the window by rubbing her hand over it, but it was useless. Our breath stuck to the windshield and made it impossible to see a thing. From time to time, I had to park the car and scrape the ice off the windows. Whenever I pulled over, Linda would park, too, and she kept watching us through her rear-view mirror.

When we finally arrived the event, it had already started. We were very shy, but Linda introduced us to some Canadian writers. It was quite funny. We all talked, but we couldn't understand each other.

Jalal at the Changing Together conference in Edmonton, 1998. A translator (left) reads his work to the English-speaking audience.

Some of the people I was introduced to could barely pronounce my name correctly, and saying their strange-sounding names was even harder for me. As I struggled with the names, I wondered how our English as a Second Language (ESL) teacher managed to learn the names of twenty students from around the world in a few days. I remembered how at high school we had a teacher who by the time the school year ended hadn't even learned the names of half of the students in his class. Still, even though we barely understood each other, I suddenly felt overjoyed to be among the community of writers in Edmonton.

Linda Goyette did an extensive interview with me and Sabah and sent it to Satya Das, who was a columnist for the *Edmonton Journal*. Being recognized like this by the writing community in Edmonton boosted my confidence and gave me the courage to start writing again. I joined a local group called the Stroll of Poets, as well as the Writers Guild of Alberta and the International Canadian Writers' Association. I have since read my poetry, in both English and Kurdish, at numerous literary conferences.

Two years after arriving in Canada, my friend Dilshad Abdullah in Hawler sent me some Kurdish journals. It was wonderful to rejoin the literary conversation with those I had left behind. In 2003 I published my poetry collection, *An Exile's Memoir*, in Kurdish, and in 2006 I published a fourth volume of poetry, *Call Me Home*. I also began to publish numerous poems and articles in online newspapers. This new freedom to write was a dream come true.

At about the time that I received the magazines and journals from Dilshad, I also bought my first computer. My daughters helped me to set up an e-mail address. Because it was the first time I had ever used a computer, it took me quite a while to become familiar with it. But soon I was reading Kurdish newspapers online. It was quite a struggle to find a font that would allow me to read Kurdish online and use it in a word processor. Eventually, I found and installed a Kurdish font and learned how to type. The first poem I wrote on the computer was called "Even in Fall there is no Place," and it was published online in a paper called *Dengekan Voice*, which is based in Toronto. Since then, I have read my poems in Kurdish and in English at a number of conferences.

Even though I was writing again, I had to do so in the little spare time I had. Then, early in 2007, I heard that I had been asked to be Edmonton's first Writer-in-Exile. The year-long residency was organized by PEN Canada, the Edmonton Public Library, and the Writers Guild of Alberta. I was given an office in the public library and told I would be paid a salary to write. Such luxury was beyond my wildest dreams.

A Death in Exile

We soon settled into our new lives in Edmonton, but I missed being around other Kurdish people. I knew there were many Kurds here in Edmonton, but we never seemed to be able to get together. And so, in 2000 I founded the Canadian Kurdish Friendship Association. In 2004 the Association received the RISE Award in recognition of its important contributions to improving community relations.

Jalal reading a poem at a Nowruz (New Day) party in Edmonton, 1998.

Jalal and the Nigerian author and Nobel Prize-winner, Wole Soyinka, 2001.

Through the activities of the Canadian Kurdish Association, we made many new friends among the Kurds living in Alberta and elsewhere in Canada. Among the strongest supporters of our Association was Hakim. Hakim came from the mountains of Kurdistan and was forced to flee his village during the second Gulf War. He had spent five years at a refugee camp in Van, Turkey. Four of his children were born in the camp. The Iraqi regime did not want to open schools in Kurdish villages because it wanted to keep the population illiterate. Hakim was one of those. He could neither read nor write.

Eventually, Hakim was granted political asylum in Canada, where he became a legendary pioneer in the Kurdish community. Coming from a village that consisted of a mere twelve families to a bustling Canadian city without any way to communicate and with no previous exposure to this lifestyle was an unimaginably difficult adjustment. He attended many semesters of ESL classes to learn English, as he was determined to learn the language. In the end, however, he gave up. He told his friend Rahman how this upset him. It made his life really difficult. Whenever he was asked for his address, he would flash a piece of paper with his address written on it.

There were many stories about Hakim. Like the time when he forgot to put out his cigarette. Soon a raging fire was devouring his place. He went to some agency for free furniture, but he was told they didn't have any except five toothbrushes. So he took them and went home. No gift was too small for Hakim. Even this fire could not destroy Hakim's will to live. The only thing he ever complained about was Saddam Hussein.

Even though Hakim had been in Canada for fifteen years, he still had to take the citizenship examination with the help of an interpreter. But by the time his Canadian citizenship papers finally arrived, he'd been dead two weeks. The news of his death sent shock waves through the Kurdish community. Hakim's death was like a wake-up call to the Kurdish community. Kurdish men have never been encouraged to do exercise and the change in diet when they arrived in Canada caused many health problems for them. They put on weight and soon developed many problems. Hakim paid for his habits. The night before his death, he had stuffed himself with his favourite meat, lamb. His freezer always contained a couple of carcasses. He was just crazy about lamb.

After Hakim's death, everyone in their fifties began to worry about what they ate and began visiting the doctor regularly and going to swimming pools. At the memorial service, one of the attendees, Sepan, said, "I will buy a treadmill."

A few months later, I asked him, "How is the exercise going?"

"I have only used the treadmill twice," he replied. Many of the other Kurdish men bought treadmills and got recreation memberships, but because it had never been part of their lifestyle none of them continued with it for long.

Another attendee at the memorial service, Borhan, was quite blunt: "I will die if I don't eat meat, lamb. But if I eat it, I might die or not die. So I think I will take my chances."

Following Hakim's death, there was also a marked change in the way Kurdish teenagers treated their fathers. Fearing that they, too, might become fatherless, they started treating them better. Again, this was a lesson they learned from Hakim's family. Hakim's eight children, like many other Kurdish youngsters growing up in Edmonton, had quickly learned English and had forgotten their mother tongue. This annihilated the relationship between the children and the parents and led to a lack of respect for each other. Straight after Hakim's death, his children regretted that they had not been very nice to their father. Only his oldest son, who was seventeen and was constantly busy on his cell phone, didn't seem to have been affected by the death at all.

The family didn't have anyone to decide what to do about Hakim's body, which was still being kept in the city morgue. The issue of what to do with his body became the main topic of conversation at his memorial service. His son-in-law didn't consider it practical for him to accompany the body all the way to Kurdistan—he didn't want to be away from work for a month. He said, "Going home is hard enough for the living. Imagine how much harder it will be on the dead."

Some members of the Kurdish community didn't want to set a precedent by burying Hakim in his adopted country. This was also their way of saying they expected their bodies to be taken back to

Kurdistan. The discussion continued for a long time. Eventually, *Mam* Nadir, a respected old man in the community, said, "But Canada is also Khuda's land. Hakim spent fifteen years here. He never went back to visit Kurdistan. It seems he liked it here. His children all have grown up here; they have little or no connection to Kurdistan. In our first four years together here, Hakim used to talk a lot about the village where he came from, but after that he hardly mentioned it."

Eventually Hakim's son-in-law decided to bury the body in Canada. Even after his death, Hakim would remain a pioneer by becoming one of the first members of the Kurdish community to be buried in this country. Arrangements were made with a mosque. Most Kurds had not seen a hearse before, for in Kurdistan the mourners transported the body to the gravesite in whatever vehicle was available. A vehicle dedicated to transporting bodies was a novelty. The men gathered around the vehicle in amazement. Smo's father said, "It is such a nice automobile. Truly, here they have a plan for everything."

For the Kurdish community, going to the cemetery was a new experience. On the way, some of the cars were left behind because of heavy traffic. Hakim's oldest son was in one of those cars. He was trying to videotape the procession for the family back home in Kurdistan. But because he was constantly on the phone, no one could reach him. Meanwhile, the men from the mosque were getting impatient and wanted to be done. So they went ahead with the burial without the son's presence.

Hakim's burial marked the start of what would become the cemetery for Kurds living in exile. Two years after his death, Hakim's children decided to go and visit their father's grave. They went to the mosque for directions, but because this was their first visit and the grave still had no tombstone, they couldn't find it. Apparently, the grave had become one with the ground.

On the way back home, they all went and ate at McDonald's.

Somewhere In-between

Following Saddam Hussein's downfall and the end of the Kurdish civil war in 2003, I decided it was time to return to Kurdistan for a visit. I knew this first visit back to my home country was going to be very special. After I bought my ticket, my wife and I went on a gift-buying spree. I also called our various Kurdish friends in Edmonton, asking if they had any messages or gifts they wanted me to take for their families. As news of my visit spread through the Kurdish community, some people, like *Kaka* Rush, wanted me to talk about nothing else but the trip. After many discussions, he decided that he would rather go back for good than just for a visit. He lived in a low-income rental house that was too small for his family because he refused to buy a house. He thought doing so would tie him to Canada. Every month, he would save money for a ticket back home. But like many other people in exile, he was transformed by his experiences in his new country and he never has left it, not even to visit the neighbouring United States.

In the end, I left with bags of gifts and messages for friends and family in Kurdistan. Four big suitcases, stuffed to bursting-point. And only one of them contained my clothes! Sabah wanted me to take a fifth one, but I put an end to the madness. "Do you think I'm going from here to Hawler and Koya by truck or by plane?" I asked.

Even as I sat on the plane, after an absence of seven years, I still couldn't believe that I would soon be reunited with my family and friends, not to mention a wealth of memories. At the time, because flights to Kurdistan were not yet available, the trip had to be through either Turkey or Iran. I chose Iran, because I was told the Turkish border police didn't treat Kurdish travellers very well. They took away Kurdish books and music and insulted people just because they happened to be Kurds.

At each airport where I had to check in my luggage—Edmonton International, Frankfurt in Germany, and Mehrabad International in Tehran—the airport authorities charged me for my overweight luggage. In Tehran, I tried to pay in American dollars, but they would not accept it, so I had to find a foreign exchange. In the end, I suspect I paid double for all the gifts I took along.

From Tehran, I flew to Kermanshah in Iranian Kurdistan and from there I took an inter-city taxi to Marivan on the Kurdish border. I paid the driver my $50 fee and asked him not to take along any other passengers, as I had plenty of luggage. It was a four-hour drive and I

Above: Peshtewan, Jalal, Kamaran. Three brothers on the highway between Hawler and Koya, close to Ashkaftsaqa, 2005.
Right: Looking at the ruins of Ashkaftsaqa, evening, 2005.

tried to talk to the taxi driver to find out a bit more about life on the ground for Kurdish people there. However, he wasn't interested and instead we talked about the weather. He had brought plenty of tea with him and he offered me some, too. It made me sweat and I opened the window, but the heat coming in from outside was even worse. When I was thirsty again, I asked for water instead.

We arrived in Marivan around sunset. I was a little worried, as I still had to get my papers from the Iranian police before I would be allowed to cross the border into Kurdistan. Before leaving Canada, I had called my family and told them I would enter Kurdistan at the Bashmaq border post in Hawler.

I explained my problem to the taxi driver, but he said, "Don't worry. I know the chief of the secret police in Marivan and he is the person in charge of issuing border passes. If you give him some money, he will take you to his office and process your paperwork even when he is off duty."

"I'm ready to pay him," I replied.

"Do you have a personal photo ready?" the driver asked. I did not. He must have seen the worry crawl over my face, because he added. "Even if you have a family photo, that is fine. Just find it. We will cut out your face and use that."

"How much money do I have to give him?" I asked next.

"Two hundred dollars," came the answer. This was becoming an expensive trip.

I handed over the money right away. I had compiled a family album to show to relatives in Kurdistan and I took one of the pictures from it and gave it to the driver as well.

The driver took me to the official's house, which was just a few blocks away from his office. He knocked at the door. A man in a flowing *dishdasha* opened the door. They spoke for a bit and then the taxi driver returned and drove me to a grey house nearby, which turned out to be the offices. The official did not come with us and I was getting worried. He arrived a little while later. It took the man ten minutes to process my papers and hand them to me.

The driver took me to the checkpoint, but stopped about a hundred metres away.

"Could you take me a little closer, please? I have many bags to carry," I said.

"This is my limit," he replied. "I am not allowed to go any closer."

The driver helped me to unload all my bags and then he left. I stood there, wondering how I was going to manage this. There was no way I could carry all the bags to the border crossing, and I did not want to leave them unguarded while I carried them one-by-one. Just then, a group of people came by and offered to help me carry my bags. I accepted their offer gratefully. I paid them in American money, for which they were very grateful.

It was the first time since I had left Turkey that I had seen so many police. Maybe it was my past memories of Turkish police, or maybe it was the images of them beating people to subdue them, but I was very nervous about crossing the border. My bags were filled with Western clothing and I was, after all, a Kurd.

At the Bashmaq border to Kurdistan my brothers Jamal, Peshtewan, and Kamaran were waiting for me. With them were my brother-in-law, Karwan, and his wife, Srwa. They had all come to see me. It was a happy moment. It made me forget my troubles and the gruelling twenty-hour flight. Many Kurdish people complain that the reception they get when they go home is not all that warm. That was not my experience. On the way back to Hawler we talked non-stop, jumping from one topic to another. We stopped briefly for dinner in Suleimaniya before continuing on our journey. The drive went by so quickly that we barely noticed that almost five hours had passed. There was just so much to talk about! We got home around midnight. People were coming from every side, kissing and hugging me. All my close relatives and members of my family were there. I did not recognize some of the children because I had never seen them before. It was wonderful to be among family again.

After saying hello to everyone, I opened the suitcases with gifts. Everyone was very pleased with the presents. Sabah's nephew's only reaction was: "Oh my God, even in Canada everything is made in China." We all laughed about that and settled down with some tea. We stayed up all night, talking.

It seemed so unreal to be together again in Kurdistan. Two weeks into the trip, people were still coming in droves every night. I also visited with Sabah's family. They, too, were very happy to see me and were eager to hear about Canada. I gained quite a bit of weight from all the rice, kebab, lamb, kofta, dolma, and other dishes I was served daily. At one point, I remembered Hakim's sudden death, and I realized I needed to keep an eye on my cholesterol. But it was so hard with all the good food that everyone was feeding me!

I was eager to find out what had happened to those prisoners with whom I had spent so much time. My brother, Kamaran, for instance, was having heart problems, which the doctors ascribed to the typhoid he contracted while in prison. He told me of the many of the prisoners he saw at the hospital where he went for his check-ups. They were all suffering from physical and mental health problems, but like the thousands of other prisoners under Saddam's regime, they received no assistance.

One day I went to the Sheikh Allah Bazaar and found Hamza working as a street vendor, selling rice. He said the Kurdistan government had not helped him in any way after his release. He said he was told he was had been just a detainee not an actual prisoner.

"I guess our confinement in thirty-five centimetres of space for all that time means nothing to them," I said.

But Hamza added, "*Mamosta*, what can I say? At least this is a government that doesn't throw us in jail just because it can. No more Anfal. No more chemical weapons. At least now we don't have to live in fear like we used to." He looked around and then called me closer. "Look," he said and showed me a Kalashnikov he kept hidden in his cart. "If Kurdistan falls into danger again, I am ready," he explained.

On the days when the prisoners felt especially down, some would say: "The moment we are released, we will start running: running from this prison, from our homes, from this fascism. We will not stop until we've reached a place where peace and security and freedom are the norm."

On the day of our release, Chapuk and Pala, two young men who were imprisoned because their fathers were *peshmerga*, did exactly that. I still remember how quickly they took off the moment they were released. I can still picture them running with one hand clasping the side of their sherwals. I couldn't understand how, after all that time in prison, they still had the energy left to run. Maybe being released gave them back their energy. I was curious to find out what had become of these two. Because they ran through the district where many members of the secret police lived, I thought perhaps they had been stopped and arrested a second time, or even killed, for that was what the secret police chief had said he would do to us as we were about to be released.

I ran into many of the people I was imprisoned with. We would talk about our prison days for hours. About how afraid we were and how we slowly forgot about freedom, and how we began to think that the only life there was, was within the four walls of our prison. But no one had the slightest idea of what became of Chapuk and Pala.

The prison days, however, were now a distant memory. Saddam's regime was no more but the prison walls remained standing. What the prisoners had written on them with their blood was still there. Saddam was gone, but the reminders of his brutality still remained for everyone to see. Seeing him behind bars was great news for those of us who had suffered under him.

Towards the end of my stay, I went to visit some of the places I often dreamed about while in Canada. The Sheikh Allah Bazaar was even more crowded than before and it was harder to work there and make a living. But you still could buy anything from hair colouring to Viagra. The library and the station were there, but smaller and more rundown than I remembered. I soon realized the childhood I had left behind in the alleys was not there anymore. Most of the places had changed. In some places, high-rise apartments had gone up, though not as nice and as high as the ones I had seen in Canada.

For the most part, I was pleased with what I could see the Kurdish government was doing. With very few exceptions, there was no more censorship. But there were new realities that people were not prepared for. Government investment in culture and education seemed to be lacking. When you go to a city, you can learn a lot about the people from the city's architecture and museums. Back in Edmonton I had gone to several museums and art galleries. Other places, too, seemed to care about preserving the past. When I went to the University of Alberta Press offices to talk about the publication of my book, I expected to find them in some big ultra-modern high-rise. But the publisher was housed in an old building that the university had maintained. They obviously realized how important it was for the past to be preserved. But here in Kurdistan, I could see our heritage slowly disappearing and falling apart.

I thought and reflected a lot while in Kurdistan. It would be nice, I thought, if a democratic system, based entirely on love and compassion, could be found. If you do not love your country, you cannot serve it. But creating a good system requires wisdom, planning, expertise, and honesty. I could tell my country was not the way it used to be; it had no room for dreams anymore. I had changed, too; otherwise, why would I have forgotten to visit the graves of my father and my brother, Salaam? Sheikh Ahmed Cemetery was only a five-minute walk from my mother's house.

This first trip back to Kurdistan helped me uncover some secrets about myself. It made me raise so many questions, questions that would take more than one visit to answer. Before I arrived, I felt my dreams would come true and I would reconnect with my childhood. But I found myself thinking more about the lack of electricity and respect for the law and the overall backwardness of the lifestyle than anything else. I was always saying how living in another country changed other people, and now after doing so myself for seven years, I could see the change in myself. This was the reason why sometimes I felt like an outsider. Before returning to Canada, I felt that continued exile in many cases was the only option for people like me.

On the return trip to Canada, the Iranian police turned out to be just as bad as their counterparts across the border, even worse. They took my passport, locked me up for a day, and kept me at a hotel for nine days without any explanation. I called Sabah from the hotel, and she quickly spread the word about my ordeal among the Kurdish community in Edmonton. Mahtab, who was originally from Iran, called a woman she knew who was working for a major contracting firm in Tehran. She in turn sought the help of a prominent businessman, who came to see me two days later. The next day I was let go. I never found out why I was detained in Iran. My friends joked that it was because my beard made me resemble the novelist Salman Rushdie.

When my plane took off, I knew it was heading westward. I was surprised that I felt as free and as elated as I did when I left Turkey for Canada in 1998. I noticed how other passengers also changed the minute they were on the plane. As soon as the women got on the plane, they removed their head coverings. They seemed to appreciate their sudden freedom.

Many of those I had come to look for in Kurdistan I never found. *Perhaps I'll go and look for them when I come to visit for a second time*, I thought, even though I had my doubts it would happen. My wish was to see my past and present as two neighbours. And I was somewhere in-between. But I still struggle to find that in-between state, because sometimes I feel as though my legs are separated by the Atlantic Ocean and the distance makes it difficult to take a step to one side.

Justice at Last

On the morning of January 1, 2007, I rose early and went and stood at the window with a cup of coffee in my hand. It has become a habit of mine to get up early. Sabah says this is an indication of growing old. This may be so, for I'm now fifty-five, which by Kurdish standards is fairly old. The coffee is a habit I have acquired in Canada. I have become addicted to coffee. The doctor says it is not good for my blood pressure; he has given me pills. I take the pills, but I just can't be without coffee.

I was still in my new blue pyjamas, contemplating the world and waiting for the sun to rise on the new year. It just so happened that for the first time in many years, the celebration of the new year coincided with the first day of Jazhni Qurbane, when Muslims commemorate the willingness of Abraham to sacrifice his son to God. It was a good day, I thought, and I looked forward to the coming year.

My meditation was broken by the ringing of the phone. It was a Kurdish friend of mine.

Jwamer's birthday party, Edmonton, 2000. Left-to-right: Niga, Ewar, Jwamer, Sabah, Jalal.

"You don't know yet?" he asked in disbelief.

"What are you talking about?"

"They're about to execute Saddam. Both Kurdish satellite channels are covering the story."

I didn't wake anyone. I decided I would break the news to Sabah and the children when they woke up. I switched on the television and watched. I saw some masked men chanting, *"Allah u Akbar Muqtada."* I didn't know if they meant Muqtada al-Sadr, the Shi'a cleric, or some other religious figure. I hoped neither man was involved. I wanted Saddam to be brought to justice, but I didn't want the outcome to be revenge on behalf of one ethnic group or another.

All I could think of in that moment was seeing five innocent children being shot in front of their parents right before my eyes on the night the police arrested me. The television flashed back to a scene from Saddam's trial. A string of witnesses told their stories. They were Anfal survivors. Some had survived the massacre at Dujail, just north of Baghdad, in 1982. These witnesses were brave, I thought: in simple but passionate language, they confronted the dictator. I looked at Saddam sitting in the stand. He was still the same old Saddam: arrogant, belligerent, out of touch with reality, showing no remorse for his many crimes.

As I listened to the eyewitnesses, I kept hearing my own experiences repeated over and over again. The story of my life, I realized, was part of a larger narrative. Slowly, the idea for this book took shape. I wished my book to be one of the reminders of these crimes that were committed against Kurdish people and humanity.

I turned away from the television and walked over to the kitchen window, from where I could get a better view of the sun rising over Edmonton. As the new day dawned, a line I had heard some time back popped into my head: "It is hard to live in the same world forever, isn't it?"

I don't remember who said that, but I, too, like to say the same thing.

Chronology

624 CE Battle of Badr; 319 followers of Islam triumph over 900 non-believers.

762 CE Abu Jafar-al-Mansour founds Baghdad and becomes the second Abbasid caliph.

1775   Qasim Agha Abdullah builds the ancient *hammam*.

1953   Jalal Barzanji is born in the spring.

1958   Military coup brings an end to the Hashemite dynasty. Abdul-Karim Qassim becomes president of the Republic of Iraq.

1961   Fire spotted on Mount Korader; *peshmerga* enter village. Kurdish Revolution begins.

1963   Author's family leaves Ashkaftsaqa and flees to Hawler. Abdul-Karim Qassim assassinated in February; the Ba'ath Party under Ahmed Hasan-al-Bakr gains power. In November, Abdul Salam Arif topples the Ba'ath government and becomes president. The Haras Qawmi arrest Jalal's father.

1968   Ba'ath Party comes to power. Hawler Public Library is turned into a prison.

1970   Jalal starts writing. He reads his first poem in public and his first publication, "The Ripped-out Cemetery," appears in *Rahela*.

The Iraqi government negotiates a ceasefire with *peshmerga* forces under the leadership of Mustafa Barzani on March 11.

Jalal finishes high school.

1971   Jalal enrols in teacher's institute.

Bakour Tea House is bombed; Jalal's friend Farhan dies in the explosion.

1973   Suicide bombing attempt on Mustafa Barzani.

1974   Ceasefire ends; November Revolution begins.

University of Suleimaniya relocates to *peshmerga*-controlled Qat'al Diza in January. The University of Suleimaniya is bombed on April 22, leaving hundreds wounded and dead.

1975   Kurdish Revolution collapses.

Jalal Talabani founds Patriotic Union of Kurdistan.

Massoud and Idris Barzani re-organize Kurdistan Democratic Party.

Shah of Iran brokers the Algiers Agreement on March 6.

1976   Jalal begins teaching at primary school in Sktan. The attack on Sktan takes place on Jalal's first day there.

1978   Jalal's father dies on April 17. Jalal is transferred to Smakshirin (teaches here until arrest in 1986).

1979   Jalal gains permission from censors to publish *Dance of the Evening Snow*.

Saddam Hussein forces his second cousin, Ahmed Hassan Bakr, to resign the presidency and Saddam takes the helm.

1981   Jalal meets Sabah.

1982   Jalal proposes to Sabah; Jalal and Sabah marry.

1983   Birth of Ewar, Jalal and Sabah's eldest daughter.

Jalal, Abbas Yusuf, and Dilshad Abdullah are denied permission to publish a joint collection of poetry.

1985   Jalal publishes *No Warming Up* with Al-Hawadith, Baghdad.

1986   Jalal is arrested in March, along with other members of his family.

Birth of Niga, Jalal and Sabah's second daughter.

Jalal's mother, Zerin, and his sister, Ruqya, are released from prison in November.

1986-89   The start of Operation Anfal, Saddam's brutal chemical warfare and attacks on Kurds.

1988   Ayatollah Khomeini launches a campaign against Kurds of Iran.

Iraqi regime enforces evacuation of villages to depopulate rural Kurdistan.

Halabja gas attack (Bloody Friday Massacre) occurs on March 16.
Jalal, and his brothers Jamal, Kamaran, and Peshtewan are released
from prison with general amnesty on Saddam's birthday in May.

1990   Saddam Hussein invades Kuwait on August 2.

1991   Saddam Hussein and the *peshmerga* agree to a ceasefire at the beginning of February.

On February 24, the US leads assault on Iraqi forces in Kuwait.

Kurdistani *Rapareen* (Uprising) starts on March 1. By March 10, *peshmerga* and uprisers control all cities in Kurdistan except Mosul and
Kirkuk. The following day, March 11, Kurds control Hawler. The rest
of Kurdistan follows.

The situation soon reverses itself and by March 20, Kirkuk is once
more under Saddam's control. Hawler is retaken on March 31.

Jalal and family flee Hawler in April. There is a mass exodus of Kurds
to Iran and Turkey.

A no-fly zone is created beyond the 36th parallel in late April on the
initiative of France's François Mitterand.

1992   Birth of Jwamer, Jalal and Sabah's son in April.

1996   Civil war between PUK and KDP starts in August. On September 25,
the parties arrange a ceasefire. On November 24, both parties sign a
peace agreement.

Jalal leaves Kurdistan.

1997   Jalal flees to Turkey and is granted asylum in Canada. Sabah and
the children join him later that year. Jalal and family stay in Sivas,
Turkey, while they wait to leave for Canada.

1998   Jalal and family leave Sivas for Canada on February 28.

2000   Jalal founds Canadian Kurdish Friendship Association.

2003   Jalal publishes *An Exile's Memoir* in Kurdistan.

Saddam Hussein is ousted from power; Kurdish Civil War ends.

2004   Canadian Kurdish Friendship Association wins RISE Award.

2005   Jalal returns to Kurdistan for the first time since fleeing the country
in 1997.

2006   Jalal publishes *Call Me Home*.

2007   Kurdish families move from citadel ghetto to The New Citadel in
Hawler.

Jalal is appointed as the first PEN, WGA, and Edmonton Public
Library Writer-in-Exile.

2010   Massoud Barzani is re-elected president of Kurdistan.

Glossary

aba: woman's outer garment that often conceals European-style clothing

agha: chief of the village

Al-Anfal: "the spoils of war," title of the eighth sura in the Qu'ran

Allah u Akbar: Allah is the greatest

Anfal: a campaign of terror utilizing chemical warfare against Iraqi Kurds and led by Ali-Hassan al-Majid

arrack: strong alcohol

Ba'athism: the offical policy of the Ba'ath Party in Iraq

baba: father

barani: outer hall of the *hammam*

bxor: cyclamen

darbandi gomaspan: Valley of Gomaspan

dishdasha: more commonly known as a *thawb* or *thobe*, this is an ankle-length garment, usually with long sleeves, similar to a robe

dolma: rice, spices, and minced meat rolled into a vine leaf

doshag: thin, cotton, roll-up mattress

Eid-al-Fitr: a three-day fast-breaking Muslim celebration at the end of Ramadan

Gali wasman kujray: the name of a peak on Mount Bawaji, "the place where Wasman was killed"

hammam: public baths

haraam: something not allowed in Islam

Haras Qawmi: Secret Police, militia

Hawdang: literary magazine on whose editorial board Jalal sat

Iraqi Turkmen Movement: political party for Turkmen people in Iraq

Jahanam: a level of Hell to which idol worshippers are sent on the Day of Judgement

Jash: a Kurdish mercenary group

jawani: the inner hall of the *hammam*

Jazhni Qurbane: when Muslims commemorate the willingness of Abraham to sacrifice his son to God

Kak!: an exclamation

kaka: brother

kapr: campsite

karkhana: red-light district in Ankara

kofta: a meatball, mixed with herbs and spices, coated in breadcrumbs and fried

Kurmanj: the majority clan/tribe of Kurds

Kurmanji: the language spoken by the majority of Kurds

lahm hajon: pita with ground meat in the top

madrasah: a Muslim educational institution, school

Mam: uncle

Mamosta: teacher

mom: candle

muezzin: man who calls the faithful to prayer from the minaret five times a day

nawser: deep-fried flatbread eaten during Ramadan

Nowruz: the New Day, March 21

Nuseri Kurd (The Kurdish Writer): a journal of the Kurdistan Writers' Union

peshmerga: the Kurdish Freedom Fighters

Rahela (changed later to *Beri Newe*, or *New Idea*): the magazine Jalal and high-school friends created and in which Jalal was first published

rapareen: uprising

Rebazi Newe (New Path): a literary journal Jalal edited

Salaam: a greeting

Sayyid: a title of respect

Shakh: a subversive, underground magazine

sharbat: juice

sherwal: traditional Kurdish trousers

shifta: deep-fried veal patties

shurakan: a left-wing radical movement established after the uprising in 1991

tawli: backgammon, trictrac

Wahabi: an Isalmic religious movement among Sunni Muslims

wasta: master

wastani: middle hall of the *hammam*

247

Index

Ramadan and Eid-al-Fitr, 33-35,
176, 222

Winter in Fireland
A Patagonian Sailing Adventure
NICHOLAS COGHLAN
400 pages | 4 maps, 48 B&W photographs, suggested
reading list, index
978-0-88864-547-0 | $34.95 paper
Adventure Travel/Memoir/Sailing

Bosnia
In the Footsteps of Gavrilo Princip
TONY FABIJANČIĆ
264 pages | 45 B&W photographs, maps, index
978-0-88864-519-7 | $29.95 paper
Travel Writing/Politics/World History

Under the Holy Lake
A Memoir of Eastern Bhutan
KEN HAIGH
296 pages | B&W photographs, map, notes, suggested
reading list
978-0-88864-492-3 | $29.95 paper
Adventure Travel/Literary Memoir